PROUD TO SAY
I AM A
UNION SOLDIER

—Sergeant Richard J. Foley
Company B
Sixth Kentucky Cavalry

The
Last Letters Home
from
Federal Soldiers
Written During the Civil War
1861-1865

Franklin R. Crawford

Franklin R. Crawford

HERITAGE BOOKS
2005

HERITAGE BOOKS

AN IMPRINT OF HERITAGE BOOKS, INC.

Books, CDs, and more—Worldwide

For our listing of thousands of titles see our website
at
www.HeritageBooks.com

Published 2005 by
HERITAGE BOOKS, INC.
Publishing Division
65 East Main Street
Westminster, Maryland 21157-5026

COPYRIGHT © 2005 FRANKLIN R. CRAWFORD

Cover: *The News* by Carlton Alfred Smith, 1853-1946

International Standard Book Number: 0-7884-3189-7

Where do we get such men?

"The Bridges of Toko-Ri"

Table of Contents

Dedication...5

Acknowledgement..6

Introduction..8

Chapter I
Major Sullivan Ballou – 2nd Rhode Island Infantry............10

Chapter II
Colonel Thornton Brodhead – 1st Michigan Cavalry...........15

Chapter III
Private Elijah Curtis – 92nd Illinois Infantry.......................24

Chapter IV
Colonel John Cromwell – 47th Illinois Infantry.................30

Chapter V
Private Isaac Overall – 36th Ohio Infantry........................41

Chapter VI
Private Pliny White – 14th Vermont Infantry.....................51

Chapter VII
Private John Adkinson – 95th Illinois Infantry...................66

Chapter VIII
Private Meritt Simonds – 41st Illinois Infantry...................75

Chapter IX
Private George Culbertson – 127th Illinois Infantry............82

Chapter X
Second Lieutenant James Bayne
      106th New York Infantry..93

Chapter XI
Private Ernst Damkoehler – 26th Wisconsin Infantry..........99

Chapter XII
Private Thomas Brown – 1st United States Sharpshooters...109

Chapter XIII
Corporal James Raymond – 4th Massachusetts Cavalry......124

Chapter XIV
Colonel Matthew Starr – 6th Illinois Cavalry...................131

Chapter XV
Quartermaster Sergeant Edward Boots
      101st Pennsylvania Infantry...............................141

Chapter XVI
Private Thomas Morrison – 22nd Wisconsin Infantry.........150
Chapter XVII
First Lieutenant Rufus Ricksecker – 126th Ohio Infantry....172
Chapter XVIII
Private Lyne Brown – 55th Massachusetts Infantry.............183
Chapter XIX
Sergeant Richard Foley – 6th Kentucky Cavalry............…190
Chapter XX
Private Spencer Williams
        3rd Tennessee Cavalry – USA..........................…198
Chapter XXI
Private Thomas Horan – 65th Indiana Infantry...............207
Bibliography...215
Index..218

Dedication

For my parents, Charles and Harriet Rutherford Crawford, and my brother, John, who started me on my journey.

For my wife, Velma and our children, Nena and Charles, who accompanied me every step of the way.

For Kathryn Elizabeth Vincent, "May all your paths be peaceful and pleasant, charged with the best fruit, the doing good to others." Jefferson C. Davis

Most of all, for my best friend, "Elmer."

Acknowledgements:

Before thanking the many that have been responsible for so very much of the contents of this project, I would like to thank two individuals who are uniquely responsible for its ultimate completion. Doctor Shin Chin, the perfect physician perceived a major problem and undertook the solving. Doctor Baron Harper, the craftsman that demonstrated to me, in a multitude of ways, that there is indeed not only life after the Civil War but, more importantly, life rather than the Civil War. To both this project is especially dedicated and a "hearty" Thank You is submitted. You are, more than you may realize, responsible for the results found within these pages. I hope, in some small way, they are worthy of your efforts.

Thanks are also due to many others. For their help and guidance regarding the acquisition of these fine letters I would like to thank Cheryl Schnirring and the staff at the Illinois State Historical Library in Springfield, Illinois. Also of great help was Douglas Brown, Lawrence Kestenbaum and Eric Wittenberg as well as the staff at the Burton Historical Collection at the Detroit, Michigan Public Library. Eric T. Davis and The Rare Books Library of the Ohio State University, Columbus, Ohio was a great assistance as was Margery Strong at the Vermont Historical Society. Likewise, Eric Mundell at the Indiana Historical Society was very helpful. The staff at the Rare Books Library, Northern Illinois University Library was of great help, also. Individuals like Edwin Boots, the Damkoehler family; Katherine Dahle, Shirley Garrepy, James Joplin, Arthur Lillibridge and Gary Overall were gracious in allowing me access to their private collections of family materials. DeAnne Blanton at the National Archives in Washington, D.C. proved, beyond doubt, that there is absolutely no question to which someone on the staff there can not find the answer.

To all members of "my" Civil War Round Tables, Northern Illinois, McHenry County and Lake County, in Illinois as well as Manasota and Sun Coast in Florida, I offer my sincere thanks. Without you, I often would have been out here all alone with no one to share my troubles.

Individuals that not only offered their research skills but added to that invaluable help with a huge amount of encouragement and creative suggestions were Benton McAdams, author of **REBELS AT ROCK ISLAND**, David Noe, author of **FIREARMS FROM EUROPE**, Erik Gene Salecker, author of **DISASTER ON THE MISSISSIPPI**, and Barbara Freund, author of **AMONG THE THINGS THAT WERE: LETTERS FROM A VERMONT FARM FAMILY (1830 – 1874)**, all excellent works in their own right. Others who also were of great assistance were Dr. Ronald L. Cope, Illinois State University, who read every word of this many times, and Jayne McCormick who provided so much assistance with her internet knowledge.

I also want to thank Dr. William Glenn Robertson, the command historian of the United States Army Combined Arms Center at Fort

Leavenworth and the deputy director and chief of staff rides at the Combat Studies Institute of the United States Army Command and Staff College and a true authority of the entire Civil War who, unknowingly, at a small crossroads at Murfreesboro, Tennessee, gave me the primary inspiration to do this project.

Last and last only because one should always save the best for last, will be my wifey, Velma, who has read and corrected this more times than I can count. You have indeed shown that you are "the last surviving widow of the Civil War" in many ways. I truly thank you for everything.

As all of the above know, whatever mistakes there are within are indeed mine. No one can hold any of you responsible for my not making changes that you suggested nor will I pass blame for your not finding my mistakes within these letters.

Introduction

Volumes have been written analyzing skirmishes, battles, triumphs, failures and leaders of both sides of the hauntingly tragic era of America's history, the Civil War. The red and blue lines, boxes and arrows drawn upon battlefield maps depict troop movements and placements but glaze over the harsh reality of war. At the point of every arrow on each battlefield map was a father, a son, a brother or a husband whose family back home anxiously awaited his return. Prayers, hopes and dreams of such good fortune were often dashed upon the bloody fields of combat, death coming to the soldiers by the hundreds of thousands and, when observed today, almost 150 years later, these statistics continue to reveal the numerical horrors of that war.

From the comparatively few casualties suffered at the battle of Mill Springs, Kentucky, January 19, 1862, (795 by both the north and the south) to the disastrous 51,112 killed in the three days battle, July 1, 2, and 3, 1863, in and around Gettysburg, Pennsylvania, the fatalities of the American Civil War are still awesomely staggering. In total, 373,458 deaths and another 412,175 wounded were sustained in the four brutal and passionate years of combat according to the United States Civil War Center. During the course of war, many men had premonitions they were soon to be in the presence of death. They spoke of it in their daily conversation and alluded to it in their correspondence. It seems the longer they were away from the safety of their home the more they realized the possibility of not returning increased with every passing day. There were also men who fully understood they were about to die. These men had received wounds which were known to be fatal. Theirs was an even stronger sense of commitment to their family. Counsel and requests of the family at home regarding the final disposition of their mortal remains filled the pages of their last correspondence. However, seldom did the appearance of resignation find its way into the same communication. There was a steadfast resolve to fulfill the manly duty of a soldier in combat and be successful in the execution of that duty.

Somehow, and sadly, these grim realities seem to have given way to the complacency of time. Such deaths, before the expected mortality of old age, touched families in a multitude of ways. Many loved ones were brought home for burial in family plots and large memorials were erected in their memory. Multitudes more were left where they fell, to be cared for by their nation and their God. National cemeteries now exist relatively near the location of these battlefields and the men were simply and reverently interred there.

A frequent practice of the bereaved was to retain the last common bond in remembrance of the deceased soldier, the last correspondence sent by the now departed. Whether killed in action during some far away battle, lost in a prison camp in a distant land or whether they died a stranger without even a name at the lowest ebb of their lives, these men and boys would be missed by their generation as well as the next. Their memories became enshrined forever not in the frame of a photograph or painting but more often, in a cardboard box to be eventually set aside in a trunk or a larger container, to be discovered anew, generations later, and once again attain the glory and pride in the eyes of a new generation, only recently aware of their long ago fallen hero.

It is uncertain how often these individual letters were removed from their shrine to be reread or even if they were at all. It is entirely possible that they were simply held tightly to the mother's, wife's or daughter's breast and further tears shed over them. Fathers and sons, in an era when the shedding of tears was not considered the mark of a true man, may have simply stared at the letters and cried within. It is not beyond reason to think that they would have been taken in hand on either the date of birth of the deceased or the anniversary of the death, or both. What is certain, beyond doubt, is that they were passed on to the next generation and then the next; each being told somberly of the significance of the letters. These new owners would have been charged with the task of guarding those letters from destruction as the whole had been guarded in the past.

Many of these packages were eventually deposited into college or university libraries with the hope that they would be available for study by any and all interested while others found their way into state and local historical libraries or museums for the same purpose -- both because the surviving descendant really did not want the responsibility, perhaps, of being the curator of such an important piece of history. Others would continue to remain as they were, still wrapped carefully, often bound together with a small ribbon, still encompassed in the same small box, even the box or container becoming part of the treasure trove of the family.

There are literally thousands of letters and sets of letters from Civil War soldiers hidden away in university libraries, historical society libraries and private homes, waiting to be discovered. This compilation of letters is just that. They are all located in obscure depositories, or in private collections, known by few. These were men whose lives were offered at the altar of freedom and, unlike so many others, that offer was accepted by their country. They left their families, their friends and their homes, and went to war for an idea or a concept. They did their jobs and some of them, these in particular, never returned.

These letters, some accompanied by photographs of their authors, once again make these individuals unquestionable heroes of a distant but not forgotten war.

United States Army Military History Institute
Major Sullivan Ballou
2nd Rhode Island Infantry

"to help maintain this Government"
Major Sullivan Ballou
2nd Rhode Island Infantry

Major Sullivan Ballou was a rather tall, partially balding, thirty-four-year-old lawyer and politician, leading a very full and interesting life when the Civil War began. He was born near Cumberland, Rhode Island on March 28, 1827, but his father, Hiram, passed away in 1833 when the lad was but six years of age. The youngster was raised by his close family members whose history stretched back to the founding of the colony of Rhode Island. His graduation from Brown University in 1852 helped pave his way to becoming a state representative and, in 1857 and 1858 he served as the Speaker of the House. Following his efforts as a state legislator, Ballou returned to his home in Smithfield, set himself up in the practice of law and settled into a life of a strong family man.[1]

Sullivan married Miss Sarah Hart Shumway of Worcester, Massachusetts on October 15, 1855 and the couple became the proud and dutiful parents of two sons, Edgar Fowler and William Bowen. The outbreak of the Civil War, however, drew Sullivan Ballou away from his domestic duties and into what he considered his patriotic duties. He enlisted on June 5, 1861 as a major in the Second Rhode Island Infantry and, on June 19, he and the regiment left Providence, Rhode Island and embarked on a journey to the nation's capitol, Washington, D.C. There they served until the plans for the advance on Manassas Junction, Virginia were formulated and the all of the regiments in the area, even those whose terms of enlistment were about to expire, began the long and in some instances the last march to the west, to the waiting Confederate Army.[2] One week before the battle of First Manassas, or First Bull Run, July 14, 1861, Major Ballou had received some indication that he and the Second Rhode Island Infantry were going into action. It was at that point he took the time to write his dear wife Sarah the following letter. He tried very hard to serve three personae; dedicated soldier, concerned father and devoted husband.

"Headquarters
Camp Clark
Washington D.C.
July 14th 1861

My Very dear Wife
      The indications are very strong that we shall move in a few days perhaps tomorrow and lest I should not be able to write you again I feel

impelled to write a few lines that may fall under your eye when I am no more. Our movement may be one of a few days duration and be full of pleasure, and it may be one of severe conflict and death to me. "Not my will but thine O God be done" if it is necessary that I should fall on the battlefield for my Country I am ready. I have no misgivings about or lack of confidence in the course in which I am engaged, and my courage does not halt or falter. I know how American Civilization now bears upon the triumph of the Government and how great a debt we owe to those who went before us through the blood and suffering of the Revolution; and I am willing perfectly willing to lay down all my joys in this life to help maintain this government and to pay that debt.

But my dear wife, when I know that with my own joys I lay down nearly all of yours, - and replace them in this life with care and sorrow when after having eaten for long years the bitter fruit of orphanage myself. I must offer it as their only sustenance to my dear children, is it weak or dishonorable that while the banner of purpose floats calmly and proudly in the breeze, underneath my unbounded love for you my dear wife and children should struggle in fierce though useless contest with my love of country.

I cannot describe to you my feelings on this calm summer night when two thousand men are sleeping around me, many of them enjoying the last perhaps before that of Death, and I am suspicious that Death is creeping behind me with his fatal dark arm communing with God my Country and thee. I have sought most closely and diligently and often in my breast for a wrong motive in thus hazarding the happiness of all that I love and I could not find one. A pure love of my Country and of the principles I have advocated before the people and the name of honour that I love more than I fear death, have called upon me and I have obeyed.

Sarah my love for you is deathless   it seems to bind me with mighty cables that nothing but Omnipotence can break and yet my love of Country comes over me like a strong wind and bears me irresistibly with all those chains to the battle field   the memories of the blissful moments I have enjoyed with you come crowding over me, and I feel most deeply grateful to God and you that I have enjoyed them so long. And how hard it is for me to give them up: and burn to ashes the hopes of future years when God willing we might still have loved and loved together and see our boys grow up to honorable manhood around us. I know I have but few claims upon Divine Providence but something whispers to me perhaps it is the wafted prayer of my little Edgar that I shall return to my loved ones unharmed. If I do not my dear Sarah never forget how much I loved you nor that when my last breath escapes me on the battlefield it will whisper your name.

Forgive my many faults and the many pains I have caused you How thoughtless how foolish I have sometimes been! How gladly would I wash out with my tears every little spot upon your happiness and struggle with all the misfortunes of this world to shield you and my children from harm but I cannot I must watch you from the spirit world and hover near you while you buffet the storms with your precious little freight and wait with sad patience till we meet to part no more.

But Sarah! if the dead can come back to this earth and flit unseen around those they love I shall be always with you in the brightest day and the darkest night amidst your happiest scenes and gloomiest hours always always and when the soft breeze fans your cheek it shall be my breath or the cool air your throbbing temple it shall be my spirit passing by. Sarah, do not mourn me dead   think I am gone and wait for me for we shall meet again.

As for my little boys they will grow up as I have done and never know a father's love and care

Little Willie is too young to remember me long but my blue eyed Edgar will keep my frolics with him among the dimmest memories of his childhood   Sarah I have unlimited confidence in your maternal care and your development of their characters. Tell my two mothers I call Gods blessings upon them   Oh! Sarah I wait for you then come to me and lead thither my children   Sullivan"[3]

Major Ballou was correct: within just a few days his regiment found itself on its way west out of Washington, D.C. and advancing to the plains near Manassas Junction, Virginia.

The brigade of General Ambrose Burnside marched along the Sudley Ford road during the mid morning of July 21, 1861 believing their movement was covered by the deep woods along side the road. They had no way of knowing that a few miles to the south, beside a small stone bridge crossing Cub Run, the Confederate soldiers were well aware of their movement thanks to the long line of dust observed while the Federal soldiers advanced to the Warrenton Pike.   This observation told Confederate General Nathaniel G. Evans of their placement as well as their intent. Evans moved the men of the Fourth South Carolina and Major Robideau Wheat's Battalion of Louisiana Tigers to Matthew's Hill which was across the valley in front of Young's Branch. With these riflemen, General Evans brought with him two 6-pound howitzer guns and the artillerymen to operate them. His plan was to meet this advancing column - repel them and drive them back to the capitol of Washington, D.C.[4]

Upon arriving on Matthew's Hill, Evans placed his riflemen in line of battle almost a mile north of the Warrenton Pike with his left flank firmly established on the Sudley Ford Road and his right extending into the field some distance. Each end of this line was anchored by one of the howitzers and its crew. Evans, known by his soldier's as "Shanks", was there by 10 o'clock in the morning, awaiting the advance of the Federal troops his front covered by yet another small wooded area of live oaks alongside the Sudley Ford Road.[5]

It was shortly after the Confederate soldiers' arrival on Matthew's Hill that Burnsides' Federal skirmishers were observed advancing and immediately were fired upon. This activity brought forward the Second Rhode Island Infantry and its six cannon to contest the field. The Second Rhode Island, which would become one of the better fighting regiments of the Army of the Potomac during the Civil War, was under the command of Colonel John S. Slocum. One of Colonel Slocum's most trusted subordinates was Major Sullivan Ballou, the lawyer from the city of Smithfield.[6]

At the outset of battle, Colonel Slocum was wounded three times, unhorsed, and left dying on the field of battle. As command passed to Lieutenant Colonel Frank Wheaton, and the integrity of the unit was becoming compromised by the short-lived absence of command, Major Ballou was at the center of the regiment attempting to shift its position and direction. While attending to his duties there, he was struck from his mount by a cannon shot which mangled his right leg and, like Colonel Slocum, he was left dying as the battle raged on. At the end of the day, when the Federal troops were fleeing to Washington, D.C. at a much quicker pace than their approach to Manassas Junction had been, and with far less organization, Major Ballou found himself a prisoner of war at the Sudley Church near the site of his wounding. He also realized he was dangerously wounded and in great pain.[7]

According to the deposition of Private Josiah W. Richardson of Co. C - First Rhode Island Infantry who served as a nurse while a prisoner of war at the Sudley Ford Church/hospital, Ballou's mangled leg was amputated on July 28th by a Confederate Surgeon but the major did not survive. Richardson's statement indicated that Ballou died at four in the afternoon on the 28th and his body was buried across the road and just a few yards south of the church the following day.[8]

There Ballou's remains, as well as those of Colonel Slocum and Captain Levi Tower who had also been killed in action at the First Battle of Bull Run, remained until the following spring. On March 23rd, 1862 at Camp Brightwood, near Washington, D.C., the men of the Second Rhode Island Infantry gathered to pay their respects to their fallen comrades whose bodies had been exhumed for the purpose of returning them to their homes. The governor of the state of Rhode Island, William Sprague, escorted the remains to the ceremony and read the following statement to the assemblage. "The Rebels supposing the remains of Maj. Ballou to be Col. Slocum disinterred the body, removed the clothing, and burned the body to ashes." Ballou's remains were removed to Swan Point Cemetery in Providence, Rhode Island where they were joined by the remains of his beloved Sarah after her death on April 19, 1917 at East Orange, New Jersey.[9]

{1}   Record Group 94, Office of the Adjutant General, Compiled
Service records. Volunteer Soldiers, Ballou, Sullivan - Pension file &
Service Record.

{2}   Ibid.

{3}   Sullivan Ballou to "My Very dear Wife" - July 14, 1861 - Ballou
Collection - The Illinois State Historical Library, Springfield, Illinois

{4}   John Hennessy, *The First Battle of Manassas - An End To
Innocence July 18 - 21, 1861,* (Lynchburg, Virginia: The Virginia Civil
War Battles and Leaders Series, H. E. Howard, Inc., 1989), pp. 41 – 42

{5}   Ibid.

{6}   Ibid., pp. 49 – 62

{7}   Ibid.

         United States War Department. *The Official Records of the War
of the Rebellion. A Compilation of the Official Records of the Union and
Confederate Armies. 128 Vols.* (Washington: 1881 - 1902), Series #1 --
Volume #2 - Chapter IX - The Bull Run, or Manassas, Campaign, Virginia
#41 - Report of Lieut. Col. Frank Wheaton, Second Rhode Island Infantry

{8}   Record Group 94, Office of the Adjutant General, Compiled
Service records. Volunteer Soldiers, Ballou, Sullivan - Pension file &
Service Record.

{9}   Robert Hunt Rhodes, ed. *All For The Union: The Civil War Diary
and Letters of Elisha Hunt Rhodes.* (New York, New York: Orion Books,
1985), p. 60

         Record Group 94, Office of the Adjutant General, Compiled
Service records. Volunteer Soldiers, Ballou, Sullivan - Pension file &
Service Record.

Colonel Thornton F. Brodhead
1st Michigan Cavalry

II
"your children will be Fatherless."
Colonel Thornton F. Brodhead
1st Michigan Cavalry

Colonel Thornton Fleming Brodhead sat astride his horse just south of Lewis Ford on Bull Run Creek on August 30, 1862, and prepared his men of the First Michigan Cavalry and the Fourth New York Cavalry for an assault by the men of the Second Virginia Cavalry. Behind these Yanks were the cavalry regiments of the First West Virginia and the First Vermont, all awaiting the pending onslaught. As the Virginians approached the crest of the ridge in front of the Yanks, the command of "Draw Sabers" was given and bugles sounded the advance. Forward the troops moved, "knee to knee, in perfect line" one horseman wrote afterwards. First at a walk, then a quick canter and then a full gallop, the men of the Second Virginia likewise advanced and the two forces collided in a haze of gun smoke and dust. The battle of Second Manassas or Bull Run commenced for these troops here on the field near the Portici House or Lewis Farm.[1]

Thornton Brodhead had come to this juncture in his life as a result of much hard work and perseverance. Born December 5, 1820 at South New Market, New Hampshire, by the age of twenty-six he was a law degree graduate of the prestigious school in Cambridge, Massachusetts, Harvard University. On April 9, 1847, Brodhead was commissioned First Lieutenant of the Fifteenth United States Infantry and joined the ranks of the military men in the Mexican War. From May through October, his academic talents were utilized as regimental adjutant under the command of Colonel, and later Brigadier General, Franklin Pierce. Pierce would eventually become President of the United States.[2]

The military and the war wore well with Lieutenant Brodhead and in August, 1847, he was brevetted captain for "gallant and meritorious conduct at Contreras and Cherubusco." Although the phrase seems to be a general catch-all for a brevet or honorary promotion, it did not come easy. Continued exemplary service was required and that was not a common commodity among the lower ranked commissioned officers. Brodhead put forth extra effort and on December 2, 1847, the actual rather than honorary rank of captain was realized. Within seven months the war was over and young Brodhead became a civilian again.[3]

As a civilian, Thornton entered a life of politics and journalism while living in Michigan. It was June, 1849, that Brodhead joined Miss Archangela Macomb Abbott in matrimony in Detroit. Their first child, Josephine Archangela, was born April 1, 1850 and a brother, John Thornton, arrived September 13, 1851. By now the family was living in

Lansing, where Thornton represented District Six as a state senator. After serving one term for the people from Pontiac, Oakland County, he again returned to a private life as a lawyer, living in Trenton, Wayne County.[4]

Brodhead served as the Postmaster for the city of Detroit during the Presidential administration of his former commander, Franklin Pierce. While here, three more daughters were born into the Brodhead family, Mary Jeanette, Ellen Macomb and Catherine Julie. By now attorney Brodhead had become active in politics in the Trenton area and the citizens of District Three elected him to represent them in the state senate in 1859. While serving, again in Lansing, Elizabeth Adams, their sixth child was born.[5]

While his political and legal career flourished, Brodhead found yet another activity to pursue. He became editor and part owner of a local newspaper called the Detroit Free Press. It was in this capacity that Brodhead found it easiest to express his views regarding the politics of both his state and his nation. The site of his home and law office, built in 1855, is now historical site #L0577 and is located at 20604 East River Road in Grosse Isle, Wayne County, southeast of Detroit.[6]

The governor of Michigan appointed Brodhead colonel of the unformed First Michigan Cavalry on August 21, 1861. In less than one month Colonel Brodhead had recruited 1144 officers and men to the service at Camp Lyon near Detroit and on September 13, the men were mustered. With just two weeks of training the command left for the east, bivouacking near Frederick, Maryland, for most of the winter. Much of its service those first few months was in the Blue Ridge Mountains and on the Maryland side of the Potomac River. Towns like Berryville, Leesburg, Winchester, Kernstown and Woodstock and sites such as Snicker's Gap and Cedar Creek were often mentioned in reports and letters home until June of 1862. During these days Colonel Brodhead received the sobriquet "The Federal Ashby," a name meant to bestow an admiration for his courage, daring and respect.[7]

A short letter written to his mother on October 8, 1861, reveals darkness in the thinking and politics of the colonel. These thoughts would again raise their ugly heads almost a year later in a letter to his wife. He told his mother, "I have to fight harder against home enemies than I ever expect to fight against the traitors in the army." What or who these enemies were is unknown but Colonel Brodhead seemed very aware of their existence.[8]

A brief altercation arose in December between the Colonel and some wagoners who had delivered eighty-two wagons to the regiment to be used to move the First Michigan to a different location under the command of General Nathaniel Banks. Brodhead pulled rank and took immediate control of the eighty-two wagons and his regimental quartermaster, detained thirteen six-mule teams, supposedly under the order of General Banks. The teamsters were told they could use their own pleasure about returning to the city of Washington. To add further confusion to the situation, a party of men of the regiment, under the command "of a sergeant" robbed these teamsters of "saddle blankets, curry combs, brushes as well as several overcoats and blankets, private property of the men." These offended men submitted their complaints to the Office of Assistant Quartermaster located at the corner of "G" and 22nd Street in the capital city.[9]

A brief explanation from the Colonel in late December laid the situation to rest. The teamsters had refused to take orders from Brodhead as he was not their commander. Therefore, because of the need for haste, Brodhead simply took the situation in hand and did what he had to do. He confiscated the wagons and kicked the teamsters out of camp. As the wagons needed to be pulled, he authorized his quartermaster to do likewise with the livestock. One of the best qualities of a good officer is assertiveness and Colonel Brodhead had his fair share.[10]

On June 12, 1862, the men and the colonel returned to Virginia from Maryland and arrived in the area of Front Royal on the 16th. Under the command of General Nathaniel Banks who was under the direct command of General John Pope, the men engaged Confederate forces at Cedar Mountain on August 9 with the loss of four men killed, two wounded and three missing. Their opponents at Cedar Mountain were under the very able command of General Thomas J. "Stonewall" Jackson.[11]

General John Buford, Brodhead's immediate superior, on August 17, sent the men of the First Michigan and the Fifth New York on an expedition from Stevensburg, Virginia to Louisa Court House to guard some fords on the rivers in the area. This expedition began a series of events that would eventually bring General Pope's army to battle with General Robert E. Lee near a small village named Manassas Junction, the site of severe fighting the previous year.[12]

Choosing his own paths through the countryside to the assigned destination, Brodhead and his men found themselves moving cautiously toward the village or crossroads known as Verdiersville along the Orange Plank Road. At this crossroads, Confederate General James Ewell Brown Stuart was waiting for General Fitzhugh Lee and his men to join him. Stuart was an impatient man. Action was one of his strong points in all of his operations. Because of this, Major Norman Fitzhugh, Stuart's adjutant general, was sent along the Orange Plank Road to meet Lee and escort him to Stuart who was headquartered at the Rhodes house just a few hundred yards from the crossroads of the village. Major Fitzhugh did not find General Lee. Instead, Colonel Brodhead and his one thousand Federal troopers found Major Fitzhugh. The unlucky officer carried on his saddle two satchels which carried vital information for General Robert E. Lee. Those papers were now in the hands of the Federal troops and would never be delivered.[13]

Very early in the morning of the 18th at the Rhodes house, General Stuart and his men started making preparations for the day while they awaited General Fitzhugh Lee. Among those present besides Stuart was Major Heros Von Borcke, Stuart's massive aide from Prussia. Stuart's personal adjutant, Chriswell Dabney was there and a young captain, rather new to Stuart's command, was there also. This captain was John Singleton Mosby, who, before the war's end, would be a legend that was second to none.[14]

Today, however, Mosby was attached to General Stuart's command and was at Stuart's beck and call. Seeing a large cloud of dust raising on the road, Stuart sent Mosby and a young lieutenant to welcome the men he believed were General Fitzhugh Lee and Major Fitzhugh. Stuart was half right; Major Fitzhugh was returning to camp but under the subjugation of Colonel Brodhead and his Federal cavalrymen as a prisoner of war. As the lieutenant and Mosby approached the column of soldiers, not recognizing them as Yankees, they hailed them and requested that they stop. They were answered abruptly by carbine fire and a charge by Brodhead's troopers. This immediately convinced the two Confederates to reverse direction and flee.[15]

During the following ten minutes, pandemonium ruled in the Confederate bivouac. Von Borcke mounted his horse and galloped through the front gate directly into the middle of the Federal cavalry. A Federal officer, face to face with the giant Prussian, aimed his revolver at him and demanded his surrender. At the very same time, Von Borcke ducked down to his horse's neck, spurred the animal in its flanks and slapped it across its head. All of this startled the Yankee officer and he pulled back for just a brief moment. That was all Von Borcke needed; he and his horse sped away at breakneck speed followed closely by a handful of Union cavalry. In a mile or so these horsemen realized their mounts, tired from the overnight journey, were no match for Von Borcke's fresh mount and they returned to the farm empty-handed.[16]

While this was transpiring, General Stuart was also reacting to the situation. He dropped his blankets and equipment that he was carrying, and bareheaded, bolted for his horse. In a flash he mounted, jumped the rear fence and headed for the wooded area behind the house. Young Dabney, who was still in bed, was the last Confederate to leave the area. He left his bed as well as his side arms, and raced to his horse which was tied to the fence. The knot would not come undone. Frantically he tugged at the reins and, as the knot gave way, he vaulted aboard with bullets from Yankee guns zipping all around him. He too tore off toward the wooded area, trailing his commander by several yards. They united in the wooded area a hundred yards from the house and watched the Yankees swarm over the farm carrying off everything of value and many things that were worthless. Some of the items carried away were Dabney's guns, Stuart's

18

blankets, a cloak and Stuart's famous plumed hat. It was a new hat, just recently received as a result of a bet the general had won.[17]

That bet had been made with Federal General Samuel Crawford just after the battle of Cedar Mountain. At a time of truce, the two officers had wagered whether or not the Confederate victory there would be declared a Federal victory by the northern press. The press did so and Stuart had won the bet. The new plumed hat had been delivered from General Crawford just a few days previous. Stuart's staff reveled in teasing the Confederate horseman concerning the "Union acquisition" and Stuart vowed he would make the Yankees pay dearly for his loss.[18]

Colonel Brodhead left the small crossroads in haste and returned to the Federal lines with Major Fitzhugh and the two satchels which contained important official information. These papers were turned over to General Pope at Culpepper and Pope was quick to move. Troop movements were redirected, and both armies concentrated near Manassas Junction, Virginia, for the second time during the war.[19]

During the battle of Second Manassas General Pope found himself in the unenviable circumstances of trying to extract himself and his army from the front of both General James Longstreet and General "Stonewall" Jackson, located near Henry House Hill, the Warrenton Pike and Matthew's Hill, all prominent landmarks from the campaign of First Manassas. A mile and a half to the south, at Lewis Ford - a crossing of Bull Run Creek - the First Michigan, First West Virginia, First Vermont and the Fourth New York were about to become involved in their own quandary. Their adversary was the very able Colonel Thomas T. Munford and his Second Virginia Cavalry.[20]

As the opposing forces collided with dust and gun smoke clouding the area, Munford quickly realized he was greatly out numbered. He was also decidedly surprised. Before this, Federal Cavalry had been, at best, apprehensive. These Yanks were anything but apprehensive; they were advancing briskly. As the troopers crashed together, the momentum carried these blue and gray lines past each other. Munford realized his Virginians were outnumbered and outmatched. He broke off combat and hurried back to their comrades. Joining with other Virginia commands, such as the Sixth, Seventh and twelfth Virginia, they all threw themselves immediately into combat.[21]

The Federal units from West Virginia and Vermont by now had separated themselves from the New Yorkers and the men from Michigan and only the latter two regiments stood, in line, almost as on parade, awaiting the next Rebel charge. The Twelfth Virginia plowed headlong into the First Michigan and the Seventh engulfed the Fourth New York. Now the Federal troops appeared to be falling apart. There was no organization, just a mixture of men and horses having no direction and trying to escape with their lives. This aspect of the battle was finished and the Federal cavalry was on the run. Colonel Brodhead tried gallantly to rally his men or any men at Lewis Ford making every effort to set up a line of defense. While doing so, Adjutant Lewis Harmon of the Twelfth Virginia, at gun point, demanded Brodhead's immediate surrender. This was out of the question for the colonel. He refused and Harmon immediately shot him twice. Wounded severely, twice in the chest, the colonel tumbled from his horse and was taken prisoner.[22]

The following day, August 31, 1862, Colonel Thomas Brodhead penned the following letter to his wife in Michigan.

"August 31, 1862
My dearest Wife,

I write to you, mortally wounded, from the Battle Field. We are again defeated. And as this reaches you, your children will be Fatherless.

Before I die let me implore you that in some way it may be stated, that General Pope has been outwitted and that McDowell is a traitor. Had they done their duty, as I did mine the dear old Flag had waived in triumph.

I wrote to you this morning. The letter was dated Sunday. It should have been dated as Saturday. And to-day I sink to the green Couch of our final rest   I have fought well, my darling, and I was shot in the endeavor to rally our broken battalions. I could have accepted; but would not run till all hope was gone; and was shot about the only one of our Forces left on the Field. Our cause is just. And our generals - not the Enemy's have defeated us. In God's good time he will give us Victory.

And now, Good bye, Wife and Children. Bring them up, I know you will, in the fear of God and love for our Saviour. But for you and the dear ones so dependent, I should die happy. I know the blow will fall with crushing weight on you. Trust in him who gave Manna in the Wilderness.

Dr. Nash is with me. It is now after midnight; and I have spent most of the night in sending Messages to you.

I send my silver watch to Johnny. And all my Military Equipment at home, guns, saddles & etc are his. The Rebels took my horse, saddle, pistols, and Saber from me as soon as they shot me. It is lucky that I had this pencil and paper in my pocket so as to write you.

Two bullets have gone through my Chest; and directly through the Lungs. I suffer little now, but at first the pain was acute. I have won the Soldier's name, and am ready to meet now, as I must, the Soldier's fate. I hope that from Heaven I may see the glorious old Flag wave again over the individual Union I have loved so well.

Fair well Wife and Babes and Friends. We shall meet again.
Your loving Thornton"[23]

Brodhead died on September 2, Harvard University's first casualty of the Civil War. His remains were taken to Alexandria, Virginia, where they were turned over to his brother, John, an alderman in the city.

They were delivered to his wife and family in Michigan and buried with honors in Section N, Lot # 107, Elmwood Cemetery, Detroit, Michigan. He was awarded a brevet rank of Brigadier General of Volunteers for "his actions at the battle of Bull Run (second) where he was mortally wounded."[24]

On September 10, 1862, a letter from Thornton Brodhead to his brother John was published in the *New York Times* as Brodhead's last letter. The introduction indicated that it was written as he was lying by the water as he was dying and that the "original is covered in blood." He said, "I am passing now from earth, but send you love from my dying couch. For all your love and kindness may you be rewarded? I have fought manfully, and now die fearlessly. I am one of the victims of Pope's imbecility and McDowell's treason. Tell the President, would he save the country, he must not give our hallowed flag into such hands.

But the old flag will triumph yet. - the soldiers will rebuild its poles, now polluted by imbecility and treason. John you owe a duty to your country; write - show up Pope's incompetency, and McDowell's infamy, and force them from places where they can send brave men to assured destruction. I had hoped to live longer, but I die amidst the danger of battle, as I could wish. farewell! In you and the noble officers of my regiment, I confide my wife and children. J."[25]

Colonel Thornton F. Brodhead's letter to his wife at the last moments of his life was soon made public in Washington, D.C. His comments instigated a charge of treason and a court of inquiry was convened to determine General McDowell's guilt or innocence regarding the charge. He was exonerated of the charge. The fact is that the politicians and the military seldom pulled in tandem during the Civil War, or any war. Even after his death, Colonel Brodhead's perseverance to his life commitment of "extreme effort" to succeed persisted.[26]

{1}   John J. Hennessy, *Return to Bull Run - The Campaign and Battle of Second Manassas.* (New York, New York: Simon & Schuster, 1993), pp. 430 – 434

{2}   Record Group 94, Office of the Adjutant General, Compiled Service records. Volunteer Soldiers, Brodhead, Thornton F. - Pension file & Service Record.

{3}   Ibid.

Ihling Bros. & Everhard. eds *Record of Service of Michigan Volunteers in the Civil War 1861 - 1865.* Vol. #31 (Kalamazoo, Michigan 1903)

{4}   Ibid.

{5}   Ibid.

{6}   Ibid.

{7}   Ibid.

John J. Hennessy, *Return to Bull Run - The Campaign and Battle of Second Manassas.* (New York, New York: Simon & Schuster, 1993), p. 42

{8}   Thornton Brodhead to "Mother" Oct 8, 1861 - Burton Historical Collection - Detroit Public Library.

{9}   Record Group 94, Office of the Adjutant General, Compiled Service records. Volunteer Soldiers, Brodhead, Thornton F. -Pension file & Service Record.

{10}   Ibid.

{11}   Robert K. Krick, *Stonewall Jackson at Cedar Mountain* (Chapel Hill, North Carolina: University of North Carolina Press, 1990), pp. 9, 367, 376

{12}   John J. Hennessy, *Return to Bull Run - The Campaign and battle of Second Manassas.* (New York, New York: Simon & Schuster, 1993), p. 42

{13}   Ibid., pp. 45 – 47

{14}   Ibid.

{15}   Ibid.

{16}   Ibid.

{17}   Ibid.

{18}   Ibid.

{19}   Ibid., p. 48

{20}   Ibid., pp. 430 – 435

{21}   Ibid.

{22}   Ibid.

United States War Department. *War of the Rebellion. A Compilation of the Official Records of the Union and Confederate Armies. 128 Vols.* (Washington: 1881 - 1902), Series #1 -- Volume #16 -- August 16 - September 2, 1862 - Campaign in Northern Virginia. No # 193 - Reports of Maj. Gen. James E. B. Stuart, C. S. Army, commanding cavalry of the Army of Northern Virginia, of operations August 16 - September 2.

United States War Department. War of the Rebellion. *A Compilation of the Official Records of the Union and Confederate Armies. 128 Vols.* (Washington: 1881 - 1902), Series #1 -- Volume #16 -- August 16 - September 2, 1862 - Campaign in Northern Virginia. No # 194 - Reports of Brig. Gen. Beverly H. Robertson, C. S. Army, commanding Cavalry Brigade, of operations August 20 - 30.

United States War Department. *War of the Rebellion. A Compilation of the Official Records of the Union and Confederate Armies. 128 Vols.* (Washington: 1881 - 1902), Series #1 -- Volume #16 -- August 16 - September 2, 1862 - Campaign in Northern Virginia. No. #198 - Report of Col. A. W. Harmon, Twelfth Virginia Cavalry, of Skirmish at Lewis' Ford

{23}   Thornton Brodhead to "My dearest Wife" Burton Historical Collection - Detroit Public Library

{24}   Record Group 94, Office of the Adjutant General, Compiled Service records. Volunteer Soldiers, Brodhead, Thornton F. -Pension file & Service Record.

{25}   Thornton Brodhead to "Brother and Sister"" - New York Times - September 10, 1862.

{26}   John J. Hennessy, *Return to Bull Run - The Campaign and Battle of Second Manassas.* (New York, New York: Simon & Schuster, 1993), p. 467

Author's Collection
Private Elijah Curtis
Co. D - 92nd Illinois Infantry
Danville, Kentucky, National Cemetery

III
"I have not received any letters cince I left Rockford"
Private Elijah Curtis
Co. D - 92nd Illinois Infantry

Polo, Illinois is a small city located one hundred and twenty miles northwest of Chicago. Just a few miles from Polo was the small settlement of Elkhorn and it was here that twenty-four-year-old Elijah Curtis made his home with his widowed father and his younger sister, Mary Jane. The Curtis family of three farmed a small acreage and managed to scratch out a meager living. On August 22, 1862, Elijah traveled to Polo and entered his name in the rolls of the 92nd Illinois Infantry. He stayed in the area until the end of the month when he embarked on his journey that would eventually find him north of Rockford, Illinois at a place called Churchill's Grove to muster into the regiment at Camp Fuller.[1]

He wrote his first short letter to Mary Jane just after he arrived.

"Dear Sister
            Camp Foller, Rockford
                        August 31/62
                                    I started From frepoort At ten O clock Friday knight and got to rockford of A quarter to twelve and came up to camp   I like it very well   we Marched Some yester day   we are in the pretest place I ever Saw. there is going to be Preaching in camp to day at three O clock   I Saw Cal and John white and lots of others Boys   I dont expect to Stay till Wnesday   if I cant get Away Sooner   our Barracks are in A prety place on the ground   Some of the Boys are writing   henry Smith I dont Know what he is doing   I dont Know as I have any more to Say

                        Mary J. Curtis
            Direction
                        Rockford Ill
in care of capt Preston"[2]

The men of the 92nd were mustered into the service on September 4, 1862 and Elijah was assigned to serve in Company D with other men from the Polo area under the command of Captain Lyman Preston. The men began their training in earnest and, after three weeks, young Elijah again wrote his sister:

"Dear Sister
            Camp Fuller   Sept
                               23st 1862
                                    I take My Pen in hand to write you A

few lines to you I just had time to write Before cince I come Back I feel better then when I Started up here. I Stood gard Sunday and Monday Tell ten O clock I have gote them things that Mrs Jones Brot up here She left them with Mell Doddson well I Must go to diner I have Ben to diner I must Finish this letter and write another Before two O clock the pay master was here yester day and Paid off the Seventy4 Reg and we thought he was going to Pay us to day but I heard he was run out of Money and he was gone to chigago But I dont know how it is there is So many Big lies told John whites company left before I got back I dont know as I have Any more to Say At present

Excuse All Mistakes   Elijah Curtis"[3]

When training was completed, in October, 1862, the men of the 92nd left Camp Fuller, their comfortable barracks and northern Illinois for the south, having no idea where they would finish their journey. It was at Camp Covington, Kentucky, across the Ohio River from Cincinnati, Ohio where they first encamped and Elijah wrote again to his family, describing his journey South and the hazzards of travel in those days.[4]

"Camp Covington
Oct 12/62
Dear Sister
  We got throw Safe we Started from Rockford Friday morning twenty minutes of Eight O clock and got in chigago at half past one and Marched around town till I had A Notion to throw off My Napsack and then we went in the great union Depot and Staid till about nine O clock and we Started we got to Michigan City at twelve at twelve inn the knight there is so much Sand there it looked white I Saw one fence almost drifted over with Sand just like Snow we went on and the first thing I new in the Morning we was in the State of indianna in the knight three cars got loos and we went three miles Before they found it out then one of the engines had to go back indiinna is A low flat and watery State corn aint very good nor the houses either there is Some very good But they are few and Scattering there is good many little towns on the road there is lots of land that is not taken up Some barrens & when we got to the wabash river the train had to Stop the Bridge was out of rig there was Some men fixing it when we come we Stopped about three hours and the train run Back three miles and Switched off and put the Enjines on behind and Shoved the cars across the bridge the Boys all walked across and then we had two miles to go to layfayette it is quite A town we Stayed there about two hours we got out dinner and Started on again and got to Indinaplos little after Sun down it is A fine citySity it was more like home than any place on the road it was About dark and I could not See much Between layfayette and Indinaplos is most all timber we did not Stay long in indinaplos Just as we Started Some of the cars broke loose

again But we did not go fare   we had to go Back about hald a Mile   I went to Sleep after that   Some times I would wake up and the cars would run like every thing and other times they would be Stoped to water   But I did not no much till we got to Cincinattia   it was about 4 O clock this morning this is a very large citySity But I dont think there is as pretty houses as there is in chigago   we Staid in the cars About half an hour this morning and then we Marched two miles and A half to camp across the ohio river about A mile into Kentucky to camp Covington and there I am now   it dont look much like Sunday to day   the captings are putting up there tents we will hafto Sleep out of dors to knight   our tents is not come yet   henry Smith is going on gard   he told me to tell that it depended on him to Save 15000 men   this is all to day   Direct to Camp Covington kentucky   92 reg com D in care of cap Preston   Elijah Curtis"[5]

On October 19 the regiment moved east, passing through Cynthiana to Mt. Sterling. The regiment's stay at Mt. Sterling was very short. The men spent their time guarding the city and western Kentucky from the rebel guerillas led by a cold blooded killer named Champ Ferguson. November found the regiment of Illinois farm boys camped at Nicholasville, Kentucky still training and doing guard duty where needed. Elijah wrote home, telling of his life as a soldier.

"November 19th/1862
Dear Sister
I received your letter this evening   it is raining to Knight like Sixty   it is Ben railing more or less ever Since Sunday Knight and we have been travelling all the time   we Started from Mt Sterling last Friday and went four miles north of there Sunday   we Started Back again throw Mt Sterling and Back throw Lexington   we are now encamped about half A mile from Nicholasville this Side of town   I dont know weather we will march to morrow or not   I have march this trip But I have not carried my napsack   this is A poor place to write   So never mind   I received A letter from P.W. Dodds this evening also   I have not received Williams yet   Chapter 2 November 20   I did not write much last knight   the Boys would not keep Still   Henry Smith the darned shit was the worst one   So we did not march to day and I have A chance to Scribble A little   it is raining A little yet   we have had quite A task About the negroes to Mt Sterling But I gues it will come out all right   I forgot to tell you in the last when we was to covington I saw Ephraim Kingery   he is first Lieutenant in the 115 regment ill   they were Camped A little ways from us   he wanted to know if you was married yet or not & the last time I Saw him was when we was to Lexington the first time   I dont know whare he is now   you want to know what we haft to eat   we live First rate   we have crackers Beaf pork coffee Sugar molassas and Sometimes corn cakes and once and A while A turkey and Sometimes A little honey and Sometimes

Potatoes   O I tell you we live well   the other knight I was on picket in the morning we went to a house and got our Brakfast   he did not like to give it to us But he had to   he was A rank Secsh   I suppose we will march to morrow   I can not tell you all the mistakes you made in this letter   I am quite well to day   give my best Old Specks to all my inquiring Friends   Elijah Curtis
Excuse all Mistakes and Bad Spelling and Sctibbling &"[6]

On November 26, the regiment arrived in Danville, Kentucky, where they were immediately stationed along the Louisville and Nashville Railroad to prevent damage to that line by Confederate General John Hunt Morgan's forces.[7]

From here Elijah sent one more letter home:

"Nov 29th/62

Dear Sister
I dont now as I can write much as my rist is lame yet   I aint Ben Able to do any thing Since A week ago last Sunday   I was riding on the waging and we Come to A toll gate   two other Boys was on and My Self when it come to us   I was Behind them on the load   they took holt of the gate and the weight come off the end   the Poll come down on the load and took me off and Strained my rist bad and hurt my knee   I had to ride in the ambulance wagon   we are about three miles from town   we got here yester day About three O clock   there was three regments here Before we come and there is three more coming on to Camp now.   I Suppose we will Start again tomorrow morning   I Suppose that Father got that letter that henry Smith rote when we was in Falmonth   the next town we camped in was cynthiana on the Morning of the twenty Six   So there was Snow about four inches deep or more   Sunday night we camped to Paris   Monday morning we Started to lexington and got four miles from town and we camped for the day for Some reason I dont now   yester day 28 we came Fifteen miles   I have Seen more Black men and women then any thing else from Covington to cynthiana   it is not worth fighting for But from cynthiana to Lexington is A fine country   I have not received any letters cince I left rockford   I am expecting Some every day   I feel pretry well except A cold   I dont now as I have any moore to Say as my rist is getting tired   E.Curtis Direct to me By the way of Cincinnati Company D 92 Ill"[8]

When the regiment returned, to Danville, Elijah was hospitalized, entering General Regimental Hospital #2 on January 23, 1863, with a severe case of jaundice. Jaundice is the progress of malarial fever which is a result of morbid changes to the liver. A marked yellow coloration of the body is present and is often most noticeable in the whites of the eyes. As the condition progresses in severity the tongue will usually become heavily coated or furred, and very dry during the intermittent fevers. Occasionally the tongue will turn a dark brown in color. Diarrhea becomes prominent but there are also occasional bouts of severe constipation suffered by the patient. A constant excessive thirst and vomiting accompanies severe pain and cramps in the lower abdomen. As death approaches the patient becomes delirious, develops a heavy cough and profuse sweats which are then followed by coma and convulsions.

As early as 1820 the use of heavy doses of quinine was discovered to be a temporary relief for the disease. Three to five grains given three or four times a day was the usually dosage but physicians experimented with this form of treatment according to their own individual beliefs.

The cause of malaria was totally unknown at the time of the Civil War. Such beliefs as soils undergoing the natural process of decomposition under the combined influence of heat and moisture were one such theory. Therefore the presence of swampy area, marches, river bottoms, bayous, ponds, dams and canals were to be avoided. The studies of the causes of this disease in works of the time are a fascinating study in futility and simple guessing.[9] It was not until the medical work done during the building of the Panama Canal in Central America that Doctors Colonel William Gorgas and Major Walter Reed discovered the cause and the prevention of malaria in the early twentieth century. By draining and removing the swamps and other standing waters, the cause of malaria, mosquitoes, was eliminated and preventative measures were undertaken.

Young Elijah Curtis never recovered. He died on February 16, 1863, and is buried in Section #5, grave #29 located in the Danville City Cemetery, Boyle County, Kentucky. The only surviving information concerning Elijah Curtis is included in the five letters he sent home to his sister while he was embarked on his military career. When he lost his life, it is possible that his father and sister were never informed of the final disposition of the soldier. He was hospitalized, away from the men in his regiment and the friends in his company. They continued the war and Elijah was simply one of the forgotten. Neither his sister nor his father ever applied for a pension for their Elijah, thus information about him is precious little.[10]

{1}   Record Group 94, Office of the Adjutant General, Compiled Service records. Volunteer Soldiers, Curtis, Elijah - Pension file & Service Record.

{2}   Elijah Curtis to "Dear Sister" August 31, 1862 - Collection of Frank Crawford

{3}   Elijah Curtis to "Dear Sister" Sept 23st, 1862 - Collection of Frank Crawford

{4}   Ibid.

{5}   Elijah Curtis to "Dear Sisiter" Oct 12/62 - Collection of Frank Crawford

{6}   Elijah Curtis to "Dear Sister" November 19th, 1862 - Collection of Frank Crawford

{7}   Frederick H. Dyer, A *Compendium of the War of the Rebellion - Two Volumes.* (Dayton, Ohio: National Historical Society. The Press of Morningside Bookshop. 1979), Volume #2, p. 1085

{8}   Elijah Curtis to "Dear Sister" Nov 29th, 1862 - Collection of Frank Crawford

{9}   Surgeon General Joseph K. Barnes, United States Army – *The Medical And Surgical History Of The War Of The Rebellion. (1861-65)* (Washington Printing Office, 1870), Reprinted by Broadfoot Publishing Company – Wilmington, North Carolina 28405 – 1990 – 15 vols. Vol V, pp. 129 – 190.

{10}   Record Group 94, Office of the Adjutant General, Compiled Service records. Volunteer Soldiers, Curtis, Elijah - Pension file & Service Record.

Colonel John N. Cromwell
47th Illinois Infantry

IV
"...accept a kiss for yourself and boys."
Colonel John Nelson Cromwell
47th Illinois Infantry

On March 23rd, 1830, Mr. and Mrs. Morris Nelson Cromwell became the parents of a son, John Nelson. John would spend his childhood playing and becoming educated in Plainfield, Union County, New Jersey. His grandfather, Jeremiah Wilson Cromwell had arrived in the area from England in the late eighteenth century and farmed there for years.[1]

On November 17, 1852, when John – or, as he was occasionally called, Nelson - was twenty-two years old, he married eighteen year old Miss Sarah M. Brokaw in her father's home also located in Plainfield. Two sons were born to the young family. The first, William Nelson, was born in New York City during January of 1854 and the second, Charles H., arrived in May of 1856, just after the family had taken up residence at their new home in Peoria, Illinois. As a new settler in the western frontier of this state, Nelson, a skilled silver platter and engraver, became financially well-off and highly regarded by the people in the community.[2]

On July 9, 1856, Cromwell was asked to join the local militia unit called the Peoria National Blues. Three days later Private Cromwell became Second Lieutenant Cromwell, and in one year he advanced to the rank of first lieutenant. Silver plating, engraving and assuming a leadership role in the local militia unit was indeed making life for the Cromwell family very acceptable in the heartland of the country.[3]

Committees were formed for every possible aspect of the formation of the Blues. One committee was appointed to compose both by-laws and a constitution. Yet another was formed to raise funds by subscription from citizens in the city. A small committee acquired music for the organization and yet another looked for and found a location suitable for the militia to practice and learn proper military drill and etiquette. These were all appointed on July 9, 1856 at a meeting held at Firehouse #2 on North Adams Street. Three days later at a second meeting at the same place, these duties were reported as accomplished and a muster roll of members was created. Efficiency and purpose seemed to be the watchword for these future Civil War heroes.[4].

Also at the second meeting a committee was formed to give the organization a name while another was created to give the men uniforms. Officers for the first year were elected. All four would be dead before the war was over. Chosen as captain was Charles E. Denison who would be mortally wounded on December 31, 1862 while serving as captain of a company in the Eighteenth United States Infantry at the battle of Stones River, Murfreesboro, Tennessee. Denison would die of those wounds on

January 15, 1863 at Nashville, Tennessee. First Lieutenant was John Bryner, a future colonel of the 47th Illinois. Second Lieutenant was John N. Cromwell and Third Lieutenant was William A. Thrush, yet another future colonel of the 47th Illinois.[5]

The Peoria National Blues, like so many similar organizations, both North and South in the nation at this time, served as a much needed training opportunity for many future Civil War soldiers. The Blues certainly contributed greatly to the roles of brave citizen soldiers that would serve their nation so admirably during the coming hostilities.[6]

John Bryner was one of the primary organizers of the Blues and, during the war, a Colonel of the 47th Illinois Volunteer Infantry. His service cost him his health and he eventually was forced to resign his commission. He died in Springfield, Illinois on March 19, 1865, a broken man.[7]

Otto Funk, another member of the Blues, became Colonel of the Eleventh Illinois Cavalry and, as a result of his dedication and service, he was given the brevet rank of Brigadier General at the end of the war. The Civil War history of the Eleventh Cavalry is indeed impressive; including such actions as took place at Shiloh, Tennessee and Corinth, Mississippi as well as countless other expeditions during the course of the war.[8]

Another original member of the Peoria city militia was David P. Grier who served admirably as Colonel of the 77th Illinois Volunteer Infantry and led the regiment with much pride and ability, participating in such battles as Chickasaw Bayou, Arkansas Post, Vicksburg and the Red River Campaign in Louisiana. Likewise, Colonel Grier was advanced to the rank of Brevet Brigadier General at the close of the war. Young John Hough was promoted during his service to the rank of Assistant Adjutant General and likewise was brevetted as a Brigadier General at the close of the war.[9]

Even more men from the Peoria Blues rose to officer rank during the Civil War. Joseph Barr became a lieutenant in the Eighth Missouri Infantry before he accepted an appointment to the Chicago Mercantile Battery. He was mortally wounded at the battle of Sabine Crossroads in Louisiana on April 8, 1864 and died of his wounds on the battlefield that night. Lieutenant Maurice Dee, another Blues militiaman, was accidentally shot while serving with the Eleventh Illinois Cavalry at Vicksburg, Mississippi and died at the Overton Hospital which was located in Memphis, Tennessee on November 16, 1864.[10]

John D. McClure became Colonel of the 47th Illinois as a result of Colonel Cromwell's death. Addison J. Norton advanced to the rank of Colonel of the Seventeenth Illinois Infantry. Norton saw action in the battles of Ironton, Missouri, Shiloh, Tennessee and Vicksburg, Mississippi before being raised to the brevet rank of Brigadier General at the end of hostilities. As well, William A. Thrush, yet another Peoria citizen that was instrumental in the formation of the Blues became the first colonel of the

47th Illinois and it was his death, at Corinth, Mississippi, on October 3, 1862, that created the vacancy in rank which allowed John Cromwell to be promoted.[11]

At least thirty-four members of the Peoria National Blues acquired prominent positions in several state regiments during the Civil War and one, Archibald S. Palmer, commanded a United States vessel on the Mississippi River during the war. The Peoria Blues were extremely well represented during the conflict.[12]

The political and social atmosphere which began to intensify across the United States, both in the North as well as the South, also became evident in Peoria, Illinois. After the firing on Fort Sumter in Charleston, South Carolina's harbor in mid April of 1861, an effort was made throughout the northern states to suppress the desires of the southern citizens of the country from seceding from its membership as a state within the nation. Three month or ninety day regiments were created for this assignment but they proved unequal to the task. Thus, by autumn of 1861, three year regiments were created in Illinois as well as other northern states. On August 16, 1861, the 47th Regiment, Illinois Infantry Volunteers, mustered into the country's service at Camp Lyon on the outskirts of the city of Peoria. Part of the men that were enlisted became Company A. They were raised or recruited by Captain John N. Cromwell and, as a token of their devotion and admiration, on the 22nd of the month they presented him with his officer's sword. The men of the Peoria Blues were indeed going off to war.[13]

When the regiment finished with their rudimentary training at Camp Lyon, they moved on September 23 to St. Louis, Missouri and then, in early October, further west to Jefferson City, the capitol of Missouri. Simple garrison duty filled the hours there until late December. On the 22nd the men of the regiment marched west fifty miles to Otterville where they remained for yet another month of garrison duty and further drill and training. In early February their next move took them to the small village of Commerce, Missouri where they began preparations for the National Army's operations against Island #10, in the Mississippi River, and New Madrid.[14]

The regiment's first experience under fire came at New Madrid, Missouri on March 5. According to Private Van Meter of Company B, the 47th's Captain Cromwell greatly impressed the men of the regiment by his calm behavior under this first fire. While the men all seemed to "crawl into a hole and pull the hole in after us," Cromwell stood, apart from the regiment and continued to observe one of the southern fortifications through his field glasses.[15]

After the March 5th fall of New Madrid and the March 7th fall of Point Pleasant there came more action with the capture of Tiptonville on April 8. The time between April 13 and 29 had the men pass through Fort Pillow on the Tennessee side of the Mississippi River and then to Hamburg

Landing further south. On April 29 the men were involved in the slow advance on and the siege of Corinth, Mississippi.

During these operations in Corinth, the action at Farmington, Mississippi was also written about by Private Van Meter who remembered it vividly. While the regiment waited in ambush behind a ridge, Captain Cromwell went on hands and knees to the top of the ridge and, from behind the brush, he observed every movement of the southern troops at the front. When, at last, orders were received to advance on the enemy, Captain Cromwell was the first on his feet, encouraging the men to charge and follow him. Having observed the enemy from afar, John Cromwell was aware of where to lead the troops when they reached the top of the protective ridge. For this, after the battle, Cromwell was promoted to the rank of Major. Without doubt others than Van Meter witnessed Cromwell's coolness and appreciated its effect on the enlisted men in the ranks. "A Major's place," he related, "was to the rear of the center of the regiment." As a major, however, Private Van Meter felt that Cromwell was "nettled" to be "shielded by a breast works of his own men." However, from his assigned place his "clear ringing voice could be heard cheering the boys on."[16]

From May 31st to June 12th, the 47th Illinois was in pursuit of the Confederate forces that were able to withdraw from their fortifications at Corinth, Mississippi under the nose of the new Federal Commander General Henry Halleck who had assumed command of the National troops when he was unsatisfied and, perhaps, a bit envious of the fame that General U. S. Grant gained after Grant's successes at Forts Henry and Donelson and the battle of Shiloh. It was during this time that Cromwell became ill and requested a medical leave of absence to restore his health.

On June 24th, 1862, Major Cromwell wrote a letter of resignation to General Halleck. It seems there were situations that had developed within the National Army that Cromwell was not willing to abide by or accept as the way things should be. The complicated turn of events is best explained by Major Cromwell.

"Camp Clear Creek, Miss

June 24th 1862
To Major Genl Halleck
                    Sir
                              I respectfully tender my resignation under the following circumstances, In a charge in driving in the Enemies pickets before Corinth on the 28th of May, Owing to the Extreme heat of the day I was sun struck, and rendered unfit for duty, but on the Evacuation of Corinth anxious to be with my regiment I went on duty in pursuit of the Enemy and continued on duty to my detriment to the 10th of June when I was attacked with Intermittent fever, which completely prostrated me, I

33

applied to the Surgeon of my regiment for a certificate on which to found a Leave of Absence for twenty days which was granted, approved, and forwarded, by my Lieut-Col. Comndg. but was returned citing me to appear before the Medical Director of the right wing of the Army of the Miss. for Examination which I did by being taken in an ambulance to his quarters, he fully recommended and Endorsed my application but my papers were returned a Second time disapproved. I Enlisted in the volunteer army on the 16th day of Aug. 1861 and have served faithfully as Captain of Co. A without being absent until the 9th of May 1862 at which time my Lieut Col was killed. I was appointed Major of my Regt and have served in that capacity until taken sick, anxious to do my duty in the Service of my country, my highest considerations are my family first. I do therefore respectfully decline any further service and hope my resignation will be approved.

With Respect

John N. Cromwell

Major 47th Regt Ills Vols"[17]

This letter was endorsed by Lt. Colonel Thrush and sent through the chain of command to General Halleck. On June 27th it was simply marked "Disapproved - By order Maj Gen Halleck" while Halleck was still at Corinth, Mississippi.[18]

On July 3rd the men of the 47th left Corinth, Mississippi to Rienzie, in the same state and served there until the middle of August. They then marched to Tuscumbia, Alabama in mid August and back to Clear Creek, Mississippi by early September. A very sick and disheartened Major Cromwell accompanied them the entire distance.

It was at the battle of Iuka, Mississippi, September 19, 1862, while the 47th Illinois Volunteers were under the command of General William S. Rosecrans that Major Cromwell became a prisoner of war. At the close of the day's fighting the regiment was ordered to make a counter charge into the advancing Confederate troops. After a volley fire by the men from Illinois, they advanced on the Confederate soldiers and eventually were able to drive them from the field of combat. Major Cromwell, in order to make the best possible shots with his revolver, moved to the front of the regiment. The fighting ceased and the men in the ranks laid their exhausted bodies down for a much needed sleep, their loaded guns in their hands, with guards placed to protect the resting soldiers. Major Cromwell was placed in charge of the placement of the pickets and, in doing so; he strayed into the enemy lines and was taken captive by the Rebels.[19]

On October 3rd, Colonel Thrush was killed in action at the battle of Corinth. Although Lieutenant Colonel Samuel Baker was next in line for command and, although Major John Cromwell was a prisoner of war in the hands of the enemy, Major Cromwell was promoted to the rank of Colonel. Cromwell was paroled at Vicksburg, Mississippi by his captives on

September 26th and sent with other parolees to Benton Barracks, just south of St. Louis, Missouri. After a brief visit with his wife and family in Peoria, Cromwell returned to Benton Barracks and served on a court martial board until exchanged.[20]

Just after his return from his family he wrote;

"St Louis   December 11th, 62

My Dear Wife

I arrive here safe in due time after I left you. found all things right - reported to Col Conrad - all was well - got back just in time. I do not Expect to remain here a great while. I am Exchanged and am now waiting orders from war department to return to my regt - which I think will be soon - I have my Commission in my pocket as Col. of the 47th and have put the Eagle on my shoulder. and there I Expect it will remain until I see propper to take it off. I have just met Mr Malam Vail of Plainfield he will carry this to you with my best wishes. he recognized me or I should not have known him.

Sallie I do not know what to write about there is no news in this place. All I can say is that I am well, but oh how home sick. I wish this unholy rebellion was at a close so that we could be togather once more but I hope for the best,

I have just returned from the Barracks where I have been holding court martial and will continue Daily until I am ordered to my Regt.

and now My Dear in the absence of any news I will say good bye accept a kiss for yourself and boys and believe me your affectionate Husband until death.

Nelson

Love to all - write soon and often and direct

Col J. N. Cromwell
Plantation House
St. Louis Mo

You need not say care of Oliver Hall"[21]

There Cromwell remained until his orders allowed him to rejoin his men in late February. He was included as present for duty in the March rolls of the 47th Regiment where they were located at Ridgeway Station, Tennessee guarding the railroad.

On March 12th, the men in The Eagle Brigade, named for their celebrated mascot, Old Abe, an American Bald Eagle, left for Memphis, Tennessee and the beginning of their participation in General U.S. Grant's Vicksburg Campaign. These regiments, besides the 47th Illinois were the eighth Wisconsin, the Eleventh Missouri, the Fifth Minnesota and the Second Iowa Artillery under the immediate command of General Joseph "Wolf" Mower, were also often referred to as "Joe Mower's Jack Ass

Cavalry." The brigade, in the Fifteenth Army Corps, was commanded by General William T. Sherman. When the regiment arrived at Helena, Arkansas on board the Steamer *Empress* they were disembarked and remained in that river city for ten days when they again boarded a steamer and arrived at Duckport, Louisiana on April 1st. Here they served as guards where needed and also loaded and unloaded steam boats, dug proposed canals to divert the waters of the Mississippi River and slept on any dry area found to keep out of the flood waters of the river.[22]

A rather uneventful April and first two weeks of May found Cromwell and his men of the 47th involved heavily at Jackson, Mississippi. On the 14th of May the city of Jackson was virtually abandoned by the men under the command of General Joseph Johnston, C.S.A. and the National troops took full advantage of the material and buildings in the city for the following two days. The Eagle Brigade, the 47th Illinois included, camped in the yards around the State Capitol Building where the Confederate soldiers, prisoners of war, were housed under the charge of Colonel John N. Cromwell.[23]

These men were all paroled on the following day, May 15th and the sick and wounded National soldiers were housed at the Daniels Hotel nearby under the charge of Surgeon Henry S. Hewitt. The following day Federal troops began withdrawing from Jackson, their ultimate destination being Vicksburg, Mississippi forty miles to the west on the Mississippi River. The last men to leave were the members of The Eagle Brigade.[24]

As an act of consideration for the wounded soldiers, seemingly about to become abandoned in the hospital building in Jackson, Colonel Cromwell returned to them for a few last words of encouragement and to bolster their spirits, knowing that they were soon to become prisoners of war as Cromwell had been just a few months previous. As he left the men, knowing that Confederate forces were entering the city at the moment, he mounted his sorrel mare which he had purchased from Lieutenant J. Woodworth of Company C - the Eighth Wisconsin Regiment in early March and headed west to rejoin his men and the rest of the brigade. Shortly after his departure Colonel Cromwell was cut off by an advance guard of Confederate Cavalry scouts near the public square and ordered to surrender. At this moment, the final minute of Cromwell's life is uncertain. One report stated that he wheeled his horse upon hearing the command to surrender, spurred her heavily and, in the process, was shot four times through the body by the Confederate patrol. Another narrative recounts that Cromwell simply turned his horse to face his enemy and surrendered, when he was shot by a single pistol shot fired by Lieutenant Addison Harvey, future leader of a group of southern soldiers called Harvey's Scouts who were at the time under the command of General Wirt Adams.[25]

This may well have been the first action that Harvey's Scouts participated in as a single command. Reports of their activity indicate that on May 16th, 1863, they captured twenty eight men at Jackson, Mississippi and killed one Federal officer. Those twenty eight men must have been the men in the Daniels Hotel that were sick and wounded and the one man that was killed had to be Colonel John Nelson Cromwell of the 47th Illinois Infantry. This would, it seems, make Cromwell the last casualty of the battle of Jackson.[26]

Ironically, Captain Harvey was assassinated April 20, 1865, at Columbus, Georgia by a man that Captain Harvey had caught stealing a horse belonging to a Scout. A fight started and Captain Harvey ran the thief away from the camp. Later, that same night the man returned and, finding Captain Harvey alone, slipped behind the officer and shot him in the head, killing him instantly.[27]

The deposition of Cromwell's body is, in ways, as intriguing as his demise. The body was carried by citizens of the city to the Daniels Hotel where its owner directed that it be washed and prepared for burial. Mr. Daniels, a member of the Masonic Lodge as was Colonel Cromwell, purchased an eighty dollar casket for the burial. Because the sexton for the city cemetery refused to allow the remains to be buried in the local cemetery, Mr. Daniels demanded that, since he owned a large plot in the cemetery, he had proper authorization as to who should be buried in it and so it was done. He paid an additional twenty dollars for the digging of the grave because, again, the sexton refused to allow his workers to do so. As a result of this act of compassion by Mr. Daniels, his hotel was burned to the ground the following day by angry citizens of the city.

After the war, in November, 1865, Mr. H.C. Hudson of Newark, New Jersey and a friend of the Cromwell family arrived at Jackson, at the family's request, to claim the remains of the late Colonel. After a bit of partisan hassle by a few local citizens in Jackson, Mr. Hudson, with the assistance of Major Barnes, Commander of the Post of Jackson and some 800 United States Colored Troops, recovered Cromwell's remains, escorted it solemnly through the streets of Jackson to the railroad depot. There, on November 28th they departed for Plainfield, New Jersey. Eight days later the casket arrived in New York City and was transported to Newark, New Jersey for embalming. It was placed in a handsome coffin with silver mountings and on the 6th of December it was removed to Plainfield for its final burial.[28]

On Monday morning, the 11th of December, 1865, the remains of Colonel John N. Cromwell of the 47th Illinois Infantry were laid to their final rest at Evergreen Cemetery, conducted to that grave site by the Elizabeth, New Jersey Rifle Corps, one of the oldest and best militia organizations in the state. A gallant Peoria National Blue was laid to rest by the appreciative New Jersey Rifles.[29]

Private William Van Meter of the 47th Illinois Regiment Volunteer Infantry, over forty-five years later, in a letter to Colonel Cromwell's oldest son, William, voiced his undying praise of his colonel:

"Your father, Colonel John N. Cromwell, was a Loyal Citizen, a Brave Soldier, a Perfect Gentleman, and to sum it all up in one word, A Man !"[30]

{1}   Record Group 94, Office of the Adjutant General, Compiled Service records. Volunteer Soldiers, Cromwell, John Nelson - Pension file & Service Record.

{2}   Ibid.

{3}   Editors - *The History of Peoria County* (Johnson & Company, Chicago, Illinois – 1880)

{4}   Ibid.

{5}   Ibid.

{6}   Ibid.

{7}   Ibid.

{8}   Ibid.

{9}   Ibid.

{10}   Ibid.

{11}   Ibid.

{12}   Ibid.

{13}   Ibid.

{14}   Ibid.

        Record Group 94, Office of the Adjutant General, Compiled Service records. Volunteer Soldiers, Cromwell, John Nelson - Pension file & Service Record.

{15}   Brigadier General J.N. Reece, *Report of the Adjutant General of the State of Illinois* - (Springfield, Illinois - 1900), Volume 111, pp. 405 - 453.

{16}   Letter from William H. Van Meter to William Nelson Cromwell - undated - Illinois State Historical Library

{17}   Ibid.

{18}   Ibid.

{19}   Ibid.

{20}   Record Group 94, Office of the Adjutant General, Compiled Service records. Volunteer Soldiers, Cromwell, John Nelson - Pension file & Service Record.

{21}   John Nelson Cromwell to "Dear Wife", December 11, 1862 - Illinois State Historical Library

{22}   William H. Van Meter to William Nelson Cromwell - undated - Illinois State Historical Library.

        Brigadier General J.N. Reece, *Report of the Adjutant General of the State of Illinois* (Springfield, Illinois - 1900) Volume 111, pp. 405 - 453.

{23}   William H. Van Meter to William Nelson Cromwell - undated - Illinois State Historical Library.

{24}   Ibid.

{25}   Ibid.

        The Death of Col. Cromwell - Peoria Daily Transcript, Peoria, Illinois, June 22, 1863.

        Col. Cromwell - Peoria Daily Transcript, Peoria, Illinois, June 23,

1863.

     The Death of Col. Cromwell - Peoria Daily Transcript, Peoria, Illinois. July 31, 1863.

{26}   Edwin C. Bearss & Warren Grabau, *The Battle of Jackson - May 14, 1863* (Publication Sponsored by The Jackson Civil War Roundtable, Inc., Gateway Press, Inc, 1981), pp. 3 - 34.

     Cloyd Bryner, *Bugle Echoes: The Story of Illinois 47th Infantry* (Springfield, 1905), p. 79

     Wiley Nash, *Harvey's Scouts*, 1914 - Madison Co., Ms
http://www.rootsweb.com/~msmadiso/harveyscouts/

{27}   Sue Skay Abruscato & Mary Abruscato Hara, Harvey's Scouts, 2001
http://www.rootsweb.com/~msmadiso/harveyscouts/

{28}   *The Late Col. Cromwell* - Plainfield Union, Plainfield, New Jersey, December 12, 1865.

{29}   Ibid.

{30}   Letter from William H. Van Meter to William Nelson Cromwell - undated - Illinois State Historical Library.

V

"Remain your faithful husband until death."
Private Isaac Overall
Co. I - 36th Ohio Infantry

Like far too many soldiers in the Civil War, not a great deal is known about Isaac Overall of Chambersburg, Ohio. The date of his birth can only be guessed. He gave his age, at the time of his enlistment on January 8, 1862, as thirty-two years. The rather tall, 6' ½", older soldier was a property owner in the Ohio River town as indicated by his purchase of a city lot in 1859. Isaac and his wife, the former Martha Jane Proctor, had been married on September 21, 1851 by the Reverend Hiram Newman in Gallia County.[1]

The fifty dollars the young couple paid for their property was, at the time, a fair sum of money, particularly for a family with three small children. A daughter, Florence Virginia, had been born to the laborer, born in Tennessee, and his wife in the spring of 1854. The little girl soon became big sister to two brothers, Jacob Asbury, born in the spring of 1856 and John William, born in the summer of 1858. Another son, Jasper Newton, was born in the spring of 1860.[2]

When the dark complexioned, dark haired father enlisted and mustered into Company I of the 36th Ohio Volunteer Infantry, he immediately was sent to join his regiment, then camped at Summersville, West Virginia where it had been posted since mid September 1861.[3]

The command was under the leadership of Colonel George Crook, a graduate of the United States Military Academy at West Point, New York, class of 1852. Young Crook had previously been assigned to the Fourth United States Infantry but he was requested to command the Ohio Volunteers. Shortly after the battle of Antietam, near Sharpsburg, Maryland, he would be promoted to the rank of Brigadier General of Volunteers. As an Indian fighter after the Civil War, he was engaged in the Battle of the Rose Bud in Montana which took place just before the Battle of the Little Big Horn in June of 1876. He was also instrumental in the capture of the great Apache Chiricahua Indian Chief, Geronimo, in the Arizona Territory in 1886.[4]

Private Isaac Overall posted his first letter home, February 19, 1862, at Summersville in what is now West Virginia. His health, he said, was good, with the "exception of a cold" and the men were, he felt, "well satisfied." There was, Isaac informed Jane, "a good winter qarters and good clothing and plenty to eat." Isaac was also concerned for the children; he asked that Jane inform him "how they ar and tell me how you ar geting a long."[5]

Just a few weeks later, Isaac sent another letter from Camp

41

Summersville. This letter has greatly suffered the ravages of time, making transcription tenuous in certain sections. One corner has been destroyed by age or insect or both. Nonetheless its message of boredom of camp and loneliness is clearly conveyed for the absent father. His statement that "I would like to see you all mity well" was an echo of the sentiments of so many of the absent soldiers of the time, North or South.[6]

His longing for home and family was evident in yet another letter to his "Dear Wife" written March 17, 1862. Isaac was "glad to hear that the nabors is good to you. Tell them I thank them very kindly for their kindness to you and the children."

Isaac's mail from home was, it appears, at least sufficient if not bountiful. He mentioned receiving letters from Jane as well as from other members of his far away family. Isaac mentioned, in this letter, sending articles home such as a blanket as well as his "likeness." Signing his letter, "Isaac Overall to Jane Overall and children" he finished by requesting "write soon as you can."[7]

By May, although still at Summersville, Isaac was able to report to his family some military activity. By then he had participated in a five day "scout" after horse thieves and "Booshwhackers." The efforts, for the men, had not been in vain as Isaac pointed out. "We hung to of them the 9 of this month at Sutton a bout thirty miles from Summersville." The hanging, Isaac believed, was fully acceptable because "Tha had killed a union boy a bout fifteen years oald and the mail curry that carred the mail cross Poul mountain." He simply reported "Tha cut the boy open and stuck his head in sid. I think the hanging was to good for them."

This letter was brought to a finish by Isaac expressing his hope that Jane would "take care of your money that I send home to you." A post-script tells even more of Overall's growing homesickness. "When tese few lines you read think tha are from a husband that is fare from you and my dear children."[8]

Private Overall informed his family on June 2, 1862, that the regiment had moved. They were then encamped at Camp Meadow Bluff which was located fifteen miles from "Louis Burgh"; he was still in West Virginia. He also explained to Jane why he did not participate in the "Battle of Louis Burgh." Isaac was on excused duty by the order of his Captain because he had sore feet. He further commented that he did not know when the regiment's next pay day would be but as soon as his pay was received he would send it to them. He also wrote that he wanted her to use the money to pay their taxes on the house and lot.

Almost as an after thought, Isaac told Jane that James Overall had participated in the battle of Lewisburg and had been as "brave as a man cod be." Isaac continued. "He was shot through the cape on the tope of his head and tore the cape all to pieces. He was lodeing when the ball struck his cape and nock it a bout teen feet. He pick it upe and went a head. Lucki there was not any thing the matter with him."[9]

42

Descendants of Isaac and Jane Overall have not been able to connect this James Overall as a relative of Isaac although James was also Tennessee born. James had been born in Butler County, Tennessee and had joined Co I of the 36th Ohio in August of 1861. Soon promoted to Corporal on December 14, 1861, and in September of 1862, James was admitted to the General Hospital at Georgetown, District of Columbia. Four weeks later he was transferred to the Kalarama Hospital in Washington where he died of small pox on February 1st, 1863. He is buried in the Military Asylum Cemetery in Washington, D.C.[10]

Isaac's letter to the family dated mid-June contained much the same information as before regarding his health and loneliness. He expressed his admiration for his company officers and mentions briefly a young soldier that shot off his own index finger of his right hand while serving his turn at guard duty. Overall felt the incident was no more than an accident but it was no doubt scrutinized by others as a soldier's way out of the service.

More military activity is described in Isaac's letter to Jane dated "June the 26th 1862" while they were still located at Meadow Bluffs. In another partially destroyed letter, Overall wrote "Wee left base last Sunday moring to go to Salt Sapphus Springs to attack old Heath, but when wee had reached our destination, behold and what did we find - a desolate camp. The bird had flown and we had our tramp without a fight. Wee came on his pickets some fifteen miles this side of his camp. We taken all his pickets but one that was a cavalry man. He made good his esscape and give the alarm as we could have captured all of them. It was reported here that heath had about four thousand men under his command but he took good ease to skeedadle beefore wee got in reach of him. He left all of his tents and wagons hid in the woods. Wee taken several of his hoses and wagons and five or six busele of silage and four or five buselel of crackers. We then taken about 200 head of as prety cattle as ever I seen in my life. Besides six or seven prisoners, this is all I believe that we lost except a sad accident to one of our calvary men. He was shot by our own men. They being out a scouting, seen him and thought that hee was a rebell calvary man. When they instantly fired on him three balls tuking efect on him. He lived till Sunday evening. When he dide there was one or two slightly wounded of the 44th Reg. They was shot at by some Bush Whackers." This June letter is the first that Isaac closed by reminding Jane that he would "remain your faithful husband until death."[11]

After this incident the 36th Ohio moved to the Kanawha Valley in West Virginia. Isaac wrote a letter to his wife dated July 6, 1862 but it was not post marked on its envelope until July 25th. Much took place; it seems, between the writing and the posting. Isaac mentioned that his mail from home had been sparse, having but "one letter from hom since I left Summersville." He asked about the garden as well as other things of home, perhaps hoping to inspire someone to communicate with the lonely soldier so far away, anxious to hear from his loved ones. His closing tells much about his abilities to adjust to his adverse situation and cope with the conditions that could not be changed. He wrote "I dont want you to think that I am dissatisfied for I like it as well as a person could under the circumstances altho I wouldnt like to see you and the children worry."[12]

Two more short letters to his family show that Isaac's frustration and boredom were increasing. In both he tells of the inactivity of the regiment but indicated that there was talk of more activity in the future. About this possibility he commented, "I do not care for I am getting tiered of doing nothing." His closing in one of the letters advises Jane "Give your self no trouble about me. I am sure that I am on the rite side and in the car of a merciful god and if he is on our side, who can be against us."[13]

By the time Isaac's next letter was written, the regiment had indeed moved and there was no longer inactivity for the regiment. The 36th Ohio had been assigned to General John Pope and the Army of Virginia which had been created by the Federal Government June 26, 1862. Under Pope the 36th Ohio had been held in reserve during the Second battle of Manassas or Bull Run on August 28 - 30. The men were then assigned to The Army of the Potomac under the command of General George B. McClellan. Under that command they fought in the battle of South Mountain on September 14 and Antietam three days later.

The most severe fighting for the 36th Ohio was at the battle of South Mountain, in an area called Fox's Gap. The regiment came under intense fire from the Confederate soldiers assigned to protect the gap but the Buckeyes met the challenge and were instrumental in gaining control of South Mountain for the National Army. The regiment suffered seven killed, eighteen wounded and three men missing.[14]

At Antietam, fought near the town of Sharpsburg, Maryland, the regiment was under damaging artillery fire. Eight men were killed, fifty-eight wounded and seven men missing as a result of the artillery barrage they withstood near Rohrbach's Bridge at the battle of Antietam. Since the battle this location has become better known at Burnside's Bridge because the Federal forces that were engaged there were under the command of General Ambrose Burnside. These casualties, combined with those endured by this regiment later in the war at places such as Chickamauga, Georgia, Orchard Knob, and Missionary Ridge in Tennessee and Cloyd's Mountain, Winchester and Cedar Creek, Virginia, gained the unit a place of honor in William B. Fox's REGIMENTAL LOSSES IN THE AMERICAN CIVIL WAR (1861-1865) as one of the top 300 Union regiments.

Curiously, Isaac's letter of October 1, 1862, made very little mention of the severe fighting at Bull Run, South Mountain or Antietam. Isaac clearly left that type of news to the newspapers of the time. He felt it only necessary to say he had "passed through all the recent battles come out untutched ..... I have nothing of particular interest to write this time ..."

Although they were still located at the "moth of Antietam creek" he felt the men were destined to move soon towards Harper's Ferry, Maryland because the sick and wounded of the regiment "have ben moved to different hospitals, so that leaves us free to move at a minutes notice." On October 6th they did just that. They moved, but not to Harper's Ferry.[15]

From October 6 to November 16 the regiment marched from their Sharpsburg, Maryland, camp to the village of Hancock, West Virginia. This was followed immediately by a march to Clarksburg and then, to the village called Gauley Bridge, about forty miles southeast of Charleston. At the junction of the Gauley River and the New River, forming the Kanawha River, Isaac mailed a very short note and ten dollars to his family. The march continued through the Kanawha Valley to Charleston.

Another short note was sent to Jane from Charleston on December 30, 1862, telling her of Isaac's good health and inquiring as to her receipt of some money he had sent. His regiment, he explained, was not paid regularly and, because of this, he was unable to send much money home. This was a real problem, one that existed in virtually every department during the war. The men were promised, and paid, the sum of thirteen dollars per month. They were not promised, however, that they would be paid with regularity. A man that enlisted with the understanding that he would receive this pay and thus be able to send much or even all of it home, at times became a great burden to the family at home. A smaller amount of pay, with regularity, was often better for the family than a larger amount of "promised" pay when provided sporadically.[16]

A letter dated Feb 20, 1863 must have given Jane quite a shock. Isaac now wrote from Nashville, Tennessee over three hundred and fifty miles southwest of Charleston. The letter, as usual, made little mention of military procedure and events but did contain the information that a family at home would want to hear. Isaac's health was good. He had expressed money home and hoped to send more soon. These were the subjects that Isaac realized with which Jane would be most concerned.[17]

On April 1, 1863, five weeks later, Isaac offered another letter. This was mailed from Carthage, Tennessee, east of Nashville. His ever present hope for health for his family was his usual beginning. He also mentioned seeing almost 500 rebels across the Cumberland River but he did not feel they were much of a threat to the Federal forces.[18]

A month later Isaac and the 36th Ohio were still at Carthage and Isaac was still hopeful that they would soon receive their four months of back pay. He offered a suggestion for Jane showing her that he recognized the futility of the situation: "Try and get a long the best you can." He further indicated that he understood the feelings of some of the men in the regiment that had recently deserted. "Well I think" he wrote, "them felows had but little to do to desert .... nothing going on her." He mentioned a new "coronal" for the regiment but, as he said, "I dont know how we will like him yet." This colonel, William G. Jones, was killed in action during the fall of 1863 at the battle of Chickamauga.[19]

Isaac Overall, private in the 36th Ohio Volunteer Infantry, wrote again to his wife Jane two weeks later.

"Carthage, Tenn
May 13th/63
Dear Wife,

I seat my self this Eave to pen you a few lines in regard to my health. I am well at present and believe the health is generlly good in the Regt. I sent you ten Dollars a few days ago. I was only payed for two months. Wee had our clothing accounts to settle. Consequently, I could not send you any more at this time. I think that wee will be payed a gain soon.

Thare was exceiting times heare on yesterday. One, J. Smith, a citizen of the County, was hanged on charge of being a spy. He had been carrying news from our camp to the rebels for some 2 months before he was cot. He leaves a wife and 9 children. It fell on our Regt to construct a scuffle and execute him. I think it will be a warning for the citizens in and about Carthage. Thare is some more heare that if had their just dues would go the same way.

I want you to write and let me know when you heard from Andrew last. I have no heard a word from him since I was down home last winter. I wish that you would write oftener. I have not had a letter from you for something like a month. I wish you would send me a few post stamps if you can make it convenient. We have to pay double their value heare.

Tell Sarah Overall that I received a letter sometime since that she had written to Jim on or about the 1st of February. It had went to Washington and was sent to the Regt. I opened it and burned it. James owed a little in the Co, but I think the boys will make the sum up and pay it.

I have no more to write this Eave.
My love to all   more soon,
I. Overall"[20]

It was mid June that Jane heard again concerning her husband. Hugh Nibert, her nephew, also in Company I of the 36th Ohio, wrote to her to tell her that Isaac was dead. Hugh did not know much about the conditions of Isaac's passing except that he had been ill but seemed to be improving. When the regiment left Carthage for Murfreesboro, Tennessee, Isaac was left behind. Isaac's official cause of death ranged from lung fever to pneumonia to diphtheria depending on which account is consulted. The date of his death, according to the military records, was listed June 6 while letters home indicate he died either June 10 or 11.[21]

From the diagnosis of the cause of death for Isaac, we can assume that his death was a painful and frightening experience. Lung fever was simply another name for pneumonia and pneumonia and diphtheria could have easily been mis-diagnosed by the doctors of the day.

Diphtheria, at the time, was a widespread and greatly feared disease. As late as the early part of the 20th century the disease had a death rate of close to 10% but these figures have dropped considerably with modern medicine. The symptoms generally begin with a sore throat, a slight fever, and chills. It can become very difficult to swallow and will, eventually, cause the patient to suffocate. There can, with diphtheria, be individuals that simply carry the disease but fail to suffer the symptoms or the results. If not properly treated, the bacteria will produce a powerful poison which will spread throughout the body causing serious and often deadly complications such as heart failure or paralysis.[22]

It was known at the time of the Civil War that pneumonia was an inflammation of the lungs which was caused by exposure to cold and dampness. There was, at that time, lobular and broncho pneumonia, one dealing with the actual lobes of the lungs and the other with the bronchial tubes leading to the lungs. Treatment was acknowledged to be unsuccessful to relieve the inflammation until it seemed to abate by natural causes. A process of dry or wet cupping was used until conditions improved. Cupping was the removal of two to four ounces of blood by the application of wet or dry cups to the side which seemed to relieve the pain. This method was used to a great extent to the prisoners of war at Camp Douglas, Chicago, Illinois. At the Satterlee Hospital in Philadelphia, Pennsylvania 1/6th of a grain of sulphate of morphia in ½ ounce of Mindererus spirit every three hours. Mindererus spirits were a salts formed by the union of acetous acid and ammonia, thought to have certain healing properties at the time of the Civil War.

At Hospital #8 at Nashville, Tennessee, a teaspoon of paregoric, a camphorated tincture of opium, every three hours with a drink of acetate and bitartrate of potash with poultices to the affected side of the chest were often administrated. The Rock Island, Illinois hospital regularly used Dover's Powder with camphor and quinine. None of these and several other treatments were ever considered the best method of dealing with pneumonia.[23]

However, the following information was thought to have been a contributing factor to the health of the men that did recover from pneumonia. "The patient was supported with the best nourishment which the hospital afforded and with mild stimulants and tonic remedies, while care was exercised to avoid the slight exposures that were so prone to cause relapses". The study continued by stating, "Hence, we find beef-essence, chicken broth, raw eggs, wine-whey, sherry, Catawba, whisky-toddies, milk-punch, egg nog, brandy, beer . . . appearing generally on the records at this stage of the disease."[24]

Isaac Overall was buried in Carthage, Tennessee. When the hostilities of war were over, there are indications that all of the men that died at Carthage were removed to the National Cemetery created in Nashville. There is, however, no record that the remains of Isaac Overall are there. He is also not buried by his wife Jane at her final resting place in the Clay Chapel Cemetery overlooking the Ohio River in Gallia County, Ohio where she died on July 1, 1870.[25]

We know so very little concerning the early life of far too many Civil War soldiers. Thousands like Isaac Overall, Company I of the 36th Ohio Volunteer Infantry, rest in graves in national and community cemeteries beneath a simple headstone marked "**UNKNOWN**."

{1}   Record Group 94, Office of the Adjutant General, Compiled Service records. Volunteer Soldiers, Overall, Isaac - Pension file & Service Record.

{2}   Ibid.

{3}   Ibid.

{4}   Ezra J. Warner, *Generals in Blue* (Louisiana State University Press. 1964), pp. 102 - 104

{5}   Isaac Overall to "Dear Wife" - Feb 19, 1862 - Collection of Gary Overall.

{6}   Isaac Overall to "Dear Wife" - March 9, 1862 - Collection of Gary Overall

{7}   Isaac Overall to "Dear Wife" - March 17, 1862 - Collection of Gary Overall

{8}   Isaac Overall to "Dear and affectionate" - May 10, 1862 - Collection of Gary Overall

{9}   Isaac Overall to "Dear and affectionate wife" - June 2, 1862 - Collection of Gary Overall

{10}   Record Group 94, Office of the Adjutant General, Compiled Service records. Volunteer Soldiers, Overall, James - Pension file & Service Record.

{11}   Isaac Overall to "Dear Jane" - June 26, 1862 - Collection of Gary Overall

{12}   Isaac Overall to "Dear wife" - July 6, 1862 - Collection of Gary Overall

{13}   Isaac Overall to "Dear Wife" - July 21, 1862 - Collection of Gary Overall

{14}   Lt. Col. William F. Fox, - *Regimental Losses in The American Civil War 1861 - 1865* (Press of Morningside Bookshop - 1974), p. 323

{15}   Isaac Overall to "Dear Wife" - October 1, 1862 - Collection of Gary Overall

{16}   Isaac Overall to "Dear Wife" - December 30, 1862 - Collection of Gary Overall

{17}   Isaac Overall to "Dear Wife" - February 20, 1863 - Collection of Gary Overall

{18}   Isaac Overall to "Dear Wife" - April 1, 1863 - Collection of Gary Overall

{19}   Isaac Overall to "Dear Wife" - May 1, 1863 - Collection of Gary Overall

{20}   Isaac Overall to "Dear Wife" - May 13, 1863 - Collection of Gary Overall

{21}   H. L. Nibert to "Dear Aunt" - June 15. 1863 - Collection of Gary Overall

        Wesley Martindill to Mr. Clark - July 8, 1863 - Collection of Gary Overall

{22}   Surgeon General Joseph K. Barnes, United States Army – *The Medical And Surgical History Of The War Of The Rebellion. (1861-65)* (Washington Printing Office, 1870), Reprinted by Broadfoot Publishing Company – Wilmington, North Carolina 28405 – 1990 – 15 vols. Vol. VI pp. 737 – 745.

{23}   Surgeon General Joseph K. Barnes, United States Army – *The Medical And Surgical History Of The War Of The Rebellion. (1861-65)* (Washington Printing Office, 1870), Reprinted by Broadfoot Publishing Company – Wilmington, North Carolina 28405 – 1990 – 15 vols. Vol. VI pp. 751 - 810

{24}   Surgeon General Joseph K. Barnes, United States Army – *The Medical And Surgical History Of The War Of The Rebellion. (1861-65)* (Washington Printing Office, 1870), Reprinted by Broadfoot Publishing Company – Wilmington, North Carolina 28405 – 1990 – 15 vols. Vol. VI p. 809

{25}   Record Group 94, Office of the Adjutant General, Compiled Service records. Volunteer Soldiers, Overall, Isaac - Pension file & Service Record

Private Pliny F. White
Co. E - 14th Vermont Infantry

VI
"before the fight is over we shall be called."
Private Pliny F. White
Co. E - 14th Vermont Infantry

The August 5, 1862 call for troops from President Abraham Lincoln for 300,000 militia to serve for nine months was met by different states in different manners. Secretary of War Edwin Stanton realized, or suspected, that a draft would be necessary and announced plans to initiate such activity if needed.

For the state of Vermont, as well as several other states, this was not necessary. Answering the Federal Government's appeal, Vermont quickly gathered five new regiments, numbered from twelve to sixteen, at Brattleboro in the southeast corner of the state. These nine month volunteers would become members of General George J. Stannard's Second Vermont Brigade. General Stannard had just recently become an exchanged prisoner of war, having been captured by General T. J. "Stonewall" Jackson at Harper's Ferry, West Virginia on September 16, 1862 during General Robert E. Lee's Maryland Campaign.[1]

A member of the Fourteenth Vermont regiment of Volunteers was a former seminary student, Pliny F. White, from Whiting, Vermont. Pliny, or Plin as he was sometimes called, had been eager to enlist in the call of his country earlier, but relatives persuaded him that he was desperately needed at home by his family. He was the fourth of six children, having two sisters and a brother older and two sisters younger than him.[2]

Born on April 2, 1838, Pliny led the normal life of a farm child in Whiting, which is located in the west central part of the state, until February 25, 1843 when his father, Augustus, died. From the age of five until he was ten, the lad assisted his mother, the former Julia Augustina Smith, and his siblings in the operation of the small farm they rented from the Austin family. Most of the hard labor was performed by his older brother Sidney and older sisters, Emiline and Cornelia. Julia had married Augustus on August 25, 1825 in the small town of Starksboro, twenty-five miles north east of Whiting, where Augustus' farm was located.[3]

In 1848, Julia married Hibbard Morrill, also from Starksboro, and Pliny's young life was spent living both with his mother and step-father and his grandparents in Whiting. In 1856 or 1857 the Morrills moved themselves to the Whiting farm. When Pliny was eighteen he enrolled in the New Hampton Institute in Fairfax, Vermont, not far from Lake Champlain in Franklin County where he began study in the field of Theology. Within two years he was teaching school in Starksboro and living with his brother Sidney, a farmer and almost six years older than Pliny. Plans for the future, at that time, involved returning to the New

Hampton Institute, possibly with younger sister Sarah, who was sixteen. This, however, was not to be. Pliny's mother was again widowed when Morrill passed away on October, 1860 following a lengthy illness. Pliny was needed at home in Whiting and there he stayed.[4]

While assisting his mother with the operation of the farm, two factors began to influence the young man's life. One was the desire to purchase the farm he was working, in partnership with his mother. The other was a young lady named Lemira Brown. Pliny and Lemira were engaged to be married in the near future. For a young man in the hills and valleys of Vermont, life was taking on a new and meaningful direction even though the nation was involved in a great civil war.[5]

None of White's many letters home explained Pliny's thinking regarding his joining the Federal forces when he did, but the fact that he would be gone for only nine months and those during the winter season could have been a large influence. His country called and Pliny White responded.

On August 30, 1862 several young men from Whiting journeyed ten miles north to Middlebury and enlisted for nine months. They were some of the first Vermonters to step forward. Almost seven weeks later these young men and hundreds of others gathered at Brattleboro to be mustered into the Fourteenth Vermont Volunteer Infantry. Pliny was assigned to Company E. Early October found the city of Brattleboro inundated with raw recruits. For a short time, Brattleboro served as a training ground for five regiments. Between October 7th and the 24th, close to 5,000 young, untrained recruits converged on the nation's capitol from the state of Vermont. They would serve in the same general area until they were consolidated into the Army of the Potomac for the repulse of General Robert E. Lee's invasion into central Pennsylvania the following summer.[6]

During Pliny's service in the Fourteenth, he demonstrated his abilities with the pen and pencil, by sending over forty letters to his fiancée and approximately fifty to his mother, brother and sister Sarah. There were at least two subjects always include in Pliny's correspondence. It is no surprise that he was always requesting paper and stamps, reminding all that without paper and stamps there could be no letters home. He, like so many soldiers, no matter what the era, also requested more letters and news from home. News of family, news of friends, news of acquaintances and even news of the animals on the farm was always of great interest to Pliny. Men away from home always desire to hear from home and Pliny White certainly was no different.

While at Camp Lincoln, near Brattleboro, Pliny made every effort to inform his mother and sister what military life was like, from an explanation of being served three meals a day to the size of the tables at which they sat. Each table, three to a barracks, was large enough to sit 80 men on each side. The size (fifty acres) and location (a mile from the village) of the training camp was explained. He described in great detail the manner in which each regiment guarded its own space. He made special effort to inform his family that they should be proud to know a soldier and that they should appreciate a soldier's life. From drill to guard duty as well as every day work around the camp, Pliny included every possible bit of information which he assumed his family might want to know.[7]

From Camp Lincoln on October 6, 1862, to Fort Drummer, also at Brattleboro, on October 13, White continued his correspondence. Pliny was smugly proud of the fact that he was the only one in his mess that did not make himself sick on bread and milk. He wrote, "Of all the groaning and puking and hussleing around after boots to attend to sudden calls [of nature] one can better imagine than describe."[8]

It was in his October 14 letter that Pliny explained that the men had not actually moved at all. Colonel Stoughton had created a general order to change Camp Lincoln to Fort Drummer. Pliny explained, "I don't see the propriety of calling it a Fort but it might properly be Camp Drummer in perpetuation of the name Drummer as that is said to be the name of the first settlement of Vermont." He also made an attempt to explain how the pay system of the Federal Army was designed. Although he had been living the life of a soldier at Brattleboro since October 6, he had actually enlisted on August 11. White realized he would not be paid from the date of his actual enlistment but felt they should be paid for their time spent in camp. The Federal Government, he understood, would not commence their pay schedule until they had actually mustered into the service. By October 14, that had not happened and there were hundreds of dissatisfied soldiers in the encampment. The mustering in did not happen until October 21, 1862 and many of the men resented the free fifteen days of service and some simply went home, disgruntled with the situation.[9]

These fifteen free days were spent drilling, standing guard and policing the campground. That was the daily grind until October 21, when the men actually became a regiment in the Federal Army by going through the mustering ceremony. Now they could consider themselves soldiers, ready to protect and serve their nation. The following day they left Vermont for Washington, D. C. On October 23, Pliny wrote to Sarah telling her of the regiment's activities. They had departed "Bat" at 2 p.m. on the 22nd and arrived, by rail, at New Haven, Connecticut at 11 p.m., boarded the steamer *CONTINENTAL* and arrived at New York City by 7 in the morning. Finally, Pliny stated, "our nine months is going on." The men arrived at Washington on October 25 and marched to camp which was located at "Arlington heights". In truth, the men were camped at Camp Chase which was located in Arlington, Virginia. By October 30, however, the men were relocated, encamped on East Capitol Hill, within the District of Columbia. They did not remain there long, marching to Munson's Hill on the 30th and then Hunting Creek on November 5. Both of these were also in Virginia.[10]

Their camp at Hunting Creek, called Camp Vermont, served as home for the men until November 26, 1862. While at Camp Vermont the men were informed, according to a November 10 letter to Sarah that this was where they were to go into winter quarters. They immediately became carpenters and lumberjacks, cutting timber and building barracks. These barracks were made of posts nine feet long and set into the ground two feet. Each building was to be one hundred feet long and twenty feet wide. Each was to be divided into four rooms, twenty feet long and used for lodging and the fourth room was to be forty feet long and used for cooking and eating. But Pliny was not to be fooled. "These orders would indicate that there was a certainty of our wintering here," he said, "if there is any such thing as military certainty in the future." He also mentioned that they had gone to Alexandria on Friday, November 9 to exchange weapons. They turned in their "large clumsy ones" and now had some that were smaller and easier to handle. They were now carrying what was referred to as the "Austrian Rifle", the .54 caliber Loranze Rifle. They received ammunition for them on Saturday and on Sunday each man was provided with another forty rounds. Pliny commented, "... we are prepared for war now."[11]

Food for the men in the Fourteenth Vermont was always of primary importance. Pliny told of a very impressive menu at Camp Vermont. There was salt beef and fresh beef, boiled and fried pork and bacon. To round out the larder was potatoes, sweet potatoes, rice, beans, sugar, molasses, tea, coffee, apples and "as good bread as I ever ate." Straw for their bunk and tents was not as plentiful. Each armful was ten or twelve cents a piece.[12]

War was close, however. Pliny mentioned, on November 11, that every time men returned to camp from picket duty they almost always brought in two or three Rebels. The rest of the days were spent hanging out bedding to air and sunning themselves like "four alligators." As he mentioned, "We are having a pretty lazy time of it."[13]

Nearby Camp Vermont was a place where men had been interred that had died in a hospital at a convalescent camp. "There were 30 or 40 graves" and they were "side by side in one row stretching along the top of a hill near the side. The names of the Co Reg & State of most of the occupants were marked with black paint upon boards painted white.... a few were unmarked save by the mound of gravel above them & some rough stakes driven down by the head & foot. Here they sleep & though perhaps mourned yet their resting place is unknown to their friends and the manner of their death forever a secret."[14]

In letters dated November 24 and 25, Pliny mentioned a fine two story brick home was destroyed to provide brick for the men to build fire places, floors and other conveniences for their winter quarters. White frankly stated "We are tearing down a nice Residence. There are two parts of equal size connected by a piazza about 75 feet long and 20 wide. Each of the main buildings are 20 by 40 feet. There is a fireplace in nearly every room in the house." Pliny went on to describe the rooms in the home as beautiful and wrote that the approach to the house was a spacious avenue lined with various shade and flower trees. Guards were established at the house to assure that another Federal regiment would not take advantage of the supply.[15]

Pliny was also aware of the political actions the United States government had taken in the recent past. He mentioned that nearby was a man who claimed to be a Union man but was the brother of James M. Mason who was captured along with John Slidell from a British mail steamer named *TRENT* in November of 1861 by Captain Charles Wilkes of the Federal Navy. Both men were aboard the British ship as representatives of the Confederate States of America. This situation was resolved by January of 1862 but it could have easily brought war between the United States and England. White felt that the fact that there were Federal troops guarding the man and his house was a good thing. Good, not so much for the prevention of vandalism and foraging by the troops but good because it kept Mr. Mason from spying on Federal activity and communicating valuable information to the South.[16]

Three weeks later, winter camp, so laboriously completed, was abandoned and the regiment went on picket duty at Occaquon Creek near Bull Run Creek guarding the Orange and Alexandria Railroad. An incident at Wolf Run, Virginia, where the regiment was camped, left an impression on White. Wagon trains passed by on Monday, December 1, like nothing he had ever witnessed before. It was a train of 150 teams pulling wagons and was four miles long. It was headed to Aqua Creek loaded with ammunition for the men at Fredericksburg, Virginia under the command of General Ambrose Burnside. White was very impressed, even envious of the cavalry detachment that was serving as escort for the train. He commented, and felt every man in the infantry felt the same, that he would rather belong to them than to the infantry and would join them if his time would still expire as scheduled, which was to be July 30, 1863. A return to Camp Vermont on December 5 was short lived and on December 12 they departed for Fairfax Court House, Virginia.[17]

The day the regiment left Camp Vermont Pliny wrote another letter to his sister, Sarah. "Our nine months," he stated, "will be out before we hardly know it. We came here to fight," he continued, "though I do not think we shall see a single battle for I fear there will be a miserable compromise or an ignominious peace." He commented "... we had just as soon fight a little if need be die to avert any such calamity." It was evident that Pliny felt the talents and fighting spirit of the Fourteenth Vermont nine month regiment were not being utilized to their fullest capacity.[18]

By the 14th, Pliny had time to write to Sarah again, concerned about the farm and concerned about letters he had mailed. Another letter, written on the following day, like so many others, indicated a desire for more mail from home and he even hoped for a box which might possibly contain writing supplies and a few items for consumption. To be precise, Pliny wanted "butter and cheese mostly, a few sauceges & mince pies if you think they will keep & I guess they would if they were frozen when they were packed. A few cakes would not come amiss. Tobaccoe would come in play ..." The former good meals at Camp Vermont were a thing of the past.[19]

Letters home continued through the winter months. There were six lengthy letters in November and seven during December. Five letters were sent in January and they continued at a rapid pace even after the Fourteenth had changed quarters again. From March 24 to June 25 they were first at Wolf Run Shoals, Union Mills and again on Occoquan Creek. Before leaving Fairfax Station, Pliny took advantage of the opportunity to visit his nation's capital and witness first hand the workings of the Senate and the House of Representatives. "I could not hear anything that was said in the House of Rep. there was so much confusion & hubbub but in the Senate it was stiller so one could hear most of what was said. Several votes were taken: this is done by calling the roll & each one answers aye or nay. In this way I had a good opportunity to tell who was who."[20]

With spring coming, Pliny gave intensive farming advice to his family in Vermont in a letter from Wolf Run Shoals in early April, 1863. There was advice concerning the wood pile, the planting of certain crops such as corn and wheat, judging certain areas as fit for planting or if they should remain fallow for the season. Even suggestions as to which vegetables in which part of the garden were given freely by the soldier in far away Virginia. He even passed from the advice mode with the crops to the directive mode, stating that part of a certain meadow "I want broken up & planted to beans." In this letter more than any of the others, it is apparent that Pliny would much rather be home in Whiting, Vermont than playing soldier in Virginia.[21]

The next two weeks, from April 12 till April 28, were spent on guard and picket duty and cleaning and re-cleaning his weapon. Payday came on the 28th and White found time for another letter home. His receipt of four months pay gave him the opportunity to explain how payday in camp caused money to circulate freely, everyone paying off bills and debts which had been created over the past four months. Not only were debts settled, but now items of every description were being bought and sold. Watches, pistols and other countless items changed hands often and when all was "settled up all around" Pliny found he had four or five dollars more than what he had when he was paid. He commented that money would be sent home in a few days by express but never indicated an amount.[22]

The remainder of April and the first few days of May were still the usual humdrum of camp life but on May 3, another letter to Sarah demonstrated his displeasure with army life and the boredom he suffered.

The Twelfth Vermont had left their camp and the men were doing different duty. He was not aware exactly what the duty was, but he did wish it had been the Fourteenth regiment that had been chosen to change location and duty. He was ready to be moving about being a soldier. However, he commented, it was only a couple of months and his nine months enlistment would expire and he would be returning to the green mountains of Vermont.[23]

Another week passed, a week of afternoon drills, cleaning of rifles, camp guard and picket duty before Pliny White wrote his sister again. On May 12, he sent yet another letter full of small talk about camp life, who was visiting, and a bit of farming advice for anyone who might listen. When his rather large sheet of paper was full, he abruptly commented "There I've my sheet full. Good bye. Write often. Your affectionate Pliny." The remainder of the month of May was a dull repetitious two weeks, repeating exactly what Pliny and the other men of the Fourteenth had done during the first two weeks of the month. They cleaned, guarded and served picket duty with monotonous regularity.[24]

Pliny tells a bit about the excitement in camp that happened on May 30 when he writes Sarah on June 1. The camp was stirred to activity by a raid on a train by Confederate John Singleton Mosby and his guerilla rangers. The train, cars full of forage for Stoneman's Cavalry, was captured and burned. The twenty-five or thirty men assigned to guard the train, all from the Fifteenth Vermont, "seemed to think that they had enough to do to take care of themselves so they skeedaddled." He then explained exactly how Mosby's men had performed their feat. "The way it was done they loosened a rail and attached a wire to it & just before the train got onto this rail they pulled it away being concealed in the bushes close by. The engine got safely over but the two forward cars run off & of course that stopped the train." The raiders opened fire with their artillery pieces and at least one shot went through the boiler of the engine. After some ten or twenty minutes a New York Cavalry unit arrived "and then it was the Rebs turn to skedaddle." Such was the excitement of camp life for May and it carried over through the majority of June. On June 25, 1863 the Second Vermont Brigade, including the Fourteenth regiment, marched from Wolf Run Shoals to a couple of miles beyond Centerville. Winter camp life was over.[25]

From June 25 until July 1, the regiment passed, on their way north, Centerville, Frying Pan, Herndon, a place called Guilford Station and Edwards Ferry on the Potomac River. On June 27, they were on the outskirts of Poolsville, Maryland. The following four days found the foot soldiers passing Sugar Loaf Mountain, Adam's Town, Frederick and finally, on June 30, Emmittsburg, Pennsylvania. The men arrived at the small town of Gettysburg, Pennsylvania on July 1 and they were tired. However tired they were, they were also proud of their achievement. They had marched hard and in one week averaged twenty miles a day. They referred to themselves as a "flying brigade" and they were ready to go into battle.[26]

The following morning Pliny wrote his fiancée the following letter.

"Thursday July 2d
9 o clock A.M.
Dear Lemira,
    The chances are very favorable that to-day we shall go into battle. Though it is said that we are to be held in reserve. I do not doubt but before the fight is over we shall be called. I am ready and willing to go into battle and can trust myself in the hands of Him who is our only trust. Though I do not fear, yet it may be if I go into battle this may be the last time I shall write you. Already the firing has commenced but not briskly. I would like to see you, but as I can not I thought just a word would be better than nothing. I love you as ever and think of you often, and if we meet no more on earth, I hope I shall be worthy to meet you where there will be no parting word.
Your affectionate
Pliny"[27]

On July 2nd the men of the Second Vermont Brigade, men of the Thirteenth, Fourteenth and Sixteenth regiments were instrumental in the recapturing of a battery of artillery at the personal request of General Winfield Scott Hancock. Their willingness to go into battle as well as their zealousness during their advance impressed Hancock. Thus, during the re-positioning of troops during the night of July 2 and 3, these nine month veterans, whose enlistment would expire at the end of July, were moved into the Federal line of defense just a few hundred yards south of a small copse of trees within the Federal lines. The men of the twelfth and Fifteenth, the men Pliny had once envied for their activity, had been detached from the brigade and were guarding wagons away from the battlefield. As the three Vermont regiments went into their assigned defensive position that evening, Pliny's letter to Lemira was still tucked inside a pocket, waiting to be mailed. They spent the night lying on their arms in anticipation of the activity that would take place the following day, on July 3, 1863 a short distance south of the small Pennsylvania town called Gettysburg.[28]

At 1:00 o'clock p.m. the following afternoon a Confederate artillery barrage commenced. For two solid hours one hundred and forty cannon belched their contents toward the Federal line that stretched from Ziegler's Grove to the north, almost a mile to the south. As quickly as these guns could be loaded and fired, they sent their shells into the Federal lines. The majority of the missiles traveled past the waiting Federal soldiers and wrecked havoc behind the ridge on which the men were entrenched.   Although actual wounds were at a minimum, the psychological effect on the men was immense. When the firing ceased at 3:00 o'clock the men's nerves were stretched almost to the breaking point. The artillery smoke began to clear.

What they witnessed probably was the most awesome sight of their military career.   What would forever be referred to as "Pickett's Charge" was forming over a mile to their front. The front of the advance has been estimated at over one thousand yards across with the troops which were to support this vanguard even wider.   There were four divisions, eleven brigades of soldiers, or fifty regiments. To each and every soldier lying behind the small stone wall protecting the Federal forces, they seemed to be all coming directly at him.   Some fifteen hundred brave Confederate soldiers were advancing across an open field from a ridge called Seminary Ridge towards the Federal soldiers, somewhat entrenched on a ridge called Cemetery Ridge a mile and a half away. Pliny White and the Fourteenth Vermont were a part of the object of this advancement. Headed directly for the nine month soldiers were the men under the commands of General James Kemper and General Richard Garnett. On they came.[29]

As Garnett's men passed the Emmittsburg Road, less than a half mile in front of Stannard's Vermonters, they turned abruptly to the left, passed behind Kemper's men and General Lewis Armistead's troops, where they again turned to the east, and resumed the advance into the waiting firepower of the Federals there. During this movement General Garnett was killed, knocked from his mount which he was riding because he was too ill to walk. Kemper's troops, however continued in an easterly direction still headed for the Vermont men. Very close, perhaps within only one hundred and fifty or two hundred yards, Kemper's men also swung to the left, to the north, exposing their entire right flank to the men from Vermont, still equipped with the .54 caliber Loranze Rifles. At that point the Vermont soldiers stood and fired several volleys into the Confederates advancing across their front. General Stannard then had the men change their front. With a grand right wheel the men changed from a westerly front to a northerly front and fired more volleys into the backs of Kemper's men. The devastation was great and a cheer exploded from the throats of the Vermont men.[30]

That cheer was short lived. General Stannard noticed more Confederate forces approaching from their rear. These men were the support troops for this area of the Confederate advance and they were under the commands of General Cadmus M. Wilcox and Colonel David Lang, who was commanding the brigade of General William Perry. Wilcox and Perry's brigades were approaching quickly and was met by intense fire from the Vermont men. This intense fire was met by sporadic fire from the southern troops who found themselves separated from the entire advance by this line of hard fighting, blue uniformed soldiers. After a few volleys the southerners began to seek sanctuary to their rear. The support melted away and for the southern end of the defensive line the battle was virtually over. Within minutes hundreds more exhausted, wounded and scared southern soldiers were making their way back across the field to Seminary Ridge. Pickett's Charge was over.[31]

Across the open field the evening of July 3, 1863 was nineteen dead Vermont soldiers. There were also seventy-four men from Vermont that were suffering the shock of their wounds. Among the wounded was twenty-five year old Pliny White whose right upper arm had been shattered by a musket ball. That evening White was transported to the Seminary Hospital where early the next day his arm was amputated by Surgeon A. T. Woodward of the Fourteenth Vermont Infantry an acquaintance before the war. Pliny survived the amputation well for almost two weeks, before he was attacked violently by severe fever and chronic diarrhea.[32]

The day after his regiment mustered out of the service in Brattleboro, Vermont, Pliny had the following letter written to his sister.

"Gettysburg, Pa.   July 31/'63
2nd Division   1st Corpse
(Hospital)
Dear Sister,

Through the kindness of a good brother I will tell you how I am. I would not have you mourn on account of my condition for I feel reconciled to my lot, although it is hard. You know that we are taught in Gods Holy Word that "all things shall work together for the good of those that love God. I have excellent care and good nurses, who are doing all they can for me and take a deep interest in my recovery - I have good food also. I've had some fever and my pulse is quite high yet.

Yours affectionately
Pliny White"

The kind "good brother" added the following information, probably without Pliny's knowledge.

"Kind friends

You wish to know in full I suppose the condition of brother White. I am his nurse. We are doing all we can to cheer him and although his case is a serious one, yet we have hope to save him and restore him to you. An excellent lady, a Mrs. Evingham does a great deal for him - dressing his wounds (arm) and so on. She is a good mother to him. I am highly pleased to see him so good and has such abiding confidence in Him who doeth all things well.

I will add, if I can do anything for you for him I will with the greatest pleasure.

Yours respectfully

Francis N. Bell

Please use the address given and write soon."[33]

Before this letter could be answered, Susan received the following letter from Gettysburg.

"Seminary Hospital Gettysburg
August 6th 1863
Dear Friends

Without waiting for a reply to my letter that I wrote you a few days ago, I have the painful duty to inform you that brother White is no more. He died last night at 10 o'clock. When I wrote you last he was or appeared to be at times in his right mind but soon he became delirious and remained so, I believe till death ended his sufferings. His arm was doing as well as could be expected, but the fever & diahrea, soon notwithstanding our efforts, brought him very low, and frail nature has given away. Of his care and skillful treatment you may be assured that all has been done that could restore him to health.

Yesterday he tried to talk but was too low. I vainly tried to catch some words to communicate to his friends, but I think he was unconscious of his condition. Just before he was delirious he desired the minister assigned here to pray with him. It was done, and afterwards as I talked with him on the subject of religion, he seemed to regret, <u>as we often do</u>, that he had not been able to live better since he had been a soldier. He left assurances of his acceptance of God and said he was willing to die, and Thy will be done. Jesus was precouis to his soul, and he was so reconciled to his lot, so ameiable and good that we almost envied him his happiness. He has gone to rest, to reap his reward and let me assure you dear friends that as we administered to his comforts and tried to alleviate his sufferings We felt we were doing it for a widowed mother (I think he said) and kind and affectionate brother & sisters. But I must close. He is buried in the beautiful grave a few rods west of the Seminary Hospital. I will see that a good head board marks the spot. Mrs. Everingham will also write a few lines, and you will please to write to us if all is satisfactory or not.

In conclusion let me inform the society with which he was connected, that brother White had died a christian soldier a martyr to the cause, we so dearly love, and if we are not permitted to live to see the object attained for which we labour May we be permitted to know that a grateful posterity are enjoying the blessings of civil & religious liberty and of a Free Government

Yours &c
Francis N. Bell[34]

61

A letter from Mrs. Mary H. Everingham was also written on the same day.

"August 6th 1863
Miss Sarah Ann White

I am pained to break the news to you of brother. He is no more the way of all.

He told me some days ago I must write to you, and tell you he was very sick. When he came under my charge I have done all for him, I could for an own brother but the fever had hold of him to strong. He seemed to know what we said all the time but last two days could not talk but little. He told me you were teaching school and for me to send his money to you which is twenty two but Mr. Bell says something about the wallet being sent to another person, then he will tell you as he is going to write in this. Now the Steward has ordered his money to be given in his care, and the head surgeon. That is Military rules, whether you get it or not, I can't say. But I want you should write me immediately so I will know all about it. I will send you the names of Stuart and doctor and Hospital. perhaps they will send to the regiment before you get the news from them.

Please answer soon.
                    Mary H. Everingham
                            Gettysburg
                                    Seminary Hospital

Here is a lock of his hair which is all I have to send you. I thought you would prize the little token, above all others, for its all of him that can be kept.

May God help you to bear all your sorrow. Poor girl you are not the only sister whose heart is nearly broken to day. I think he told me his Dear Mother was living.

Oh how my heart aches to think of all these dear Mothers & Sisters at home while those loved ones are groaning and dying among strangers, and all caused by this Unholy Unjust War.
                    M. H. E.

Name of Doctor in charge of Hospital   Dr. Coren
Name of Stuard   Joseph Vincent"[35]

The Reverend John Quincy A. Ware of Whiting, Vermont, a close friend of the Whites, was at Gettysburg at the time, delivering supplies gathered in the Whiting community for the many Gettysburg hospitals and brought the lock of hair and other artifacts home to the White family. The letter to Lemira, which had never been mailed, was one of the items.[36]

Pliny White, of the Fourteenth Vermont Infantry, is buried at the Gettysburg National Cemetery in the Vermont section which contains sixty-one men. Of these, sixteen are men that served with Pliny White in the Fourteenth Regiment. Pliny rests in Section B, grave # six.

{1}   Ezra Warner, *Generals in Blue* (Louisiana State University Press - 1963), pp. 471 - 472

{2}   Record Group 94, Office of the Adjutant General, Compiled Service records. Volunteer Soldiers, White, Pliny F. - Pension file & Service Record.

{3}   Ibid.

{4}   Ibid.

{5}   Ibid.

{6}   Frederick H. Dyer, *A Compendium of the War of the Rebellion - Two Volumes.* (Dayton, Ohio: National Historical Society. The Press of Morningside Bookshop. 1979), Volume #2 – 1653, 1654

{7}   Pliny White to "Dear Sister", October 6, 1862. Collection of Barbara Freund.

{8}   Pliny White to "Dear Sarah", October 13, no year. Collection of Barbara Freund.

{9}   Pliny White to "Dear Sister", Oct 14, 1862. Collection of Barbara Freund.

{10}   Pliny White to "Dear Sister", Oct 23d, '62. Collection of Barbara Freund.

{11}   Pliny White to "Dear Sister", Nov 10th, 7 P.M. Collection of Barbara Freund.

{12}   Ibid.

{13}   Pliny White to "Sister Sallie", Nov 11th. Collection of Barbara Freund

{14}   Pliny White to "Dear Sister", 13th Nov 1862. Collection of Barbara Freund

{15}   Pliny White to "Dear Sis", November 22, 1862. Collection of Barbara Freund

        Pliny White to "Dear Sister", Nov 25, 1862. Collection of Barbara Freund

{16}   Pliny White to "Dear Sister", Nov 25, 1862. Collection of Barbara Freund

{17}   Frederick H. Dyer, *A Compendium of the War of the Rebellion - Two Volumes.* (Dayton, Ohio: National Historical Society. The Press of Morningside Bookshop. 1979), Volume #2, p. 1654

        Pliny White to "Dear Sister", Dec 2nd, 1862. Collection of Barbara Freund

{18}   Pliny White to "Dear Sister", 12th Dec / 62. Collection of Barbara Freund

{19}   Pliny White to "Dear Sister", Sunday Dec 14th 1862. Collection of Barbara Freund

        Pliny White to "Sallie Dear", Monday Dec 15 1862. Collection of Barbara Freund

{20}   Pliny White to "Dear Sister", March 2nd / 63. Collection of Barbara Freund

{21}   Pliny White to "Dear Folks at Home", April 11, 1863. Collection of Barbara Freund

{22}   Pliny White to "Dear Sister", Apr 28th 1863. Collection of Barbara Freund

{23}   Pliny White to "Dear Sister", May 3rd 1863. Collection of Barbara Freund

{24}   Pliny White to "Dear Sister", May 12th, 1863. Collection of Barbara Freund

{25}   Pliny White to "Dear Sister", June 1, 1863. Collection of Barbara Freund

        Frederick H. Dyer, *A Compendium of the War of the Rebellion - Two Volumes*. (Dayton, Ohio: National Historical Society. The Press of Morningside Bookshop, 1979), Volume #2 - 1654

{26}   Pliny White Diary - entry - July 1st, 1863. Collection of Barbara Freund

{27}   Pliny White to "Dear Lemira" Thursday July 2d. Collection of Barbara Freund

{28}   Glenn Tucker, *High Tide at Gettysburg: The Campaign in Pennsylvania* (Dayton, Ohio: Press of Morningside Bookshop, 1983), p. 361

{29}   Ibid., pp 361 - 364

        Edward J. Stackpole, *They Met at Gettysburg* (New York, New York: Bonanza Books 1956) pp. 263 - 265

        Champ Clark and The Editors of Time-Life Books - *Gettysburg - The Confederate High Tide* (Alexandria, Virginia: Time Life Books 1985), pp. 139 - 140

{30}   Glenn Tucker *High Tide at Gettysburg: The Campaign in Pennsylvania* (Dayton, Ohio: Press of Morningside Bookshop, 1983) pp. 361 - 364

{31}   Ibid.

        Clark, Champ and The Editors of Time-Life Books - *Gettysburg - The Confederate High Tide* (Alexandria, Virginia: Time Life Books 1985) pp. 139, 140

{32}   Record Group 94, Office of the Adjutant General, Compiled Service records. Volunteer Soldiers, White, Pliny F. - Pension file & Service Record.

{33}   Pliny White (by Francis N. Bell) to "Dear Sister" July 31 / '63. Collection of Barbara Freund

{34}   Francis N. Bell to "Dear Friends" Aug 6th, 1863 - Collection of Barbara Freund

{35}   Mary H. Everingham to "Miss Sarah Ann White" Aug 6, 1863 - Collection of Barbara Freund

{36}   Record Group 94, Office of the Adjutant General, Compiled Service records. Volunteer Soldiers, White, Pliny F. - Pension file & Service Record

Private John Adkinson
Co. K - 95th Illinois Infantry
Blain Cemetery, Boone County, Illinois

VII
"kizs little henry and the three little girls ..."
Private John H. Adkinson
Co. K - 95th Illinois Infantry

John Hazzlewood Atkinson was eighteen years old when he enlisted in the small village of Poplar Grove, Illinois to assist his nation, for three years, on July 28, 1862. The unit he joined, the 95th Illinois Volunteer Infantry, would not muster into the Federal armed forces until late September of that year. The regiment has become one of the more well known Civil War regiments, not from its military prowess but because of the future fame of one of its members, a small 5'3" soldier known at the time as Albert D. J. Cashier. After serving for the duration of the war and participating in every battle with the 95th, Albert was discharged and returned to Illinois. Much later, after becoming a member of the Grand Army of the Republic, and also voting in every national and state election, Albert's secret was discovered. After the turn of the 20th century, while living in Saunemin, Illinois, Albert was discovered to actually be a woman named Jennie Hodgers.[1]

Albert, however, was in Company G while John Atkinson and his thirty-one year old brother-in-law, James Vincent, were in Company K. John Adkinson, who was but one inch taller than Albert, at 5'4", had been born October 18, 1843, in Boone County, Illinois, just a few miles north of the tiny hamlet. He was the third child of Joseph and Mary Hazzlewood Atkinson, who arrived in the United States from England by way of Canada. Joseph and Mary would eventually parent twelve children, seven males and five females. John's younger sister, Isabella Mary, born in 1845 had already married Canadian born James Vincent and would give the family its first grandchild, James John, born in the fall of 1862.[2]

James Vincent, John's brother-in-law, was thirty-one years old, a farmer and four inches taller than John. John's admiration of the man was very evident throughout his letters home as "Jim" or "James" was mentioned in every letter John mailed home. James's health was always mentioned as well as his duties, such as picket duty or guard duty, always told. John often assured his family that James was a very important member of the company providing good advice, sound suggestions and even a great sense of humor for the men.[3]

The 95th Illinois trained at Camp Fuller, north of Rockford, by the Rock River, at an area called Churchill's Grove. When they left northern Illinois on November 4, 1862, they traveled to Jackson, Tennessee, arriving there on November 12. Their duties, while necessities of military life were far from heart pounding encounters with the enemy. They assumed the more mundane responsibilities such as camp and wagon guards and escorts for wagons carrying supplies short distances. At the completion of one of these short escort assignments, the regiment relocated at Memphis, Tennessee. They remained at Memphis for just a week and again moved, this time to Lake Providence, Louisiana, where they remained for yet another week. A very small skirmish, with no casualties, took place at Old River near Lake Providence and again the regiment moved further south, this time to Milliken's Bend, Louisiana, on the Mississippi River, arriving there April 12, 1863.[4]

John Adkinson had a fair education during his formative years but his spelling had been learned phonetically which was constantly demonstrated in his letters. Bare footed was written bare "futid" and "contrey" passed as country. A piece was usually "a peas", pleasure was "plesher", preserves - "persarves" and fortune teller became "fortchunteller." The state of Kansas was "Cances" and Christmas was written "Crismez." Many intelligent people have been notoriously poor spellers and even though his spelling was not good, John was not an unintelligent or ignorant person. He understood the family and neighbors back home wanted news of himself, James and others in the company and he endeavored to supply them and the surrounding neighborhood with the activities of the company. He once requested that his family inform the neighbors that the men were "backsolated so we woodn git the smole pox."[5]

While the 95th Illinois was at Milliken's Bend, they made preparations for their ordeal ahead. That ordeal would be the final approach to take Vicksburg, Mississippi, the much needed key to the puzzle of making the great Mississippi accessible to the northwestern Federal states as well as cutting the availability of much needed supplies for the Confederacy. These men, as well as the nation, realized what they were about to attempt. But neither they, nor the nation, had any concept of the ordeals they would suffer or the time it would take to achieve that goal. On April 25, 1863, the movement commenced with the advance on Bruinsburg, Mississippi and the turning of the Federal Army across the Mississippi River at Grand Gulf on April 30. What would become known as the final Vicksburg Campaign had commenced and John Adkinson was a part of it.[6] It was near Port Gibson, on May 1, 1863, the men of the 95th Illinois heard their first combat of their Civil War experience and actually saw the results of war as they passed over the battlefield with the wagonloads of supplies they were guarding. It seemingly was not impressive to John Adkinson as he simply mentioned their twelve mile march in the very hot weather. As a result of this march and the hot weather, John had decided that his captain, Gabriel E. Cornwell, a farmer also from the Poplar Grove area, was the best captain in the regiment. Captain Cornwell had somehow acquired a wagon which he made available to the men of company K to carry their heavy knapsacks and other accouterments on the hot march. This must have been greatly appreciated by all of the men in the company and greatly envied by the rest of the men in the regiment.[7] During the spring months of 1863, John's feelings regarding the black race were relayed home several times. He commented that he did not believe "hee cud bee a slave older. I cudent for I woodnt have the black devills a round me." He also felt there was a progression of importance in the Federal army. "mules is the first, nigers the next then a soldier the next." He was, he told his mother and father bluntly, "sick and tirard of seen nigers." It seemed from John's comments that these feelings were at least company and possibly regimental in magnitude. He commented, "the old soldurs sez when they get home if their is eney nigers their they will shoot all they see." He commented that he believed that would be a fine idea. It was also John's opinion in a letter dated April 14, 1863, that "the rebills is kiling all the nigers they can so wee cant get them for soldurs." However, John was not above using the services of these oppressed people. A comment directed to his mother in response to a question asked, as mothers are prone to do, about how John got his laundry done. He replied, "I git the darkeys to do it. they will wash a shirt for 5 cents and a pair of draws for 5 cents and that is better than washing them my self."[8] On May 6 while on march during the Vicksburg Campaign, John's health began to suffer a bit. Brother-in-law James was very well but John had "catched a cold." It was, he felt, a result of the men sleeping on the ground during their march without tents. The weather had been fine and they "ante bin in a battle yet but wee can hear the old canin bark pruty loude." This would all change in two weeks.[9]

It was on May 23, 1863 John Atkinson took the opportunity to write his parents again. At this time, the 95th Illinois felt they were seasoned veterans with more than enough combat experience to last them a lifetime. Their first combat took place May 19, 1863 in the grand assault on the Confederate fortifications surrounding Vicksburg. The 95th, as well as all of the other regiments involved, went through "the awfullest place that ever you seen." But, according to John, the assault of May 22, over the same ground, was worse: "it was the ardest battle. wee charge banet on the rebills brest wurks and wee got on top of a big ill and I tell you that is afful. the bulets came like ale stone and wee all lade down on the ground and they throude shells at us. the first battle wee had 18 killed and I think their was 62 woond but that ante the worst of it. hower caption Cornwell is dead. he was kild in the last battle." John continued; "he was shot thru the head. it kild him dead ... I was right a side the captin when he fell. I tell you I never hugd the ground so ard in my life as I did this time. every Man that held up his head he was eather killed hor woonded but I ham thankful that I was spared thru the to battles." John was indeed lucky. The 95th Illinois, in the two assaults on the Confederate works, had an aggregate loss of killed, wounded and missing of 171 men, more than any other Federal unit involved. There was a total of twenty-six killed, one hundred thirty-seven wounded and eight men missing.[10]

On May 27, John wrote home to his older brother, Robert. After his usual comments answering questions in letters from home, John returned to his personal observations of the situation at Vicksburg. He believed that the River City would be in Federal hands in a few days and that the hardest fighting would be over, at least in the west. He also had found a new officer to admire; Colonel Thomas Humphrey, a grain farmer and dealer from the small community of Franklin, in DeKalb County, just a mile south of the Boone County line. He believed that Humphrey, who was destined to be mortally wounded and die on the field of battle at Brice's Cross Roads, Mississippi on June 10, 1864, was not only a good colonel, but "the best their is in brigade." He explained his rationale for this belief - "that day that wee had the fighte the cirnell of the 72 he was so drunk it tuck to men to caret im of the battlefied. hower cirnell dont drink nor youze tobacco. he is as nice a man as ever walk."[11]

By early June, John was still optimistic about the war and its outcome and felt he would be home some time in the coming fall. He felt the Confederacy was indeed in a tight place and commented that General U. S. Grant felt their soldiers were already prisoners and were providing their own board. Of the five Confederate Generals within Vicksburg, John was convinced that three of them, including General John Pemberton, wanted to surrender. He also commented that at the battle of "Champineshill" on May 16, 1863, the Confederate forces had lost over 1,300 men killed and wounded as well as well over 3,000 taken prisoner of war. It was, he felt, well worth the effort to save "hower Contrey that hower fore fathers fote and bled and dide for and their noble sons ante a goin to let the kirsed rebills rule it if it takes the last man that wee have got in the field."[12]

A clairvoyant, who was a fellow soldier, had informed any of the men who would listen, that indeed the war was on the ebb. He told them "that peas will bee declard on the 23 day of June and the soldurs arms will all be stack at cairo ill." Fortune-telling was no more accurate in the nineteenth century than it is in the twenty-first. John assured his family that he would indeed be home in the fall.[13]

On July 4, 1863, Vicksburg fell and on the 13th John wrote his family that Port Hudson had also surrendered. The men of the 95th left Vicksburg in mid-July and headed further south to Natchez. Adkinson and a few other men of the regiment had been placed on temporary detached duty to remain behind to guard the supplies and equipment that were not able to be transported with the regiment. He immediately took the time to correspond with his family. He mentioned his health was much improved, that James Vincent's health was also hearty, and things were better than ever before. Some of the information that he relayed home was not accurate, however. John had heard that in the east the Federal army had been very successful, capturing Robert E. Lee's entire army and that they had even killed "old lee." John understood that Lee had gotten into the

69

state of "Pencillvaney" but was under the belief that Lee had asked Jefferson Davis, the President of the Confederacy, for reinforcements and that Davis had refused to assist Lee because Richmond, the capitol, was under heavy attack. It had, John mentioned, come to the point where they would see no more fighting and the men would all be home by Christmas.[14]

Another long letter was written on July 15, 1863, and John again talked about Vicksburg. His loneliness and inactivity was beginning to develop into melancholy, depression and thus home sickness. He wrote and rewrote of missing his home, parents, sisters, brothers and even his horses. The absence of bread and a bowl of milk, a common item in Illinois, for which he yearned, were greatly missed. He took several lines to tell all of them that he looked forward to his return to them as quickly as possible.[15]

John and the men that had been left at Vicksburg rejoined their regiment at Natchez by August 2. In a letter on that date, he made specific mention of gifts for his brothers. There was a twenty-dollar Confederate bill for older brother Robert. As John mentioned, "hit ante eney good" but he wanted his brother to see what the Confederacy was using as currency. There was also a ten cent piece of paper money for six year old Henry. He informed his sisters that their gifts would follow in the next letter home.[16]

John fulfilled this promise in the letter of August 6, 1863. He included ten cent papers for his twin sisters, Alta and Alice, who were two years old. He added that he, along with almost one hundred other men, had taken a boat down river some twenty-five miles to forage for food. This particular endeavor was very successful as they returned with fat cattle, fat chickens and lots of corn. He questioned all, asking their advice regarding their opinions of his reenlisting in the army when his term of duty was finished. Should he remain for another three years to see the war effort to a completion or should he finish his agreement and return home?[17]

Another short letter written August 16 continued the soldier's thoughts regarding his past and enjoying the memories of life with his brothers and sisters at home. He also expressed his decision regarding the present by telling them that he was not going to re-enlist for another three years simply because he wanted to come home and stay home. He even contemplated his future and the joys he would have with his family, especially the younger children that had grown so much during his absence.[18]

Four days later he wrote:

"Natchez Missizsippi   August the 20 / 63
Well dear brother I Set down to write a nuther letter to you to let you no that me and James is well and I hope thease few lines will fiend you the Same as it leaves me at present. well dear Brother you sed that you thought that I Sed you cud have that Steer for what I ode you. Well dear Brother I dont no   I have for got wether I did or not but it is all rite and I

think that you got a good price for im and dear Brother when I cum home you and me will make it all write. well Edward if you no how much I ow you I wish you wood write and let me no how much it is and I want you to no how my colt is getting a long and I want to know wether you have got im broke in yet and Edward you can have in to ride when you go to See the girls. well dear Brother I all most for got to tell you when I received your letter. Dear brother I received your kind letter August the 19th and I was glad to hear that you was all well. well dear Brother I think you can write pruty good. you can write now prutineer as good as I cud when I left home and if you keep a writen you will improve in a little while. dear Brother ask robert if he pade old Mr Tirner that I ode im. he sed he wood when I left home. if he did write and let me no. Edward I rote a letter to you Just a little wile before I got this letter. dear brother I was on picket yesterday and last night wee ad a good old time. wee ad all the bread and milk wee cud eat and wee honley pade 10 cents a quart for it. dear brother you sed that you think if I shud come home that odsen cud jump sum ire than he did before. I wood like to see obsen now and little henry and my 3 Sisters. well dear mother I must tell you the dream that I drempt won dark and raney nite when I was Sleeping all a lone in a plase that I bilt in sum boards, well I will tell you the dream now. dear mother I drempt that you was dead and I thought I was on guard and the boys was talking a bout their folks and I thought I felt very bad a bout it and I thought it was dark and raney and I thought I sed to the boys well boys this is a ard life to lead but I thought that mother was dead and I thought that I ad no home now and when I waked up it was thunern and litenen and ranen and dark as it cud bee and I razed up and thought it was so for a while and when I found out that it was onley a dream I tell you I was glad dear Mother. this what I drempt. dear father I wish I ad that tobacco and dear mother I wish I ad them cirence for they wood go good, Dear Brother I was glad of the Postage stamps that you Sent me. it is a ranen to day. Give my kind love to father and mother and to robert and all the rest of them and kizs little henry and the three little girls for me and please write Soone as you get this. So now I must bring my letter to a close. So good day
Edward Y Adkinson   from John H Adkinson Co K - 95 Regiment Infantry"[19]

Six days later, the Joseph and Mary Atkinson family in Boone County Illinois, was sent the following letter from their son-in-law, James Vincent, the brother-in-law that John had mentioned in every letter home.

"Natchez   August 26 1863
My dear father and mother I am happy to inform you that I am well at presant and hope this will find you all the same. I am sorry to inform you that johnny is drowned in the river. he was - him and five or six of the other boys to take the things off the boat that was brought down

from Vicksburg and he came to his diner and was all right and went back again and the boys seen him about three o'clock and then did not see him after that. they hunted all through the boat and could not find him. this was on the 24 aug and I was on picket that day and dident know anny thing about it until the next day and then I hunted all over for him and could not find him and the next morning he was found. he floated ashore and we got him out. all his pockets was picked. He had about twenty four dollars in his pocket but it was all gone and we cant tell wether he fell over board himself or wether some body knocked him over but we buried him the best we could. the boys all feels bad about it and I feel bad but you know mother we cant help it and it dont do anny good to grieve about it as it would do you harm. I send my love to you all. Write as soon as you get this.

From your son James to my dear father and mother Joseph and Mary Adkinson."[20]

John Adkinson's body was eventually returned to northern Illinois and is now buried in the Adkinson family plot in Blaine Cemetery in northern Boone County.

James Vincent died of dysentery at the Regimental Hospital in Vicksburg on December 21, 1863, four months later, and was initially buried in the Vicksburg City Cemetery. When the Vicksburg National Cemetery was created in 1866, James's remains were transferred there and they now lie in Section I, grave # 403.[21]

{1}   Record Group 94, Office of the Adjutant General, Compiled Service records. Volunteer Soldiers, Adkinson, John H. - Pension file & Service Record.

Record Group 94, Office of the Adjutant General, Compiled Service records. Volunteer Soldiers, Cashier, Albert D. J. - Pension file & Service Record.

Gerhard P. Clausius, *The Little Soldier of the 95th* (Journal of the Illinois State Historical Society - Winter, 1958) pp. 380 - 387.

{2}   Record Group 94, Office of the Adjutant General, Compiled Service records. Volunteer Soldiers, Atkinson, John H. - Pension file & Service Record.

Record Group 94, Office of the Adjutant General, Compiled Service records. Volunteer Soldiers, Vincent, James - Pension file & Service Record.

{3}   Record Group 94, Office of the Adjutant General, Compiled Service records. Volunteer Soldiers, Vincent, James - Pension file & Service Record.

{4}   Wales W. Wood, - *A History of the Ninety-Fifth Regiment Illinois Volunteers* (Chicago, Tribune Company's Book and Job Printing Office, 1865) pp. 13 - 70.

{5}   John H. Adkinson Collection - Boone County Historical Society, Belvidere, Illinois

{6}   Wales W. Wood, - *A History of the Ninety-Fifth Regiment Illinois Volunteers* (Chicago: Tribune Company's Book and Job Printing Office, 1865), pp. 70, 71.

{7}   John H. Adkinson to "dear Father" - May the 3 1863 - John H. Adkinson Collection - Boone County Historical Society, Belvidere, Illinois

{8}   John H. Adkinson to "dear father and Mother" - April the 14 1863 - John H. Adkinson Collection - Boone County Historical Society, Belvidere, Illinois

John H. Adkinson to "dear Brother Robert" - May the 6 1863 - John H. Adkinson Collection - Boone County Historical Society, Belvidere, Illinois.

{9}   John H. Adkinson to "dear Brother Robert" - May the 6 1863 - John H. Adkinson Collection - Boone County Historical Society, Belvidere, Illinois.

{10}   John H. Adkinson to "dear father and Mother" - May the 23 1863 - John H. Adkinson Collection - Boone County Historical Society, Belvidere, Illinois.

Wales W. Wood, *A History of the Ninety-Fifth Regiment Illinois Volunteer*s (Chicago: Tribune Company's Book and Job Printing Office, 1865), pp. 73 - 80.

Lt. Col. William F. Fox, *Regimental Losses in The American Civil War 1861 - 1865* (Dayton, Ohio: Press of Morningside Bookshop - 1974), p. 437.

{11}   John H. Adkinson to "dear Brother" May the 27: 1863. John H.
Adkinson Collection - Boone County Historical Society, Belvidere, Illinois
          Record Group 94, Office of the Adjutant General, Compiled
Service records. Volunteer Soldiers, Humphrey, Thomas - Pension file &
Service Record.
          Wales W. Wood, *A History of the Ninety-Fifth Regiment Illinois
Volunteers* (Chicago: Tribune Company's Book and Job Printing Office,
1865), pp. 110 - 112.
{12}   John H. Adkinson to "dear father and Mother" June the 5 1863.
John H. Adkinson Collection - Boone County Historical Society,
Belvidere, Illinois.
          John H. Adkinson to "Dear Father and Mother" June the 14 1863.
John H. Adkinson Collection - Boone County Historical Society,
Belvidere, Illinois.
{13}   John H. Adkinson to "Dear Father and Mother" June the 14 1863.
John H. Adkinson Collection - Boone County Historical Society,
Belvidere, Illinois.
{14}   John H. Adkinson to "dear father and Mother" July the 13th 1863.
John H. Adkinson Collection - Boone County Historical Society,
Belvidere, Illinois.
{15}   John H. Adkinson to "dear Father and Mother" July the 15 1863.
John H. Adkinson Collection - Boone County Historical Society,
Belvidere, Illinois.
{16}   John H. Adkinson to "dear Brother" August the 2 1863. John H.
Adkinson Collection - Boone County Historical Society, Belvidere,
Illinois.
{17}   John H. Adkinson to "Dear Father and Mother" August the 6
1863. John H. Adkinson Collection - Boone County Historical Society,
Belvidere, Illinois.
{18}   John H. Adkinson to "well dear Brother" August the 16 /63. John
H. Adkinson Collection - Boone County Historical Society, Belvidere,
Illinois.
{19}   John H. Adkinson to "well dear Brother" August the 20 ' 63. John
H. Adkinson Collection - Boone County Historical Society, Belvidere,
Illinois.
{20}   James Vincent to "My dear father and mother" August 26 1863.
John H. Adkinson Collection - Boone County Historical Society,
Belvidere, Illinois.
{21}   Record Group 94, Office of the Adjutant General, Compiled
Service records. Volunteer Soldiers, Vincent, James - Pension file &
Service Record

Private Merritt Simonds
Co. K - 41st Illinois Infantry

VIII
"I suffered considerable for want of care"
Private Merritt Simonds
Co. K - 41st Illinois Infantry

It was hot. It was dry. Merritt Simonds had had nothing to drink other than the tepid water in his canteen for almost a week on September 25, 1863. Just a few days before, the weather had been unseasonably cool and Merritt had written in his diary, on the 19th, that it was a cool morning. The night of the 19th, however was not cool. According to Merritt's entry on the 20th, the night before had been very cold.[1]

Merritt and the 42nd Illinois Infantry had just taken part in the first day's battle of Chickamauga and they had marched, on this cool Saturday at nine o'clock in the morning, from bivouac at Crawfish Springs, north a few miles, Merritt thought at least five, rested a brief time and then went into battle on the double quick. The men had done their job well, although they were nearly repulsed. The ground was held and the battle, lasting until dark, was over. The night of the 19th was filled with picket duty and attempts to sleep. Both activities were filled with anxiety, with the realization that the next day would bring more gunfire and more killing.[2]

The morning of the 20th saw the 42nd being moved back almost a mile to a high hill. There they remained until almost 11:00 a.m. On the double quick again, the men moved into the furious battle raging to their front. It was then that nineteen year old Merritt Simonds was wounded. His diary entry simply stated, "I am struck in the right leg just above the knee. shatters the bone some. I try to get off the field but cannot." The diary entry then made note of the other men in Merritt's regiment.[3]

"Captain Foster is wounded in the face . . . William Mott is wounded in the thigh . . . Frank Sunder is wounded in the right leg below the knee . . . George Palmer and John Edmonds are killed." The young soldier was very concerned about his friends and stated that he "lay here until night. The rebs promise to take me off but do not."[4]

For the next six days the young man from Sycamore, Illinois made entries in his diary explaining the situation. It was grim, the Pawlet, Vermont native knew, but he had hope. His entry on the 20th indicated the enemy dead were carried off to be buried, but the Federal wounded remained, all suffering from the sun and the lack of water. The kindhearted of the enemy provided a few blankets and a little water for these men but it did not seem like much for a badly wounded man far from home, in great pain, and hungry.[5]

After a long and restless night, Merritt appeared to become somewhat resigned to his fate: "God help us to endure it. His will be done whether we live or die."[6]

On Wednesday, the 23rd, after three nights and four days, there was no sign of relief. Merritt's situation was still bleak. He and the others were all lying on their back which was very hard on the rough ground. They continued to put their trust in God and were willing to abide by the consequences. His last entry for the 23rd was simple. "May his Holy Will be done"[7]

The morning of the 24th saw the much hoped for relief for the men of the 42nd. A Federal Doctor came to see and assist them that day. The wounded were gently separated from the dead and it was then Merritt learned that his good friend Sherwin King had been killed; shot through the head. Merritt wrote that he "hope to God that he was prepared." Merritt's hope to be removed from the battlefield seemed to intensify by the hour but it was not to be. The final entry for the day was concerning his wounded leg. It was much swollen and very painful.[8]

Friday the 25th found the men still lying on the battlefield, just a few hundred yards north of the Widow Glenn's burned out home. The entry in his diary set the tone for Simonds' feelings. "Still alive." He was bearing up under his suffering as well as he could with the belief that God would help him. He found some solace in the fact that there were others in misery with him.[9]

Finally relief arrived. After six days enduring pain and agony, a small amount of coffee and soup were brought from a hospital and there was a promise of being taken off the following day. That promise was not kept. On the evening of the 26th of September Merritt Simonds was still where he had been for almost a week. He was lying on the field of battle with very little nourishment and no medical care for his badly wounded leg. Merritt and the others had waited patiently and no relief had arrived.[10]

After the battle of Chickamauga several hospitals were created for the care of the wounded. Before the battle there were only enough supplies in Chattanooga, Tennessee to accommodate no more than 500 soldiers. Doctor Israel Moses was presented the formidable task of creating space and ordering supplies for well over 5,000 men and he did so in the following manner. He commandeered thirteen buildings which he estimated would be able to receive 1,000 patients. He also turned the Crutchfield Hotel and its beds which he believed would house about 500 to a hospital. Three churches were taken to house about 200 of the wounded. Lofts over commissary storehouses were transformed into hospital rooms which, he felt, could receive at least 300 men. The buildings near the commissary buildings would accommodate another 400. A large brick building was used as Officer's Hospital #1; it would hold at least 100 officers. Officer's Hospital #2 was a large private mansion and served to accommodate 35 men. Shelter for almost 200 wounded was made by simply taking private homes to be used as hospitals. Those men not seriously wounded were sent as quickly as possible to Stevenson, Alabama by ambulances. On October 1st, Doctor Moses also requested that, due to the increasing risk to the patients with suppurating wounds being crowded, new temporary pavilions be constructed for use as hospitals.[11]

Eventually the suffering soldiers were removed to hospitals in Chattanooga, a few miles north of the Chickamauga battlefield. Merritt penned the following letters while hospitalized there. His spelling was not the best. His punctuation was lacking. What were present were the young soldier's hopes and the young soldier's fears.

"Gen. Sheridans Div. Hosp.   Chattanooga, Tenn.
Oct 8th 1863
Dear Father;
    I write to you in different circumstances than ever before. I have been severely wounded in the right leg just above the knee and very close to it in the fierce battle of the (Chicamog-gin) I believe they term it. Which was fought on the 19th and 20th of last month. I was wounded on Sunday the 20th about noon and remained on the field until the next Saturday night when I was taken off about four miles to a hospital. I suffered considerable for want of care etc. The rebs helped me some for the first four days, then they let one of our doctors and some of our men come to see us, they removed from the dead bodies, dressed our wound a little gave us something to eat etc. Still we did not get off the field until nearly the end of the seventh day. We could have but little care then as there were so many of us and we drew nothing but meal and a little beef from the rebs. The next Wednesday we were taken in ambulances and taken to our present place which was very hard for us being a rough road of thirteen miles. I have as good care as can be taken of me here. I have had a fever nearly every day since I was wounded. It has brought me down pretty low and weak. The doctor thinks he has broken it know. The doctor says my leg will be stiff when it gets well. I rest middling well with it. I am resigned to abide the kind will of our Heavenly Father. I read my testament and pray to Him that whether I live or die I may do all to His glory. Pray for me. Sherwin was killed instantly on the battle field near me. I shall write often and let you know how I am. Give my love to all inquiring friens. write immediately Direct to the Regiment Chattanooga, Tenn. If we never should meet again on this earth may we meet in Heaven is the prayer of your unworthy
        Son in Christ
        M. J. Simonds
    I will send my photographs, one of which give to Horace and Mary, one Uncle Justin and Emma, one to Mr. Tappan's people and one to Uncle Ralphs folks and the other to Uncle Alvin's folks.
        Good bye until you hear from me again
        Merritt"[12]

Several days later, Merritt Simonds wrote.

"Gen. Hosp. No. '2'
Chattanooga, Tenn.
Oct. 27th   1863
Dear Father,
　　　　Since I last wrote I have been growing worse, my leg is now mortifying above the knee and the Dr's say I cannot live more than two days at the longest. You must not take this to heart but look to a higher source for comfort, for it is God's will and I feel resigned to my fate. I hope to meet you all in a better world.
　　　　I would like to have my body taken home and buried beside my mother.
　　　　I am comparatively comfortable at present there is no pain in my leg. I have some things which I authorize Wm. Mott to take home and some others I authorize Geo. Write to sell and send the money to you. I am owing Sherwin King $2.00 two dollars. will you please pay his father as poor Sherwin is no more. Father my mare and colt I wish you to keep them in remembrance of me. My love to all my family connections & tell them I would have written to many of them if I had thought sooner
　　　　I now bid you all a kind good Bye
　　　　M. J. Simonds"[13]

　　　　Private Simonds' leg had become gangrenous. Gangrene was a condition that had several names, all of which were frightening. Known as mortification and sphacelus, it was also known as dry gangrene, moist gangrene, hospital gangrene and gangrenous phagedaena. Whatever the name, it was feared because the survival rate was not good and, if there was survival, it was painful and debilitating, often resulting in the loss by amputation of the afflicted area.   Of the total number of gangrenous circumstances that developed in one particular study during the Civil War, 2,642 cases, only 1,361 recovered. This death rate, 45.6%, was considered severe.   Very little was known, however, research and speculation concerning gangrene was great. It was a common belief among most physicians that it developed most rapidly in any vicinity where odor from latrines or sewage was present. Also, it was known that a severe odor of rotting flesh soon permeated the entire area where the patient lay.[14]
　　　　"In the early stages it appeared as a dusky, almost black, mass of dead and rotting flesh, ... surrounded by a reddish ring of slightly swollen integuments ... while the adjacent tissues do not appear to be affected by the disease."[15]
　　　　Very little could be done regarding the treatment of this mysterious condition. The cauterization of the wounded or inflicted area by either nitric acid or acid nitrate of mercury was possible. The mercurial based treatment was, it seemed, far less painful to the patient but both

needed to be applied by puncturing the afflicted region and probing the area thus allowing the solution to do its work close to the uninfected flesh. A simple mopping of the locale did not allow the medication to penetrate to the actual soft tissue that was still alive and healthy. Another treatment tried by many surgeons was a treatment of hot creosote which often seemed to work well. The only other accepted form of treatment was amputation considerably above the gangrenous or mortifying area. Nothing was certain regarding its treatment.[16]

A few days later the following letter was sent off to Illinois from a friend of Merritt's, Private George H. Wright, also from Sycamore, Illinois.

"Chattanooga, Tenn.
Oct. 30th/63
Mr. Simonds,
Dear Sir

I am very sorry to inform you of the sad intelligence that your much beloved son Merritt is no more. he died last night. I cannot make it seem that he is dead. Poor boy! how much he anticipated and hoped to enjoy himself on returning to his dear friends at home after the close of this conflict. But his conflicts are all over, and I trust he is now in the enjoyment of perfect bliss. I seem hard to give him up, and yet we must not murmur. Although we cannot see him again in this world we can prepare to meet him in another and better world.

Merritt was a good soldier he always done his duty cheerfully and as a brave soldier.

we will bury his remains tomarrow and mark his grave distinctly so that they could be found if wanted.
Yours with respect
Geo. H. Wright"[17]

Merritt's wish to be taken home and buried beside his mother, Minerva Dayton Simonds, who had passed away in 1846 before the family moved to Illinois, was not to be. He was buried in grave #234, Section A, at the Chattanooga National Cemetery, Chattanooga, Tennessee.[18]

{1}   Merritt Simonds' Diary - September 19, 1863. Merritt Simonds Collection, Northern Illinois University Library.

{2}   Ibid.

{3}   Merritt Simonds' Diary - September 20, 1863. Merritt Simonds Collection, Northern Illinois University Library.

{4}   Ibid.

{5}   Record Group 94, Office of the Adjutant General, Compiled Service records. Volunteer Soldiers, Simonds, Merritt - Pension file & Service Record.

        Merritt Simonds' Diary - September 21, 1863. Merritt Simonds Collection, Northern Illinois University Library.

{6}   Merritt Simonds' Diary - September 22, 1863. Merritt Simonds Collection, Northern Illinois University Library.

{7}   Merritt Simonds' Diary - September 23, 1863. Merritt Simonds Collection, Northern Illinois University Library.

{8}   Merritt Simonds' Diary - September 24, 1863. Merritt Simonds Collection, Northern Illinois University Library.

{9}   Merritt Simonds' Diary - September 25, 1863. Merritt Simonds Collection, Northern Illinois University Library.

{10}   Merritt Simonds' Diary - September 26, 1863. Merritt Simonds Collection, Northern Illinois University Library.

{11}   Merritt Simonds to "Dear Father" Oct 8th 1863. Merritt Simonds Collection, Northern Illinois University Library.

{12}   United States War Department. *The Official Records of the War of the Rebellion. A Compilation of the Official Records of the Union and Confederate Armies. 128 Vols.* (Washington: 1881 - 1902), Series I – Volume XXX/1, p. 344

{13}   Merritt Simonds to "Dear Father" Oct 27th 1863. Merritt Simonds Collection, Northern Illinois University Library.

{14}   Surgeon General Joseph K. Barnes, United States Army – *The Medical And Surgical History Of The War Of The Rebellion. (1861-65)* (Washington Printing Office, 1870), Reprinted by Broadfoot Publishing Company – Wilmington, North Carolina 28405 – 1990 – 15 vols. Volume XII, pp. 823 – 851.

{15}   Surgeon General Joseph K. Barnes, United States Army – *The Medical And Surgical History Of The War Of The Rebellion. (1861-65)* (Washington Printing Office, 1870), Reprinted by Broadfoot Publishing Company – Wilmington, North Carolina 28405 – 1990 – 15 vols. Volume XII, p. 845.

{16}   Surgeon General Joseph K. Barnes, United States Army – *The Medical And Surgical History Of The War Of The Rebellion. (1861-65)* Washington Printing Office, 1870. Reprinted by Broadfoot Publishing Company – Wilmington, North Carolina 28405 – 1990 – 15 vols. Volume XII, pp. 823 – 851.

{17}   George Wright to "Dear Sir" Oct 30th/63. Merritt Simonds

Collection, Northern Illinois University Library.

{18}   Record Group 94, Office of the Adjutant General, Compiled Service records. Volunteer Soldiers, Simonds, Merritt - Pension file & Service Record

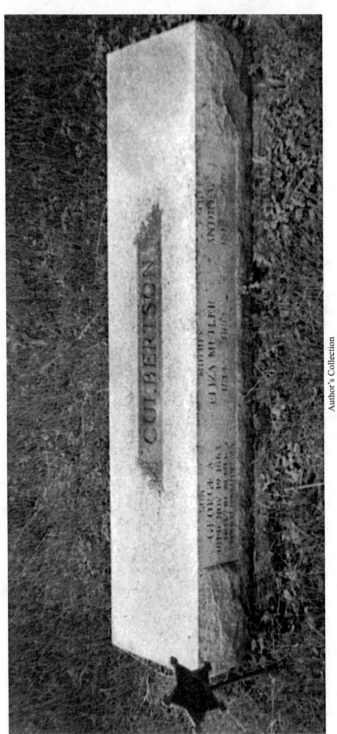

Author's Collection

Private George Culbertson
Co. I - 127th Illinois Infantry
Garden Park, Illinois Cemetery

IX

"I was about gon up"
Private George A. Culbertson
Co. I - 127th Illinois Infantry

George Culbertson was a hard working twenty-four year old who had spent his life assisting his fifty-year-old father, Andrew, and his forty-nine-year-old mother, Eliza, in the support of his two sisters and the working of their small rented farm. George was the middle sibling of the three children. Their small farm, in Spring Township, was being rented with the hopes of eventually purchasing more acres, to provide the family an even better life.[1]

George had been a contributing member of the work force on the farm and before the war he had found a special lady who seemed to have caught his eye, by the name of Laura Thorne. He mentioned her often in his several letters home while he served in the 127th Illinois Volunteer Infantry. Perhaps this made his thoughts of enlarging the property more than a simple economic adventure for the family.[2]

Young Culbertson left his home in Garden Prairie, Illinois, a small farming community some one hundred miles northwest of Chicago and traveled to Elgin, some twenty-five miles to the east to enroll in Company I, of the 127th Infantry on August 11th, 1862. He returned to his home to wait until September 6th, to muster into the unit at Camp Douglas, a few miles south of Chicago. This gave him ample time to finish the fall's harvest, gather hay for the winter and help the family to settle in for the cold and often hard winter season.[3]

Culbertson's first duty was the rather easy, although boring, duty of guarding the prisoners of war at Camp Douglas. These men, many from the battles on the Tennessee and Cumberland Rivers such as Forts Henry and Donelson, were ill-prepared for the stay in Northern Illinois and were encamped very close to the shores of Lake Michigan. While at Camp Douglas, letters to Garden Prairie reveal that life was relatively pleasant for Culbertson and the men of the 127th. Much time was spent watching two artillery batteries drill. The Elgin Battery and the Chicago Mercantile Battery trained daily with their guns. Each gun, it was noted, was equipped with six horses which was quite a sight for the infantry guard.[4]

Life for these young recruits also allowed time for visits to the city of Chicago. On one occasion the men - primarily from Cook, Grundy, Kane and Kendall counties - were invited to a lecture by a lady at Briant Hall. The price of admission was fifty cents for citizens and free for soldiers. After the event, the men were "Invited Into a Restarant and an Ice cream supper set before us." Culbertson was quite pleased with the fact as he then stated in a letter dated September 18, 1862, "O dont We Putt On

Airs."[5]

Supplies and living conditions were at least acceptable to George. He mentioned food as sufficient and it consisted of such fare as pork, potatoes, coffee, tea, and molasses. Of great importance to him was the abundant supply of good water. In fact, almost every letter young George sent back to Illinois makes some mention of the plentiful food.

By September 18th, full uniforms had been issued; a "full Black Dress Coat and blue pants" accompanied the usual supply of two shirts, a pair of drawers, an overcoat, two pairs of socks and a pair of shoes.[6]

On November 9th, after two months of guard duty, the regiment headed south to participate in the Central Mississippi Campaign under General Ulysses S. Grant. This was followed almost immediately by General William T. Sherman's ill-fated Yazoo Expedition near the city of Vicksburg, Mississippi. George, however, was still in Chicago. His very close friend, Charles H. Duck, Hospital Steward for the 127th, wrote the Culbertson family on November 2nd and informed his sister, Mary, that George was quite ill and recommended that his father should come to aid him if possible. George had requested Duck to open, read and answer Culbertson's mail "just before he became insensible."[7]

A letter following, by the same soldier, on November 6th, indicated that the regiment would be on the move and that George's condition would only worsen if he were to accompany it. It was with sadness that this friend was leaving George behind. Duck was concerned regarding $23.00 that George wanted to send to his family and he informed them that he would keep the money safe until either the family arrived or the regiment left. If the latter were to be the case the money would be sent home by express mail.[8]

George Culbertson's illness was not quickly shaken. By January 5th, 1863, Duck wrote the family again, indicating that George still had not returned to the regiment but that Duck still had George's watch which had been given for safe keeping in November. Duck had forgotten to turn the watch over to the family in all the hustle of the regiment's leaving but he assured them that it was very secure and would be sent to George as soon as possible.[9]

George rejoined the regiment in March, at Memphis, Tennessee. His health was much improved and his comments to his family were certainly upbeat and showed much promise. Talk of peach trees with blossoms and green grass growing made the area "just the country for me." He mentioned that his father should make a special effort to see the area of the Illinois Central railroad to confirm that it was indeed the area where George would like a farm some day. He predicted it to be the future garden of the west, stating there is "lotts of cenery for the I." His dismay and sadness regarding how the land looked where the army "Has bin Buildings ar diserted and all looks Hard" were the comments of a true lover of agricultural ways.[10]

His letter sent after the move from Memphis to Vicksburg, in April, 1863 showed a bit of change in George's feelings and health. He was beginning to get homesick by his own admission, but his back pay of $73.65 did seem to make the hardship a bit more acceptable. Stating that this pay was all in one dollar bills, it made "quite a pile of greenbacks." He sent home $55.00 by the Adams Express Company for the aid of the family. Although it cost $2.00 to do so, George believed it was worth the expense to assist his family in northern Illinois. He missed planting time and working the ground and he also wished he could be of more help to his family.[11]

Of almost equal concern for this farm boy was his consideration for the livestock. He asked about the colts and even his favorite work horse, "Old Bill." The young horses that had been rented out were also of concern to George. He reminded his father that they were the finest available and that they must surely have weighed at least 1300 pounds by now. Culbertson, a true horseman, would discuss his animals in almost every letter home.[12]

Military matters were not high on Culbertson's priority list. In fact his military comments, for the most part, revolved around the hope that the war would soon be finished and he would "be able to come Home to Help you put in your grain." But the war did continue and George remained with his regiment.[13]

The experiences George witnessed in the taking of Vicksburg are the same as was expressed by the thousands of other young Midwestern lads far from home. War was boring, home was so very far away, and his letters were a never ending train of thought pertaining to home life which he missed very much and military life which he realized was what the home folks wanted to hear about. In his letter of April 24th, 1863 George said the regiment had moved from some 25 miles up river and were now located 16 miles south of the city. He described the regiment's duties: "we are detached from Our brigade as a pioneer core to work on the new canal from miligan's bend into a bayou which leads to the mississippi Somewhare about warington. it is no failyer we think it is a grand good thing." Again, speaking of the bayou, he wrote of the cutting of trees and stumps to allow the boats to get through. He explained they downed the trees while standing on rafts, cut them up and hauled them out with mule teams. Culbertson further explains the finishing touches very simply "take saws and cut the stumps six feet under water. it is quite a piece of work but we do a lot of it in a day." With that statement, George began another long description of the fine homes and the abundance of peaches, strawberries, collards and the various foodstuffs in the area.[14]

One month later, George informed his family that he was at "Post Chickasaw" and carefully detailed his journey from Richmond, Louisiana on May 6 to Grand Gulf where they crossed the river below Vicksburg into Mississippi. In the attempt to cut off southern supplies, which according to

George, they had "done to a charm" the men had marched more than 200 miles in a hot and dusty climate on 3/5th rations. He said, with a hint of pride, "I never took off my clothes for two weeks" and he "pulled his own weight almost all of the distance." His only engagement with the Southern forces he illustrated as follows: "we Had no skermish with the enemy for some ways and at last they made a stand and we pitked in so then and liked them lik thunder and captures all off there artilery and lots of prisiners, that was near raymond."[15]

George's narration of the assault made by federal forces at Vicksburg on May 19th 1863, just a few days before this letter was written, is vivid: "we wer formed in line of battle in the woods and out of sight of them and then we had to rais a bluff right in range of there guns O it was awful the thout of starting but we did and we did it nobely but it was a day long to be remembered by me we went Over the bluff on a double quick firing as we ran there was lots of them Killed and wounded before they went five rodds O to see your one Boys fall all around you and to Here the shreaks of the wounded was awful they had cut all the trees off the side Hill and left them for us to climb over I felt no more fear than I would to go out on a rabbit hunt after the first shot was fired on we went fireing as we run under the most deadly that Had bin in the western army I Had got down the Hill about half way when Ora duglas was wound in the thy, right close by whare He fell and Nelson Merril and me laid down Our guns and dressed his wound Nels had some lint and we stopped the bludd and bound it up and went on and left him untill we came back there were two killed within a rodd of him the Colonel Kept marching his men on to the fort and pretty soon the officers wer as far as we could get them but there was not many men up with them (I - your Only son) was the first of our company to bring up the cullars with the colonel He said I was the bravest Man He Had I never got a Scrach no whare."[16]

Corporal Ora B. Douglass of Elgin was severely wounded and suffered greatly until his death at St. Louis, Missouri on July 28, 1863 and Nelson H. Merrill, also from Elgin, was recognized for his ability and soon after the siege at Vicksburg was promoted to first sergeant, first lieutenant and eventually became captain of the company.[17]

The 22nd of May, 1863, the date of the second assault on the Vicksburg fortifications, saw some of the men of the 127th, including Culbertson, serving as guards for the prisoners of war that had been taken on the 19th. George was not sad to have missed the second assault.[18]

The 127th Illinois Regiment spent the months of the actual siege of the river city at "Post Chicka saw" at the rear of Vicksburg. It seemed to be nothing but guard duty at the landing at the river and every fourth or fifth day, a stint of picket duty. Not much happened except now many of the men were developing fever and ague and the only pleasantness came from time picking "BlackBerries."[19]

George's health was not good again. He wrote he was "taking

quinine by the Bushel" as the physicians did not "stop to way it out." George was determined to not allow the fever to get the advantage of him again. He was unsuccessful, as were many of the men, and by mid June the entire regiment had moved to a healthier place. This move seemed to have been successful as the men soon began to demonstrate better vitality. Culbertson felt his three attacks of the shakes were of little consequence and he stated he was as well as ever. Mistakenly, he also believed the fighting was almost done for the summer.[20]

When General John Pemberton surrendered his Confederate forces at Vicksburg to Grant on July 4th, 1863, a new front was chosen and within a few days many of the troops, the 127th included, found themselves bound for Jackson, Mississippi to confront the Confederate forces under the command of General Joseph E. Johnston. An area called Walnut Hills became the next camping area, at least for the 127th Illinois Volunteers. While there, George found time to send another letter to his father. He was not included in action on the city of Jackson, but was left behind to assist the many sick - as was his dear friend, Charley Duck, the man that had served as George's spokesperson while George had been sick seven months earlier. George's health was first rate at this time.[21]

The livestock, more particularly the horses, became the mainstay of Culbertson's letters to his father. He had questions regarding many of the animals and suggestions regarding others. It was obvious that he missed home and life on the farm a great deal. George even hinted that perhaps a trip north might be in store for many of the men. It was not to be.[22]

By the 21st of July, George was back at Vicksburg and not in the best of spirits or health. He simply states "well Pa if I live to get Home again I never shal leave you a gain to trudge and tail from morning till night to obtain a livelihood but I felt it my duty to go and fight for my country but god Knows that I love my parents and it gives me manny sad thotts to know that they Have to work so Hard but maybe it is all the Best but get along as well as you can pa the more I think a bout the farm the more I want it"[23]

In early August, 1863, George Culbertson and the 127th Illinois were camped at Camp Sherman on the Big Black River fifteen miles east of Vicksburg. His correspondence to home is full of family questions with an emphasis on the livestock and farm work. George still missed the everyday freedoms of farm life and the joys of being around family and promises were made to assist more on the farm as well as to provide financial assistance. His only request was that he be provided with a "fine pair of double souled french calf boots, size eight."[24]

It was on August 12th, 1863, that George wrote a brief note to his father because another soldier in the regiment, William Holden, was writing to him. George included his note in the envelope with Holden's letter. The letter itself, although short, showed George's anxieties. He assured his family the food was both good and plentiful. The meal that day consisted of "tea vigitable soup Stewed Peaches warm Buiskets Butter." He then followed by saying, "I shant complain." Culbertson made one of the rare mentions of sick men within the regiment: "we Have men detailed to wait on the sick .... we lost one man last Night   he died of feaver   He wasn't sick but a few days   He was a nice young man   He carried our mail." George finished this brief note by stating that he did not think that he was going to be very sickly the rest of the summer.[25]

As summer gave way to fall, the 127th Illinois found themselves still at Camp Sherman on the Big Black River. In a letter dated September 8th, 1863, George wrote his concerns and wishes had not changed. He was, in his own familiar way, becoming homesick again. He was happy the girls were having such fine times attending caravans and dances and stated, "well dash away   enjoy yourself as well as you can while young for I can't." He then indicated good health for himself as well as a grand "apetite". George attributed this to the fact that "I work like a niger every day and I think it is the best thing that I can do". He also stated "the boys that lay around camp are the Ones that are the most sickly   we Have 25 sick in Hospital and it gives us boys lotts to do". Questions and advice to his father concerning the livestock and farm take up the remaining space in this letter which he ends with a short, blunt "no more   wright soon.   Geo A. Culbertson"[26]

When George next communicated with the family, he and the regiment were in Memphis making preparations to advance on Chattanooga, Tennessee, hundreds of miles to the east to relieve the Union forces under siege as a result of the loss at the battle of Chickamauga on September 19th and 20th. George was to be included in that move. On October 6th, 1863, George informed his family that the boots had arrived as well as the shirts and everything "fit first rate." He then mentioned that he had been quite unwell but he felt he was "a good deal better so I do duty all the time." His experiences were, he felt, "enough to make anybody sick." He was particularly happy to have received a cake baked by his mother. George had shared it with his friends and indicated he had made special mention to them that it had been made by his mother. Even a tear was shed, according to George, at the serving of it.[27]

The weather at Memphis was not to George's liking. He informed his family "it is awful cold Here   I liked to froze last night coming from such a warm climate   it is over 400 miles from Here to vicksburg   that makes considerable difference" His good friend Charley Duck was still home very sick and had been there for quite some time. Culbertson informed his family that Duck had made an attempt to return to the regiment but had only made it as far south as Cairo when he took sick again and had to return home. If only George's health would improve, he would be ready for the upcoming trip across the long state of Tennessee.[28]

In a short note from LaGrange Station, Tennessee, George told his family the regiment was on the move. He believed they were on their way to Corinth, Mississippi. He had "cot a very Heavy cold and it settled in my chest but Doc clark Keeps me all right" The young soldier was sure he would be better when he arrived at Corinth. After all, he would only be driving a team of mules pulling supplies.[29]

On November 23rd, George Culbertson sent the following letter to his family.

"Dear Friends at Home,

How are you? I have a Hard job on Hand   I am very sick again you know I told you when we started On the march that I was going to drive the ambulance team   well I did and the trip was to Hard for me   I drove about One weak and Had to give up muy team   November 25th and ride all the way through as far as they could take me   they did not dare to leave for fear the Rebs would get me   I tell you I was about gon up after riding 15 days On my back Over mountains and stones and the worst roads I ever saw   nothing but rocks   they left me in a Hospital at bridgeport till I get better   I Have the chronick diariah but am feeling better and am a good deal better   I am as poor as I was last winter almost but still Have Hopes yet   I will get Home sometime this winter if I live   I sent you thirty Dollars from Iuca Springs   did not Here from it yet   I will try and Keepp you posted How I get along   I am in hopes I will get well soon   we get postal fare Here   we are within Hearing distance of the front whare they ar fighting   well I must close   good by

Geo A Culbertson"[30]

Just a little over a month later the Culbertson family - Andrew, his wife Eliza, and their two daughters, Mary Ann and Sarah - received the following letter.

"Camp 127th Ill Vol
Bridgeport Ala
Dec 21st 1863
A. J. Culbertson
Dear Sir

It becomes my painfull duty to announce to you the death of your son, George who died at this place the first of the month in the hospital where we were compelled to leave him as we stopped through on our way to Chattanooga last month. He was in hopes to reach some of his friends, I believe in Kentucky when we parted with him. On our return however a few days ago we learned the sorrowful news that he was no more. That he had gon from among us to another and better world. His effects consist of one pair boots two shirts one pr pants one over coat. The above mentioned articles being so bulky and transportation so difficult to obtain its our coustom to sell. I will forward you their value, in monie as soon as disposal of. with it is 60c in monie. a calendar His watch I will send you the first opportunity I have. Wm Holden will write you all the particulars of his sickness.

Yours Truly

Capt F. A. Raymond"[31]

The day before Christmas William Holden wrote the following letter to the Culbertson family.

"Dear Friend Culbertson

This is Christmas Eve and it finds me in the Army. Still enjoying good Helth But Mr. Culbertson we are all called to morn the loss of a Dear Brother Soldier. I supose that you have herd of the Death of your Dear Boy but to make it sure I will Send you a line from my Hand. I should of writen long before this But I was not where I could here of his Death for three weeks after he Died. I Supose you will think it Strange of me not writing to you before he Died But my Dear Friend you must not Blame me. I will give you my Reasons why I Did not no it. while our Regt was at Lagrange Tenn, I was up at our Hospatall one Day and I noticed that George was Sick I Sat Down and talked with him for a few minutes I thought then that I would sit Down and write you a letter I Spoke to George and told him what my intentions were and he rather me not to Do it for you would feel so bad to know that he was sick but I thought for shure that it was Best that you Should know it so I wrote a letter to you but George Beged so hard for me not to send it that I tore it up and I have Been sorry Ever Since that I did it well after that he got Better for a while and I was in hopes that he was going to get well and I think he would if he had of Done as the Dr. wanted him to Do. You See that after we left Lagrange we Marched through to Iuka Springs. george Rode through in the carts but I thought that George was getting well and I think So now but you See that when we got to Iuka our Regt Drew two Ambulances and George had the promis of Driving one of them well when the Reg left Iuka for Chattanooga George was not able to Do it and the Dr told him that he had Better Stay and go Back to Memphis to a Hospatall I told George that he had not better come for I thought that it would not be good if he come but he thought that a March would do him good well he Drove the Ambulance for Days and was obliged to give it up I was sorry for him but could not help him well we Marched through to Bridgeport and hear we had to leave him in the Hospatall when we marched to Chattanooga we was gone one month from the time we left till we came Back and I never herd of the Death of George untill we came Back here Taz told me that he had Been Dead 3 weeks I was not Much Surprised to here of it but I was very Sorry. George was a good soldier and a good Boy much beloved by all the Boys in this Company and they all feel as though they have lost a Brother. I want that you Should write as soon as you get this give my

love to all your Dear Family   with this I Remain
Yours very truly
William H. Holden"[32]

George would have been buried in the hospital cemetery at Bridgeport, Alabama, but when all of the remains there were removed to the National Cemetery in Chattanooga, Tennessee, after the war was over, his identification was lost. George Culbertson is probably buried in one of the thousands of unknown graves. In the small country cemetery at the edge of Garden Prairie, Illinois is a simple headstone at the final resting place of Andrew and Eliza Culbertson. Also on this stone is inscribed: **In Memory of George Culbertson - Died in Alabama**.

{1}   Record Group 94, Office of the Adjutant General, Compiled Service records. Volunteer Soldiers, Culbertson, George A. - Pension file & Service Record.

{2}   Ibid.

{3}   Ibid.

{4}   George Culbertson to "Dear Friends at Home" Aug 30, 1862. Collection of Velma Crawford.

{5}   George Culbertson to "Dear Sister Mary" Sept 18, 1862. Collection of Velma Crawford.

{6}   Ibid.

{7}   Frederick H. Dyer, *A Compendium of the War of the Rebellion - Two Volumes.* (Dayton, Ohio: National Historical Society. The Press of Morningside Bookshop. 1979), Volume #2, pp. 1099, 1100.

Chas H. Duck to "Miss Mary Culbertson" November 2, 1862. Collection of Velma Crawford.

{8}   CH Duck to Wm Culbertson Nov 6.   Collection of Velma Crawford.

{9}   Chas. H. Duck to Mr. Culbertson Jan 5, 1863.   Collection of Velma Crawford.

{10}   Record Group 94, Office of the Adjutant General, Compiled Service records. Volunteer Soldiers, Culbertson, George A. - Pension file & Service Record.

George Culbertson to "Dear Friends at Home" March 16, 1863. Collection of Velma Crawford

{11}   George Culbertson to "Dear Father" April 15 1863. Collection of Velma Crawford

{12}   Ibid.

{13}   Ibid.

{14}   George Culbertson to "Dear Father and Mother and sisters" Apr 24/63. Collection of Velma Crawford.

{15}   George Culbertson to "Dear Parents and sisters" May 24, / 63. Collection of Velma Crawford.

{16}   Ibid.

{17}   Brigadier General J.N. Reece, *Report of the Adjutant General of the State of Illinois* - (Springfield, Illinois: 1900), Volume VI, pp. 507 - 509

{18}   George Culbertson to "Dear Parents and sisters" May 24, / 63. Collection of Velma Crawford.

{19}   George Culbertson to "Dear Father & Mother and sisters" June 19/63. Collection of Velma Crawford.

{20}   Ibid.

George Culbertson to "Dear Father Mother and sisters" June 24/63. Collection of Velma Crawford.

{21}   George Culbertson to "Dear Father" July 10, 1863. Collection of Velma Crawford.

{22} Ibid.

{23} George Culbertson to "Dear Father" July 21 / 63. Collection of Velma Crawford.

{24} George Culbertson to "Dear Sister" Aug. 10, 1863. Collection of Velma Crawford.

{25} George Culbertson to "Dear Father" Aug 12 / 63. Collection of Velma Crawford.

{26} George Culbertson to "Dear Sister" Sep. 8, 63. Collection of Velma Crawford.

{27} George Culbertson to "Dear Friends at Home" Oct 6, 1863. Collection of Velma Crawford.

{28} Ibid.

{29} George Culbertson to "Dear Sister" Oct 13/63. Collection of Velma Crawford.

{30} George Culbertson to "Dear Friends at Home" Nov.23, 1863. Collection of Velma Crawford.

{31} Capt F. A. Raymond to A. J. Culbertson Dec 21st 1863. Collection of Velma Crawford.

{32} Holden, William to Dear Friend Culbertson dec 24. Collection of Velma Crawford

2nd Lieutenant James Bayne
Co. B - 106th New York Infantry

X

"we hope to march to Victory or to a glorious Death."
Second Lieutenant James Bayne
Co. B - 106th New York Infantry

James H. Bayne was born in Scotland and while quite young immigrated to the United States with his parents, John and Jayne A. Bayne, his two older brothers, Andrew and Donald, and a younger sister, Marianne. The Eighteen year old James committed himself to three years of service in a New York regiment on July 19, 1862, at the city of Morristown. Before his enlistment, the blue-eyed Scot had worked as a merchant in the village and had also worked at The Manufactory of Walcott and Campbell's New York Mills located in the city of Oneida. While employed at The Mills, young James consistently contributed income for his family, providing many of the funds on which the family survived.

When war erupted in the Charleston, South Carolina harbor, all three of the Bayne brothers rushed to assist their new country. Andrew became a member of the Sixteenth New York Volunteer Infantry and rose through the ranks, becoming a second lieutenant in September and a first lieutenant in October of 1862. By June of 1864 he was a first lieutenant in the Volunteer Relief Corps and received a promotion to captain by May of 1864. He mustered out of the service in September of 1866 having transferred to the 42nd U. S. Infantry. His service as regimental adjutant lasted until April of 1869 when he was transferred to the Sixth U. S. Infantry. By the end of May he was appointed Regimental Quartermaster. Andrew retired from the service with that rank on March 25, 1871, and died on October 12, 1893.

Donald, the second brother, became a member of the 57th New York Infantry, was made captive by the Confederate forces and eventually taken to Andersonville Prison in southeast Georgia. It was there that Donald died of small pox on July 4, 1864. His grave is #61 in the National Cemetery there.[1]

James joined the 106th New York Infantry, "The St. Laurence County Regiment" and was assigned to Co. B for mustering ceremonies on August 27, 1862, at Ogdensburgh, one hundred - fifty miles north of his hometown of Oneida. The following day the 106th began its journey to Baltimore, Maryland, and the war. Training would be provided on a need-to-know basis and at that time all that was needed were warm bodies for guard duty on the Upper Potomac River at New Creek, Virginia. James, or Jim, as he was called, was promoted to sergeant on March 7, 1863 while the regiment was guarding the railroad line there.

There was an eight-day expedition for these foot soldiers to an area called Greenland Gap in mid-April and, on the 29th, they marched to Fairmount and then Martinsburg, West Virginia. On June 14, the 106th saw its first combat in the Battle of Winchester, Virginia and were forced to retreat to Harper's Ferry, West Virginia, arriving there the following day.

The regiment, still with a minimum of military training, moved into Washington, D.C. on July 1 where they guarded buildings for five days until assigned to the Army of the Potomac immediately after the Battle of Gettysburg, in Pennsylvania. They joined that army at Frederick, Maryland on July 5 to take part in the pursuit of General Robert E. Lee's retreating Confederate army. A brief action at Wapping Heights, Virginia on July 23 was followed by two months of duty on the Rappahannock and Rapidan Rivers.

It was during this time that the five-foot five inch teen lost some of his military accouterments. On June 15, he was charged for the loss of one knapsack, one gum blanket and a canteen. All were objects very much needed by a foot soldier on the move.[2]

Sergeant Bayne was, however, a good soldier and on October 21, 1863, he was promoted to second lieutenant. With the promotion came more pay which enabled him to express more money home to his family. Two shipments of money arrived in Oneida from James. The first, delivered by The Adams Express Company contained one hundred and fifty dollars and, by the same express company, another package arrived with four hundred and twenty dollars. In 1863 for a rather poor immigrant family in the state of New York, these were both very large amounts of money and undoubtedly greatly appreciated.[3]

The remaining months of 1863, the men of the 106th New York Infantry, as well as the entire Army of the Potomac, were kept busy. They were involved in action on the Bristoe Campaign from October 9 to 22 and then served on line along the Rappahannock River at such places as Kelly's Ford and Brandy Station. During the final week of November and the first two days of December these same men were also involved in the Mine Run Campaign which was considered less than a grand success for the Federal troops. However, the men were successful in preventing General Lee's Army of Northern Virginia from leaving central Virginia for the winter. Bristoe Station turned those forces back into central Virginia and the Mine Run activity kept them there for the winter months of 1863 - 64. December and January were not months fondly remembered by the men of the Army of the Potomac. However, in a letter James wrote to his friend, ex-Sergeant Styles in late March, it seems something good did indeed happen to the army.

"Headquarters   Co B - 106th Regiment N. Y. Vols
Brandy Station, Va.
March 26th 1864

Ex Sergeant Styles

You must forgive me for not writing you before now, but I hope you will be lenient enough towards me as to Say that you are Satisfied if I do better in the future.

I like Soldiering first rate and it agrees with me bully. I am even growing fat as I grow old and Should I continue to grow in this manner I will be wider then I am long. The weather is very cold today. We had a heavy Snow Storm on the night of the 23rd and as the Snow went away it leaves us in the mud knee deep, and I never Saw such mean mud as this Sacred Soil of old Virginia farms.

General Grant is with us now So we may look for active Service on a large Scale this Summer. It will be the most desperate campaign to record, but with the Successful hero of the Southwest to lead us, we hope to march to Victory or to a glorious Death. This may be the last time you hear from me for it may be my lot to fall in defense of the glorious cause which a million humans are fighting to maintain, and which is made Sacred by the life blood of two Hundred thousand Patriots and Maertyers.

The army is being reorganized and the Corps are being constructed into three grand Corps de Armee, namely the 2nd, 5th and 6th Corps, the 3rd and 1st are to be broken up and distributed amongst the other three. Our Division is to be transferred to the 6th Corps, and the best Commanders are appointed to command them. The intrepid Hancock will command the 2nd, the impetuous Warren the 5th and the Chivalrous Sedgwick; the 6th.

How I long for the active Service to begin, when I can listen to the Sweet Sounds of the booming cannon and be Serenaded by the rattling Musketry and dashing arms. But enough of this.

The boys are all well at present, that is Such as are here. Little Ben is a half bigger then he was when he left and makes a tip top Soldier. Frank Taylor is nearly Six feet high and will girth nearly Seven feet. There is no braver boy in the army. He has already killed Rebels enough to exempt the rest of his family from the draft.

I hear that Bird Conroys lady has made him a present of a pair of twins. And yet he is exempt from the draft. Now I think a person that can do such good Service at home that he Should be able to do Something for his country in the field.

There is not much to do at present, and how I wish I could get Some of Mrs Styles Splendid cigars. But I must close. My love to Mrs. Styles and I remain your friend Jim Bayne.

The compliments of F. M. Taylor

Address Lieut Jim Bayne

106th Regt N. Y. Vols

2nd Division   6th Army Corps

Washington, D.C."[4]

The arrival of General U. S. Grant was not only perceived as a great improvement in leadership by Bayne but almost the entire Army of the Potomac realized there would be a great change in strategy and the pursuit of the war. On May 3, 1864, The Army of the Potomac began to move south. This time, it was indeed "On To Richmond." From the 3rd to June 15 the men moved south, from the Rapidan River to the James. On May 5 - 7 the slugfest battle of the Wilderness pitted men against each other on wooded terrain that defied all attempts at tactics, strategy or organization. When finished, the armies moved south again. The Army of the Potomac left behind more than 17,000 casualties; 2,246 of them were dead.

The two armies squared off once again at a small Virginia crossroads village called Spotsylvania from May 8 through 19. On May 10, a Federal assault on the "Mule Shoe" salient, specifically at an area called "The Bloody Angle", penetrated Confederate lines briefly. Twelve regiments under the command of Colonel Emory Upton made this assault and one of the regiments was the 106th New York. Lieutenant James Bayne was indeed listening "to the Sweet Sounds of the booming cannon" and was "Serenaded by the rattling Musketry and dashing arms." When the serenading was finished at Spottsylvania, another eighteen thousand four hundred were listed as casualties of the battle and two thousand seven hundred and twenty-five of these were fatalities.

Again the armies moved south. The North Anna River was reached by May 23 and three days later, crossed. The armies were still moving south. The Pamunkey River on May 28 and the Totopotomoy on the 31st, both crossed in a southern movement.

By June 1864 the Army of Northern Virginia under the command of General Robert E. Lee had formed defensive positions to repel the continued southern advance of the Army of the Potomac which contained the 106th New York Infantry from St. Lawrence County. Here on the first day's battle of Cold Harbor, the final engagement of what has become known as the Overland Campaign was fought. At the crossroads village of Cold Harbor, Federal General Horatio G. Wright's Sixth Corps and General William F. Smith's Eighteenth Corps combined for an attack on Confederate lines under the commands of Generals Richard H. Anderson and Robert Hoke. The furious assault was momentarily successful; a small breakthrough at one spot in the Confederate defensive line was created but a quick and decisive counter attack quickly remedied the situation and the Federal army withdrew leaving over 2,600 dead and wounded.

One of those men who perished on the Field of Honor at Cold Harbor, Virginia on June 1, 1864, was twenty year old Lieutenant James H. Bayne of the 106th New York Infantry. For Jim, listening "to the Sweet Sounds of the booming cannon" and being "Serenaded by the rattling Musketry and dashing arms" was over. Bayne's body was recovered and buried with the others that had perished in the battle. After the war, his remains were taken to the New Fork Mill Cemetery located in Oneida, New York.[5]

{1}   Record Group 94, Office of the Adjutant General, Compiled
Service records. Volunteer Soldiers, Bayne, James - Pension file & Service
Record.
{2}   Record Group 94, Office of the Adjutant General, Compiled
Service records. Volunteer Soldiers, Bayne, James - Pension file & Service
Record.
{3}   Record Group 94, Office of the Adjutant General, Compiled
Service records. Volunteer Soldiers, Bayne, James - Pension file & Service
Record.
{4}   Lieutenant Jim Bayne to Ex-Sergeant Styles, March 26, 1864,
Collection of Frank Crawford
{5}   Record Group 94, Office of the Adjutant General, Compiled
Service records. Volunteer Soldiers, Bayne, James - Pension file & Service
Record

Private Ernst Damkoehler
Co. I - 26th Wisconsin Infantry
Andersonville, Georgia, National Cemetery

XI
"Thousand kisses for your and the children."
Private Ernst Damkoehler
Co. I - 26th Wisconsin Infantry

The enlistment papers for Ernst Damkoehler indicate that he was born in the small village of Haffensteff in the province of Braunschweig in Germany. He came to the United States in the late 1840s after spending time in the Prussian Army, and in the French Foreign Legion in North Africa. He first settled in East Troy, Wisconsin, a small farming community located thirty-five miles southwest of Milwaukee.[1]

When his sweetheart, Mathilde, from Celle, Germany, joined Ernst in matrimony at her father's home in Milwaukee, on July 13, 1851, the young couple traveled north by ox-cart to Sturgeon Bay in Door County. While farming there during the next ten years, the Damkoehler family was blessed with four children. Agnus was born in 1852 and Walter in 1854. Five years later, 1859, the family celebrated the birth of Ernst, his father's namesake and then in 1861, Clara was born.[2]

Like so many others, Ernst, not a young man of the times as well as a family man, did not rush to the recruitment offices when President Abraham Lincoln issued his calls for volunteers to put down the rebellion of the southern states. No one in the north believed it would be a difficult task nor did they believe it would take long to put down the southern rebellion. The insurrection was a whim and would be ended almost before it began, or so they believed. Also the initial three month enlistment of the patriotic volunteer heroes would be more than adequate to squelch the resistance. This would not be the case.

By September of 1862, the nation had been rudely awakened regarding the resolve of the wayward states to leave the country and create another nation; one the south felt would better suit their political and social needs. The Federal administration by then had taken an equally firm resolve regarding the prevention of that establishment. By September, 1862, the population was well aware that there was a full scale war on their hands, against fellow Americans - even fellow family members.

The battle of First Bull Run, or Manassas, July 21, 1861, was a thing of the past. The casualties of Wilson's Creek, near Springfield, Missouri, on August 10, 1861 were tallied. This tally of dead quickly rose when the battles of Shiloh, Tennessee on April 6 & 7, 1862 and Pea Ridge, Arkansas on May 7 & 8, of the same year were added to those of Perryville, Kentucky on October 8. This combat gave a gruesome total of casualties for the nation to consider. The country was indeed at war and that war's outcome, at that time, was very much in doubt as far as the Federal Government was concerned. Desperate times demanded desperate measures and the Federal Government issued yet another call for men to assist in preserving the nation and its way of government. It was heard all over the nation - as far away as Sturgeon Bay, Wisconsin. Ernst Damkoehler responded to this call on August 19, 1862 when he volunteered in a new regiment that was forming in Green Bay. He signed his enlistment papers in Sturgeon Bay as did several other German-born Americans and prepared to journey south some fifty miles to muster. The German farmer, when he left his wife one month pregnant and with four young children, was thirty-eight years old, born January 11, 1824.[3]

Ernst's first letter home, dated September 11, 1862 was mailed from Milwaukee and it revealed to her a strange turn of events. The Sturgeon Bay men had traveled to Green Bay with full intention of joining the roster of a Green Bay regiment but it appeared that the regiment was filled with "all kinds of trash from the city" and they were unwilling to join. They decided to travel yet another one hundred miles to the south to search for another German regiment, which was forming in Milwaukee. The proud Germans, with a little deception and a small broken promise that they would join the Green Bay Company in a day or two, instead, traveled by wagon and boat to Milwaukee. Ernst Damkoehler and his friends all became members of Company I of the 26th Wisconsin Volunteer Infantry, known as "The Sigel Regiment" after the German-born General Franz Sigel so much admired by the German immigrants in America.[4]

Soon after their enlistment they received their twenty-five dollar bounty and, for the following two weeks, enjoyed the life of a "citizen" soldier. Although the men had not officially mustered into the service, they had received at least part of their promised bounty payment and they felt honor bound to serve as soldiers. "After each drill we march into a beer hall where we are treated by the officers with the money we are cheated out of. It is still better than an American Regiment, where the officers keep everything." Ernst was quickly learning the ways of the American military and he had already decided he had made a huge mistake. He would have, he said in a letter to his wife, "been just as smart to stay with you and would have risked it to be drafted like all the neighbors, but now its to late." His decision to enlist, prompted by his being away from his wife and four children, haunted Ernst then and it would haunt him many more times during the war.[5]

On the other hand, Damkoehler was impressed by the German leadership in the Federal armies. He often mentioned such generals as Carl Schurz, Franz Sigel and Adolph von Steinwehr in his letters home. An interesting comment, made in a letter dated November 10, 1862 stated, "It was the same at the last Bull Run affair where Sigel beat the enemy with 15 thousand and the next day had to retreat after M. Dowell [McDowell], the traitor, was pushed against him." Although McDowell did indeed serve poorly under General Pope at the Second Battle of Bull Run, General

Sigel assuredly did not have defeat thrust upon a victorious performance there. His performance was, at best, barely mediocre. However, Ernst believed in his Prussian heroes, thus Sigel's contribution was great in Damkoehler's eyes.[6]

The following day, November 11, 1862, Ernst made another reference to his volunteering. He wrote, "The war is only a humbug and had I known as much three months ago as I do now I would not have enlisted under my own free will." Private Damkoehler, however, soon learned to adjust to the military way of life. He mentioned that friend George Bayer was driving ambulance wagons for the regiment and was receiving an extra $ .25 per day for the effort. Ernst was, at that time, not convinced that he should take such a job. However, by the 22nd of December, he had seen the advantage. Not only had he accepted a job as a carrier in the ambulance corps, he hoped to be accepted in the brigade commissary department. As a carrier, his only job, according to him, was to assist at a certain wagon and make sure some five gallon buckets were kept filled with fresh water. He mentioned that "at times I don't know what to do for pastime." With the cutting of the slight bit of "red tape" Ernst soon moved into the commissary department with a raise in pay of $.25 per day. He admitted there was plenty of work, but he was satisfied with the change in his responsibilities.[7]

Hardships at home were a constant concern for this older than average Wisconsin soldier. A wife at home providing for herself and her soon to be family of five was a constant weight on his mind. Did she have enough money? Was she receiving her fair share of the assistance being provided by citizens in the community? Was she receiving the money he could occasionally send home to her? Could she and the family handle the physical aspect of the hard work required to survive the winter in northern Wisconsin? Could she provide herself with firewood enough for the home during the winter? Could she not only provide for the provisions required to survive, but could she also acquire them from the store? All of these questions, and more, weighed heavily on Ernst's mind and consumed much of his written word in his letters home. He does attempt to reassure her that he was as safe as possible with his new job and was not exposed to the dangers of battle.[8]

By February of 1863 Ernst developed concern about yet one more predicament at home. His fifth child was close to birth and he, of course, would not be there. Mathilde's health was not the best, thus his concerns were great. In a letter dated February 2, to Agnus and Walter, his oldest children, Ernst requested that they continue to be good children and also continue helping their "mama" as much as possible. He thanked them for their lasting support and told them that their reward would come. Once again he mentioned he should have waited for the draft in Wisconsin rather than volunteering.[9]

In a letter written on February 23, 1863, from Stafford Court

House, Virginia, Ernst explained his work to his wife and family. Rolling heavy kegs and moving large boxes while sloshing around in snow that was one and one half feet deep over ground soaked with heavy rains had taken its toll on all of the men in the commissary department. Every evening, he wrote, he was so tired he could not sleep due to the exhaustion and pain. He had considered returning to his regiment but reminded himself daily that he was earning more money there and thus was providing better for his family. His hope for a respite from the hard work the coming spring was foremost in his mind.[10]

News from the Midwest did reach the Midwestern soldier in the east. In the fall of 1862 the legislature in the state of Illinois became prominent in the nation's news. The November elections in that state had resulted in a sweeping victory for the Peace Democrats and the state legislature came under Democratic control. The *Joliet Signal* proclaimed in its November 11, issue that "The party which triumphed two years ago in every Northern state and by sectionalism and slavery agitation provoked secession in the Southern States, and hurried us into a dreadful civil war, and caused our land to be drenched with the blood of its citizens, has been ignobly vanquished." This political victory was seen as a huge rout of abolitionism and a proper rebuke to the party that was making every effort possible "to Africanize the north."[11]

Even Republican leadership seemed to be wavering in its support of Illinois' favorite son, President Abraham Lincoln. The war effort in Illinois appeared to be at low ebb. This gave further impetus to the Democratic efforts in the Sucker State and that party's leaders acted swiftly. Resolutions denouncing the federal administration, urging an armistice with the south and a National Convention at Louisville, Kentucky, were passed by the House of Representatives and barely blocked in the Senate. All of this and much more was viewed throughout the nation with astonished eyes. It was also observed by soldiers in the Federal Army - many about to enter combat risking their very life, all for a national policy that could change, even reverse itself, soon. Damkoehler's reaction to this, written to his wife, was straight to the point: "You probably read about the decision of the Illinois Legislature, but I hope you don't believe in it. I hope that you have enough patriotism to bear our longer parting instead of seeing me coming home to such an eerie peace. I am still as good a patriot as I was the first day of my enlistment."[12]

On April 11th, 1863, there was a Presidential review of the Army Corps at Stafford Court House, Virginia. Damkoehler observed the ceremonies from a hillside just opposite the Presidential reviewing stand. The weather was beautiful, the new uniforms were tip-top and of course all of the men appeared to be very well fed. He got to see President Lincoln and his family, all of whom returned to Washington, D.C. as soon as the ceremonies were finished.[13]

Of primary importance to Ernst in a late June letter to Mathilde was the birth of his son: "that you will call the little boy Henry or Harry I like very well, but I would like it much better if I could see the youngster once. Who knows if the little one is allowed to get to know his Father."[14]

Melancholy, loneliness and a trace of bitterness prevailed in letters home during the fall of 1863. The men of the regiment had participated that year in the infamous "Mud March" under General Ambrose Burnside. They also took part in the resounding defeat of Federal troops under General Joseph Hooker at Chancellorsville. The Gettysburg Campaign was climaxed with a three day battle, but Damkoehler, in the commissary department, was in no immediate danger at any time.[15]

By August 4, 1863, from Warrenton Junction, Virginia, Ernst again lamented the day he volunteered. He missed his wife, he missed his children and he particularly regretted not being able to see his newest addition to the family, Henry, who was now almost five months old. Two letters from home had particularly saddened him and he commented, "How many times I have cursed the moment in which I determined even to risk my life to help our government. If I had remained at home I could have helped you in your sickness, and could have looked after the children so they wouldn't become wild." Damkoehler's commiseration was no doubt, echoed throughout the army by thousands of men likewise concerned about their families at home.[16]

Later, in yet a further effort to earn more money to send home, Ernst undertook a responsibility which certainly did not fit his character. He became a servant, a hostler, for Captain M. Schmidt of the 58th New York Regiment, also known as the "Polish Legion". A hostler looked after the needs of a horse; feeding, grooming and taking care of its equipment were all part of his responsibilities. Damkoehler took the job but certainly not for any professed love of the animal. He realized this position would give him an extra income of ten dollars a month which would be paid by Captain Schmidt. He was spared much of the hard work of the commissary. This was quite a favorable trade in Damkoehler's eyes. During the hard physical work in the commissary department, his weight had dropped from one hundred and fifty pounds to a mere one hundred and twenty-six. His physical description at the time of his muster, had listed him as "slight" but slight would now be an over-statement.[17]

It must have been quite a surprise for Mathilde to receive Ernst's next letter dated November 8, 1863. Instead of originating in Virginia, the soldier mailed this letter from Chattanooga, Tennessee near Lookout Mountain. The 26th Wisconsin was part of the most extensive transportation of army personnel by railroad that took place during the Civil War. From Alexandria, Virginia, through West Virginia and Ohio and finally to Indianapolis, Indiana, the trains proceeded. At Indianapolis, the men, all members of the XI and XII Corps, detrained and boarded other railroad cars and headed south, through Kentucky and into Tennessee, finally stopping at the capitol city, Nashville. From Nashville, under the combined commands of Generals Oliver O. Howard and Henry Slocum, the soldiers headed even further south, finally arriving at Chattanooga, on the Tennessee - Georgia line. They were there to reinforce the Federal Army.[18]

While waiting for the final consolidation of all the troops that had left Virginia, Ernst found himself even more upset with his new position. For two days his constant waiting on Captain Schmidt and his horse became almost more than the German soldier could endure. He had no time for himself and he came very close to surrendering his "position" to another and joining the ranks of a common soldier with his regiment. However, ten dollars a month was a lot of money and he could send it all to his loved ones at home. He remained on the job.[19]

The remainder of the year 1863, and the first three months of 1864, was very typical for Damkoehler. The daily grind of the commissary department, the personal chagrin at being a servant for an officer (even if it meant an additional ten dollars a month), and the constant gnawing at his heart, that his wife was over eight hundred miles north of him with five children he longed to see. One of these children, he continually reminded his wife, he had never seen. Ernst Damkoehler was not a happy soldier.

While serving in the Army of the Cumberland around Chattanooga, Tennessee, the 26th Wisconsin took part in the battles of Wauhatchie on October 28 and 29 and Orchard Knob on November 23. These were followed by a battle at Tunnel Hill on Missionary Ridge on November 24 and then the battle of Missionary Ridge on November 25. It also marched to Knoxville, Tennessee to relieve General Burnside from the pressure applied by General James Longstreet and his Confederate Army from November 27 until December 8. All of these experiences the unhappy German missed because of his assignment to the commissary department.[20]

In the spring of 1864 there was a great reorganization of the Army of the Cumberland. In the preparation of General W. T. Sherman's coming Atlanta Campaign, Ernst Damkoehler was out of a job. His commissary department was eliminated, absorbed by other like departments within the army. Damkoehler explained this in a letter to his wife written at Whiteside, Alabama, on April 17, 1864.

"My Dear Mathilde !
Received your beloved letters from March 20th, also from April 1. It is impossible for me today to answer both your letters, but I sure will send you a few lines to let you know that I am alive and in good health.

The news I have to write to you today is not very good. Our Brigade and also the 11th and 12th Corps are dissolved, and named 20th Brigade. With the dissolving of our Brigade the Commissary Department is also out of existence, and in a few hours we have to report to our

Regiment. I was supposed to go this morning to the new Regiment but through the influence of Captain Schmidt, I have to stay till the new Regiment arrives and transfer the goods to them. We have our hands full to straighten everything out and make a final report.

I have a lot more clothing now then I can use in the new Regiment. I have permission from our Commander to send the clothing home by Adams Express, two blankets and other goods. It cost plenty money to send all that stuff home but I think it is worthwhile, otherwise I have to throw it away.

I think it will be hard for me in the new Regiment, then in the last year I did not march 10 miles and I am not used to marching and carrying a big load on my back.

I am sorry I can not send you any money now. The paymaster comes next month and we get paid for 4 months, and with the money I would receive from our Captain I think that I can send you quite a sum of money.

Our Regiment belongs to the Battlefieldshen Division, and the address of the 26th R. Wis. Vol. Co. I, 3rd Div., 3rd Brig. 20th Army Corps.

I will close my letter now, and will write you tomorrow how everything is.

Thousand kisses for you and the children.

Your Ernst"[21]

By May the Atlanta Campaign was in full swing. The 26th Wisconsin, and Ernst, now a foot soldier in the regiment, seeing combat for the first time, was under fire at Rocky Face Ridge and Buzzard's Roost Gap near the town of Ringgold, Georgia. On May 14, the regiment went into battle at Resaca, another twenty-five miles south and it was here that Ernst Damkoehler was wounded the following day. The exact location of his wound is not to be found in his military or pension papers. He was taken prisoner and sent to Camp Sumter in Southwest Georgia. Camp Sumter was better known as Andersonville.[22]

By May of 1864, Andersonville was receiving many of the Federal soldiers captured at battles in the eastern as well as the western theaters of the war. A simple stockade had been constructed to hold 10,000 prisoners and it received its first prisoners in February. However, by May 26, 1864, when Damkoehler and other members of the 26th Wisconsin entered, over 15,000 captives were incarcerated there. Later, during the summer, the stockade was expanded to enclose 26 ½ acres and held well over 30,000 prisoners. Conditions were not bad: they were horrible. Sanitation was virtually non-existent and more prisoners were entering the stockade every day. Food was scant and many prisoners starved to death while there. Medical supplies were scarce and the few doctors assigned to duty there were unable to properly care for the men in their charge.

Ernst Damkoehler's wound had not been properly cared for and on June 26, 1864, one month after entering the compound, he succumbed to the wound and a chronic case of diarrhea. He and eight other members of his regiment were buried in the cemetery, close to the prison site. Later, in 1865, that cemetery, containing the remains of 12,912 Federal soldiers that died as prisoners of war, was designated a National Cemetery. The proud German, who never got his wish to see his son who was but fifteen months old when his father died, is buried in grave # 2522.[23]

{1}   Record Group 94, Office of the Adjutant General, Compiled Service records. Volunteer Soldiers, Damkoehler, Ernst - Pension file & Service Record.

{2}   Ibid.

{3}   Ibid.

{4}   Ernst Damkoehler to "My Dear Mathilde" Sept. 1, 1862. Collection of W. L. Damkoehler.

{5}   Ibid.

        Ernst Damkoehler to "My Dear Mathilde" Oct 19th, 1862. Collection of W. L. Damkoehler.

{6}   Ernst Damkoehler to "My Dear Mathilde" Nov. 10th, 1862. Collection of W. L. Damkoehler.

{7}   Ernst Damkoehler to "My Dear Mathilde" Nov 11th, 1862. Collection of W. L. Damkoehler.

        Ernst Damkoehler to "My Dear Mathilde" December 22, 1862. Collection of W. L. Damkoehler.

{8}   Ernst Damkoehler to "My Dear Mathilde" Jan. 17, 1863. Collection of W. L. Damkoehler.

{9}   Ernst Damkoehler to "My Dear Mathilde" Feb. 2, 1863. Collection of W. L. Damkoehler.

{10}   Ernst Damkoehler to "My Dear Mathilde" Feb 23, 1863. Collection of W. L. Damkoehler.

{11}   *Joliet Signal* November 11, 1862 (Illinois State Register. Illinois State Historical Society)

{12}   Ernst Damkoehler to "My Dear Mathilde" Feb 23, 1863. Collection of W. L. Damkoehler.

{13}   Ernst Damkoehler to "My Dear Mathilde" April 12, 63. Collection of W. L. Damkoehler.

{14}   Ernst Damkoehler to "My Dear Mathilde" June 22, 1863. Collection of W. L. Damkoehler.

{15}   Frederick H. Dyer, *A Compendium of the War of the Rebellion - Two Volumes.* (Dayton, Ohio: National Historical Society. The Press of Morningside Bookshop. 1979), Volume #2, p. 1684.

{16}   Ernst Damkoehler to "My Dear Mathilde" August 4th, 1863. Collection of W. L. Damkoehler.

{17}   Ernst Damkoehler to "My Dear Mathilde" Sept 7, 1863. Collection of W. L. Damkoehler.

{18}   Ernst Damkoehler to "My Dear Mathilde" November 8, 1863. Collection of W. L. Damkoehler.

{19}   Ernst Damkoehler to "My Dear Mathilde" November 25, 1863. Collection of W. L. Damkoehler

{20}   Frederick H. Dyer, *A Compendium of the War of the Rebellion - Two Volumes.* (Dayton, Ohio: National Historical Society. The Press of Morningside Bookshop. 1979), Volume #2, p. 1684.

{21}   Ernst Damkoehler to "My Dear Mathilde" April 17, 1864.

Collection of W. L. Damkoehler.

{22}   Frederick H. Dyer, *A Compendium of the War of the Rebellion - Two Volumes*. (Dayton, Ohio. National Historical Society. The Press of Morningside Bookshop. 1979), Volume #2, p. 1684.

Record Group 94, Office of the Adjutant General, Compiled Service records. Volunteer Soldiers, Damkoehler, Ernst - Pension file & Service Record.

{23}   Record Group 94, Office of the Adjutant General, Compiled Service records. Volunteer Soldiers, Damkoehler, Ernst - Pension file & Service Record.

XII

"I guess shuger wont whip the Rebs"
Private Thomas H. Brown
Co. F - First United States Sharpshooters

"... this is my Birth day and I hope before this time next year I shall be at home with you". This heartfelt wish permeated the stream of letters mailed home from Private Thomas H. Brown. At the end of this January 9, 1864 letter, Thomas requested his wife Lydia to ask his mother "if she Rembers 40 years a go to day." This comment, in one of over fifty letters from Thomas Brown, is the only clue to his age. He was born and grew up near Rygate, Vermont, a small village almost one hundred miles northeast of Rutland.[1]

Brown, born in 1824, married Miss Lydia Chandler, also from Rygate, on July 3, 1845. The sugar farmer and his wife became parents of four strong and healthy children. Their first-born, Horace Edwin, was born in 1848, and, by the time of the Civil War, was old enough and mature enough to be the proud owner of a fine yoke of young steers which he was training to perform as oxen for the family. The second child, Warren, was born in 1853 and younger brother, Carlos Heath, in 1856. The three boys welcomed a sister into the family in 1859. She was named Annette Jane but in all the family correspondence was referred to as 'Sis."[2]

Thomas Brown enlisted into the service of his country on August 23, 1862, at his hometown, to become a member of the elite group of soldiers known as the First United States Sharpshooters. He mustered into the service on September 20th and was assigned to serve in Company F just after the unit had participated in the bloodiest single day in American history, the battle of Antietam or Sharpsburg, Maryland. To become a member of this select group a demanding test had to be met. Although this test was simple it was extremely difficult to master. From a distance of two hundred yards, the "would be" sharpshooter had to group a series of ten shots fired from the shoulder in a ten inch target. Private Thomas Brown was indeed a great shot and mustered into the unit.[3]

Written from Rutland, Brown's first letter home was dated September 17, 1862, the exact date that his assigned unit was participating in the battle of Antietam. He began with a series of questions about the children and the farm that became a pattern that never ceased. "How are the children?" making sure to almost always mention each one by name and how he hoped the family would always have enough to eat. The conduct of the children was always of great concern for Thomas. He would also ask about the oxen. He told Lydia that he had had his "likness taken" and that he would send it home with his civilian clothing as soon as the men mustered in "next week and go to Washington."[4]

On September 25, 1862, Thomas wrote to his fourteen year old son, Horace. He informed the youth of forty dollars and a knife he sent home with an acquaintance. It was at this time that the men received their uniforms -- the uniform of a United States Sharpshooter. Rather than the typical dark blue jackets and light blue trousers, these men were provided with dark green uniforms, pants as well as jacket, with black gutta-percha buttons. The stylized outfit served as a camouflage for the men to do the dangerous type of work for which they were specifically trained. These men, all expert marksmen, would serve as skirmishers and marksmen in front of and on the sides of regular infantry units, thus protecting the regiment from flanking attacks by the enemy.[5]

The green clad specialists were in Washington, D.C. when Thomas wrote again to his family on October 7, 1862. His questions reflected his agricultural upbringing. "I should like to know how the corn came in and the Potatoes tirned out." The letter, as so many, was concerned with the health and welfare of the family with just a hint of news concerning the military. Now, although he still had not actually entered his regiment, Thomas stated, "thir is nothing but solders coming and going all the time ... they cars is fool evry train." Two weeks later, on the 23rd, Thomas and the other recruits joined the regiment while they were still camped near Sharpsburg. His health was good and his fare was fine. "we hav some beans and some rice and some beef and pork and a nuff of hard tack." This message also mentioned that Thomas would like to "hear a good sermon ... I hant hird even a pirair since I left home ... I had a tesatment gav me in New York when we left ... I tak Comfort in reading it." As usual, concerns about the farm, the oxen and the preparation of the home for winter were prevalent in the thoughts of the soldier away from his domicile. Thomas also advised his family that he tried hard to read "too chapters in a day" from his bible. He terminated this letter by stating "... may god grant peas to our land soon this is my prair to my god. Thomas Brown."[6]

Brown's next dispatch from "a camp in the woods" dated Nov 24th told his family that he had tried but simply "can't find out the name of this plais." "This plais" was near Fredericksburg, Virginia. With a bit of humor, perhaps, he stated that he was "well excep my old complant but I get a long well for a old man ... I am some tird this morning." Lydia had informed Thomas "the children wanted to see me but I gess they wont to see me any more then I wont to see them" Thomas Brown had been away from home only two months and he was missing everyone badly.[7]

By December 2, 1862, while still near Fredericksburg, Virginia, Brown told Lydia that it was "cold hear now" and, of more importance, at least to himself, he had finished making three rings, two for "Sis", little three year old Annette, as well as one for Lydia. He was concerned about the sizes of these three bits of handiwork and instructed his wife that if they were not the correct size he would "send hir another." Again, mention

110

was made in this rather short note that his religious pursuit was suffering from a lack of Sabbath observance and he would attend service often if he were able. He explained, "no Sabbath days hear but the tim I can get I read my testment." He found it "strang ... that we cant have some preatching hear but I hant hird a sirmon since I left home."[8]

After the battle of Fredericksburg, Virginia, on December 12, Thomas's first combat, he again wrote, but this letter was sent to his oldest son, Horace. His description of what he saw, as a sharpshooter, concerning combat was simply put. "I will tell you a bout the fite we had at Fredricksburgh ... it was a hard fite ... the way the shelds flu want slow on both sides. I stood wher I cood see shells fly tick and fast our Reg stood ready to go in and try our Rifles but it was most dark and we dident cros the River till the next morning then we went over to the City and stayd won day and too nits. the Rebs shot some shelds into the City this is a bout all I can tell you a bout the fite at present." Further explanation concerning the Federal assaults on the Confederate works before Marye's Heights and behind the now celebrated stone wall was not mentioned. The carnage of the Federal troops on this Confederate stronghold was not discussed. Perhaps Thomas Brown saw no benefit in telling his New England family or, it is also a real possibility that he simply was not aware. No matter what the possible explanation, Brown's letter to his teenage son soon settled into his typical discussions concerning health, his desire to see his children and his hopes for a quick ending to the war. He closed this letter, written on December 21, 1862 by answering a question Horace had asked in an earlier letter to his father. Thomas wrote, "you wrot you wuld like to know how we coock out hear ... we coock just as we bile sap in Vt. may god bless you all so good by this is from your father."[9]

Brown's next sixteen letters, three from "near Fredericksburgh" and thirteen from "Falmoth Va" exemplify the boredom of an army private's life during the winter months of the Civil War. From January 1, 1863 until June 6, Thomas expresses his views and opinions concerning a myriad of topics. In January he is aware of the dangers of civilians in the way of an army as he wrote about a Federal doctor that went into enemy territory to dress the wounds of a woman that had been hit by Federal gunfire. On the 15th of January he told that he was aware his taxes in Vermont had been paid by a friend named James Whit. Brown thought it was "a salt tax for a poor soldier to pay but if we can fit and get money a nuff to pay our tax we will do well ... the north will need all the money they can get before the Rebs is licked."[10]

In all of his correspondence to both Lydia and Horace, Brown took special care to ask questions about and give advice to his children. He mentioned schooling for the boys and "wrings" he has fashioned for Annette. During this six month encampment is Brown's first acknowledgment of his possible fate. On January 17, while still at "Camp on the same Old Place" he informed Horace of the possibility that "This may be the last letter I ever will writ to you but I hope it will not be." He continued making comments, suggestions and hopes for the children and still asked questions concerning the farm.[11]

A note sent on February 20, 1863, tells of picket duty and the rigors involved. The men on picket left camp on Monday morning and stayed on picket until "Thirsday nit." The weather while serving this duty ranged from a beautiful day when they left camp through a snowstorm which eventually turned to a steady rain creating a condition of mud at least "ne deep." This description of the mud would change dramatically within the year.[12]

Brown also mentioned: "you wrote to me and wanted to know if I was willing to pay a tax on my dog. I dont care about the tax but you may dow jist as you see fit about keping him ... if you can give him a way you may ... if he was a good dog I should hate to heave him killed but do as you see fit a bout him ... he is not my kind of dog I like best ... if this war was settled up I should not cair about a dog tax but I think the govnmont will need all the tax they can get."[13]

Mentioning that Annette would be five years old on the coming Friday, he wished he had some sort of present to send to her. The condition of his socks or, as Thomas called them, "footins" were fine. He had mended "the toses of them ... the hels of them is good yet." and his new boots which he had had made in Rutland seemed to "set clost to my feet and that saves my footens."[14]

A short, rather serious note to Horace, dated March 11, allowed Thomas to do some parenting from afar concerning the death of a young boy in the neighborhood in a family the Browns considered close friends. Thomas wrote, "Deth is a sad thing when it coms but when it coms as sad as it did with him it seems harder still but it is the Lord dowings and we must bair with it. I whould like to know how the rest of his children is this moren." Brown continued with his lamentation that he was "sory" that one of Horace's oxen steers "had gut won of his horns hirt" but Thomas hoped "it will not hirt the loox of him." Brown concluded with questions regarding the fact that the state of Vermont was about to begin "Drafting more men to come out hear to fit." He was curious as to the general feeling of the citizens regarding this development. His final request still remained, however, "writ as soon as you get this."[15]

In the remaining letters from Falmouth, Virginia Thomas spoke of the many families left fatherless by the war and of his wishes that he could be "to home to help you tap and help you eat som of the shuger." He also told that the "government ose me five months pay now." His letter dated April 10, related that he "had the plasure of seen the Preisedent of the United States last Thirsday   he is any thing but a good lookin Man ... he has got a nose as long as a rail."[16]

As so many soldiers involved in combat, what happened, was only what they witnessed themselves. Actions one hundred yards or two miles away were not witnessed so they often were of little or no importance to the soldier. Brown's comment in a letter dated May 7, 1863 concerning the battle of Chancellorsville reinforces that aspect of the soldier's perspective of the war. "I wont to try and git some daily papers and read and see what we have been dowing out hear for fore or five days ... the first day our rigment took 470 Reb prisners ... how meny we killed I dont know as we had too wounded out of our Co but the way the balls flew was a _____ to old folks but we mad them opin up and com over to us." He continued, "while we was giting the Rebs in the front the Infantry back and ran and the Rebs got round whir our napsacks so the Rebs took our napsacks so we lost them."[17]

A statement to Lydia exemplifies the importance of certain events to the ordinary soldier. In relating the losses at the battle of Chancellorsville, a decided Confederate success, Brown stated, "I gess we had the best of it I think the Rebs lost the mose men and I ges thir is no doubt but old Stonewall Jackson is dad ... I hop he is if it is rit he shood be."[18]

In another letter to Horace, Thomas gave another comment concerning Chancellorsville, one he perhaps was not willing to share with his wife. "I sent a boll in it [this letter] that the Rebs sent to me it hit me but it was a spint boll so it did not hirt me ... I thot I wood send it ... and you coold see it ... what I mean by a spint boll is a boll that had lost it force." Brown further informed the youth "the boll and shells flew round me like hale ... I cant tell you why I did not get kild but my time had not com." Horace was also informed about the total devastation of war within the state of Virginia. "This country," he wrote, "is in a bad fix if this war was settled to day ... Va wont not git over it in a hunderd year what I mean in saying so is that our army has birnt all the fence they wanted for wood and we have fell thousands acers of wood ... a army is a hard thing for a contry." This was May of 1863 and there would be two more years of devastation cast upon the Virginia countryside.[19]

The letters of May 25 and June 6, 1863, were continuations of Brown's hopes and fears. They were full of the same hopes and fears expressed by countless soldiers away from home, not knowing what their individual fate might be but well aware of what the extreme possibilities were. He hoped, he prayed, for the war to end. He hoped, he prayed, for his life to be spared.

On June 11, the First United States Sharpshooters in their forest green uniforms and the Army of The Potomac in their blue uniforms left their campgrounds headed north. When Thomas wrote on June 18, from Cedarville, Virginia he had no way of knowing their destination. As he commented, "whir we ar goin I cant tell you." He also said "I think we shant stay long." Thomas was correct. "Whir" they were "goin" would eventually be a small town in Pennsylvania called Gettysburg. They would stay there only six days before beginning yet another long trek, dogging

General Robert E. Lee and his Army of Northern Virginia. The first three days of the six would become an unforgettable experience for Brown and the Sharpshooters as well as the Army of the Potomac and The Army of Northern Virginia that would be discussed and debated for decades.[20]

June found the regiment, camped briefly at Gum Springs, Virginia and then, two weeks later, on July 6, Thomas informed his wife "we have had a hard and tuff fite ... we gave the Rebs a hard won this time ... the Rebs left this phase and gon some other place ... our army is hard after them ... we have took a lot of priserns and killd any mount of them ... we have lost a good meny men to ... I can tell you it is hard to see so meny men slain. I went in to the fites the first day of July. The fit lasted fore days ... it was a hard won I can tell you." This, as earlier at the battles of Fredericksburg and Chancellorsville, was Brown's description of a great battle of the Civil War. What he saw he discussed and he did not see much except a lot of men killed.[21]

According to some historians, what is known as The Gettysburg Campaign began on June 11, 1863 when forces began moving out of their encampments to the north eventually meeting in full battle at the Pennsylvania town. The campaign continued, after the battle on July 1, 2 and 3, until these same troops were back in the state of Virginia. For these aforementioned historians, that campaign was culminated at an area called Wapping Heights, Virginia on July 23rd. Just five days later Thomas Brown found the time and had the inclination to correspond with his wife and family again. He told them that the United States Sharpshooters had indeed done "some tall days marchis ... I can tell you since old Lee left for Va we have follerd him snug up ... we crost into Va at harpers Fery and came to Snickers gap the same road we cam last fall ... Last Thirsday we had a hard skirmish with the Rebs ... we drove them a bout fore miles ... the Rebs crost the rive then blod up the bridge then we left and cam to Worenton ... we came hear last Sabbathday." Brown continued, stating, "I think I have sirved my time ... it soon will be a year sinc I left home." He expressed his feelings concerning the future, "... but I am willian to stay a while yet if we can save the younion I must bring my letter to a close ... tell the chilldren I long to see them so good by for this tim THB"[22]

Brown's writings, by this time, were repetitions of previous comments to this oldest son and wife. On occasion he would make a passing remark indicating that the father and husband was more than simply absent -- he was absent and at war. On August 17, 1863, the private told his family, "I am the oldest man in our Co and I gess the tuffest won ... I hant took me no medison since last October ... thir is a good meny sick hear now days but my helth is good." In August of that year he had been informed that his friend from Vermont, O. G. Morrison had been drafted and Brown stated he would fully understand if Morrison were to pay the required $300 to option out of the draft. He commented that if he were "out of the sirves and had the money I shoud pay the $300 before I wood come." By mid-September, Thomas indicated that he had "got tird taking cair of my Rifle ... it is quit a job." He wrote, "I have to keep it nise ... it looks nic ... I can tell you it is a good rifle." A few days later, on the 19th while at Sulpher Springs, Virginia, Brown again asked Lydia to tell O. G. Morrison, "I should like to see him but dont wont to see him out hear. This is a hard phase for new men ... it will be hard for him to pay $300 Dollars but if I was out of the sirves and had $300 Dollars I wood give it before I wood com."[23]

Additional letters gave sparse information concerning the sharpshooters and the military. On October 22, 1863, Thomas tells of a man being "drumd out of camp ... he was out of my Regiment ... he was drumd out for not doin his duty ... he said he was sick and the doctor sed he was able to do his duty ... they took his pay from him and let him go."[24]

In the same letter, as much as Thomas Brown missed his home, he presented a dilemma to Lydia to which he needed family input. "I wish," he wrote, "I could com home and spend this winter with you ... the tack [talk] is if the three yaers men will list for three years longer thay say thay may go home for three months then com back of three yars more ... what do you think of me dowin so ... write and let me know what you think a but it ... if I thot I should have to stay the three years I have in listed I wood in list for three years more and come home this winter and then com back a gain ... they say they will pay us $400 and fore dollars bounty if we list for three years longer." For a second time in the same letter Thomas presented this scenario to Lydia to make sure she fully understood the options and that he certainly wanted to know her opinion. Four hundred dollars, to a man that was being paid, sporadically, thirteen dollars per month must have seemed a virtual fortune. The enticement by the government was strong. So, however, was his loneliness. A partial solution seemed to be very obvious to Brown but he decidedly wanted his wife's opinion on the matter. He closed by suggesting to her that it all "comes to seven hundred and twenty dollars for three years ... you see this is a good deal of money for three years work so good by for this time ... write soon ... Thomas Brown."[25]

After the engagement at Kelly's Ford, Virginia on November 7, 1863, Thomas wrote his family on the 19th. His description of the action of the First Sharpshooters makes their military usage in combat understandable to his wife. Brown wrote, "I should like to give you a count of the last fite we had but I cant give you jest as it was the morn we brok camp ... I did not think we wood have a fit be fore nite but we did ... as soon as we got nir whir the Rebs was our Rigment was ordered to the front ... we had not go but a short distenc tell we found them ... we drowve them back into the river ... the Rebs hed Rifel pits on the other sid of the River ... we shot at them and they shot at us then we was orderd to charge a crost the river ... as soon as we wnt to go a crost the river the Rebs rose up out of thir Rifle pits and give us a voly ... we had too wonded befre we got

115

a crost the river ... won that was wonded was besed of me and the other was the next file be hind me and still I was not hit but a soon as we got a crost the river then we went on and got into thir pits and shot at them and they shot at us till dark ... we lost won killd ... he was shot throw the head ... he never knew what hirt him ... his naime was Pate Mery [Patrick Murray, Killed in Action - November 7, 1863] ... he was a good soldier but he was cailes but his time head com and he had to go ... he is the first man that came out when I did that he has been killd but thir has bin five that has did ... thir has bin a good meny discharged."[26]

On December 5, Thomas advised his family that he had made his decision concerning his future in the military by saying, "I am sur I shant inlist a gain ... I think I have done my shair to poot down the war and if I live to sirve my time out I think I shall com home and let some of my nebers com and try thir hand and see how they like to fase the Rebs ... I think I have don my shaire." Something that Thomas witnessed the day before writing this letter undoubtedly was an influence in assisting him to make his decision. His comments were rather cold and to the point. "I will tell you what I saw yestardly ... I saw a disirter shot yesteardy ... he belong to the third Meane Rigment the same Rigment that Leander Hellett dos ... I can tell you it was a hard site to see a man march behind his coffin up to his grave ... he was a very large stout lookin man ... I pited him but he was foolish to dissert."[27]

Thomas wrote just one week later on December 12th, that he certainly would not be re-enlisting. In his own unique style he stated, "I can tell you if I live to get home thir ant money a nuff in Ryegate to get me to enlist again ... I think I have don my shair of fiting since I came out here." He was through with his military life and even the previously mentioned seven hundred dollar enticement would not alter his decision.[28]

His letter, dated January 9, 1864, the one which mentioned the date of his birth, gave a brief but accurate description of the boredom associated with camp life, even in the United States Sharpshooter regiment. "I dont get much time to writ for I heve to go on picket wonce in eight days ... we heft to stay fore days and three nite then we have gard duty to do and we heft to help our offers to get ther wood and we heft to get wood of our self and you see it keeps us bisy." Brown continued to long for peace for, as he said, "you know all wars has hed a end and this wicked war must com to a end sometime."[29]

Brown's comment in a late January letter gives some concept of the problems suffered by far too many husbands away from their wives. He wrote "you [Lydia] wrot you wished after the Children had gon to baid I wood hapin home ... I wish so to ... I think I can see you siting by the stove a warm your feet before you go to bed ... I wish I was ther to nit to go to baid with you but you see I cant for a while." Loneliness was terrible.[30]

Four letters later, one dated March 23, 1864, Private Brown wrote as follows: "I long for the day to com when I can get home then we wont heft to writ so much ... you seem to think I shant git out in June ... I dont know as I shall but I shall try hard for it ... All the boys that came out when I did they all expect to get out in June and I hope we will but if I dont I dont think I shall like it very well for I know the goverment wanted to raise 75 thousand men to fill up old regments and they said thir time shood be out when this Regment time was up and I clame I cam under the coll ... now all I ask is for the govermant to do as they a greed then I shall be satisfide but won thing is if the govermant cant do without me I can stay but I think I have don my shair of fiting for uncle sam. I think thir is plenty of men out here without me and I hope I shall git out in June so I can get home to help do the haying but I dont know as I will but time well tell so we must wait and see."[31]

That same day Private Brown wrote a single letter addressed to all four of his children. Each section was addressed individually to "Wall Horace", "Wall Waren", "Wall Carlos" and even "Wall Sis", to the youngest, five year old Annette who probably, at that time had only the vaguest concept of her father who had been away for over a year. To her, Thomas Brown must have been only an idea rather than someone she could remember gently and lovingly holding her in her early childhood.[32]

In a letter dated April 6, 1864, written by Brown to his wife of nineteen years, a new characteristic revealed itself. He had continually mentioned in almost all of his letters something regarding God, religion, sermons and prayer. This trait would continue but on this particular day, as well as in his next letter to Horace, dated the 9th of April, a new bent appears. While discussing the weather, particularly the precipitation in the area, Thomas stated "The wether it is cold and rainy and it has raind and snod for a bout a week back and the mud is ass deep." The same basic expletive was sent three days later to Horace. "I will tell you a bout the wether now ... for too days back has been drie but it rains to day and is Cold and the mud is ass deep ... it is so muddy it is hard to get around." There may not have been any emotional change in Private Brown over the last eighteen months while he was away from home in the service of his country but this seemingly meaningless expression speaks volumes. His first vulgarity to home would have given both of the adults in his family reason to be concerned about their husband and father.[33]

Two more letters were sent, one on April 13th and another on the 19th. Both continued to express his dissatisfaction with the life he was leading as a soldier and both continued to express his hopes of being allowed to survive the remainder of his enlistment so he could return to his family, to assume his former life style which would also include attending Sabbath meetings with great regularity. The letter written on the 19th does give cause for somberness and concern. He tells Lydia "This may be the last letter that I ever writ to you but I hope it ant ... I hope you and I may live to writ a gain"[34]

The next day, Thomas wrote,

"April the 20, 1864
Camp Near Brandy Station Va.
Dear Wife
It is with plasur I sit down to let you know I am well and hope thes few lins will find you all the same. I red your letter to nit and was glad to here from you And to here you was all well and glad to here you was getting along so well. I am glad to here that the boys has maid so much shuger I wish I cold be home and help you eat some but if this war was closed I think I should be willing to give all the shuger I ever saw. But I guess shuger wont whip the Rebs so I must stay a while yet. I think Generl Grant is getting redy as fast as he can to give them hale and led and I gess he will give them som Cast iron to. I hope Genrel Grant will fix old Lee and I think he will. I never saw him yet but I expect to see him to morow the talk is that he is to be here to morow. I would give all the old boots I have got if you cood just see the army of the genral it would be the bigest site you ever saw it looks jest as we cold go jest whir we please but I have seen som fiting since I came out here and I never met the Rebs but they was about a nuff for us but I hope Gernel Grant will get his men in shap so they can all work to gether and I think he will. You wrot you all wanted to see me I don't know how bad you want to see me but I know I long to see you all again but how long it will be before I shall see you I Can't tell but I hope we shall all be spaird to meat agin. I hant given up but what I shall git out in June yet but it may be I shant but I hope I shall. But if I dont I hope God will spair our livs till I can git home again. God is my only hope. I can till you the army is a wicked place for a Man to be in but for me I know I try and do the best I can, but you know we may do the best there we come short but many thing we must try and put our trust in him. I long to get home so I can go to meating again as I yousted do. I often think will the day ever come when I can git home and go to meating as I have don I hope it will tell Father and Mother I ofen think of them and long to see them I ofen think of the broth that Mother has cep warm for me when I cam back from the store I wish I hed a quart of it now. I wrot you a letter Aperil the 19 the reason I wrot it was that the mail was going to stop for a while but I don't think it is so I wont you to writ jest as you have and I will do the same I sent to pickters in the last letter I sent to you I hope you will get them You said you wish you hed a nother cow for butter was so high I whish you but if butter forty or fifty cents what is a cow worth thy must be as hie as fifty dollars and you see by the time you paid for a cow butter mint be down but I wish you had a nother cow if you hed pastur for a nother one TH Brown"[35]

The following three weeks in the life of Private Thomas Brown involved an almost steady stream of close personal contact with the enemy. May 5th, 6th and 7th found the First United States Sharpshooters in heavy combat accompanying the Army of the Potomac under the command of General George Meade and guided, in the field, by General Ulysses S. Grant, the man now in command of the awesome task of coordinating the entire war effort on all fronts making a single concentrated effort for the Federal government. These activities, the combat on May 5 through 7, would be referred to as "The Wilderness" and also would be some of the heaviest fought, most talked about and least understood, of all of the many battles fought by the Army of the Potomac. After three days of furious combat in forest and undergrowth known, even before the battle fought there, as "The Wilderness," the armies moved south.[36]

On May 8th the First United States Sharpshooters were in at Laurel Hill performing their duties as heavy skirmishers. From Laurel Hill to Spotsylvania Court House on the evening of the 8th the men remained engaged on General Grant's great Richmond Campaign. A brief but bloody encounter on the Po River on May 10th was followed by the massing of the troops around Spotsylvania Court House, the political center of Spotsylvania County, Virginia. There they continued their steady pounding on the strong defensive positions created by the combat veterans under Confederate General Robert E. Lee's able command.[37]

Lee's men had created a long line of entrenchments built in the shape of a giant U or, as it was referred to at the time, "The Mule Shoe." Across the base of this salient Lee had his men construct yet another line of defense for his brave, gallant and exhausted men. In the initial assault on the "Mule Shoe", measuring well over two miles across, at an area now known as "The Bloody Angle," Federal forces under the command of General Winfield Scott Hancock began their offensive before dawn -- some accounts reporting the exact time as 4:30 a.m. on May 12, 1864. The men of Company F, First United States Sharpshooters, took their usual places at the sides and in the front of the attacking troops to serve as skirmishers. Forty year old Thomas Brown was part of that assignment. In this bloody, twenty hour, hand-to-hand combat, the Federal detachments captured two Confederate Generals, Edward "Allegheny" Johnson and George H. Steuart, over 4,000 Confederate soldiers and several artillery pieces while struggling through the blinding haze and the ceaseless downpour of rain.[38]

Even though the Confederate Army of Northern Virginia suffered intensely during the conflict that spring day not far from Fredericksburg, Virginia, this was also the fate of the men in the Army of the Potomac. Federal General Lewis A. Grant, former Colonel of the Fifth Vermont Infantry and then in command of the Second Brigade, described the action in his Official Report as follows, "It was emphatically a hand-to-hand fight. Scores were shot down within a few feet of the death-dealing muskets. A breast-work of logs and earth separated the combatants. Our men would reach over the breast-works and discharge their muskets in the very face of the enemy. Some men clubbed their muskets and in some instances used clubs and rails." General Grant's description of the same area the following day was quite graphic. "The slaughter of the enemy was terrible. The sight the next day was repulsive. Behind their traverses, and in pits and holes they had dug for protection, the rebel dead were found piled upon each other. Some of the wounded were almost entirely buried by the dead bodies of their companions that had fallen upon them."[39]

Casualties for the battle which took place May 12th at Spotsylvania Court House simply are an estimate. The butchery for the ten days of fighting was, for the Federal army, losses of 18,000 soldiers. There were, in the First United States Sharpshooters, a total of fifty-three casualties. Of these, three men were taken prisoner. There were thirty-eight men and officers listed as wounded and twelve men were killed. One of the killed, somewhere in the slaughter described by General L. A. Grant, was forty year old Private Thomas H. Brown.[40]

Where Thomas H. Brown was buried is unknown. He possibly could have been returned to his Vermont home in Rygate but this would be unlikely because of the numbers killed and the fact that he was "but a private." Possibly he was entombed in the Fredericksburg, Virginia National Cemetery located at Marye's Heights, the scene of the Federal carnage at that conflict, as simply one of hundreds interred there from the battle of Spotsylvania Court House in graves marked only, **UNKNOWN U.S. SOLDIER**.

{1}   Thomas H. Brown to "To My Wife" January 9, 1864. Thomas Brown Collection, Vermont Historical Society.

Record Group 94, Office of the Adjutant General, Compiled Service records. Volunteer Soldiers, Brown, Thomas H. - Pension file & Service Record.

{2}   Record Group 94, Office of the Adjutant General, Compiled Service records. Volunteer Soldiers, Brown, Thomas H. - Pension file & Service Record.

{3}   Ibid.

Captain C. A. Stevens, *Berdan's United States Sharpshooters in the Army of the Potomac 1861 - 1865* (Dayton, Ohio: Press of Morningside Bookshop, 1984), pp. 2, 3.

{4}   Thomas Brown to "Dear Wife" Sep the 17 1862. Thomas Brown Collection, Vermont Historical Society.

{5}   T H Brown to "Wall Horace" Sep the 25th 1862. Thomas Brown Collection, Vermont Historical Society.

Captain C. A. Stevens, *Berdan's United States Sharpshooters in the Army of the Potomac 1861 - 1865* (Dayton, Ohio: Press of Morningside Bookshop, 1984) pp. 5, 22.

{6}   THB to "Dear Wife" October 7 1862. Thomas Brown Collection, Vermont Historical Society.

Thomas H. Brown to "Dear Wife" October 23, 1862. Thomas Brown Collection, Vermont Historical Society.

{7}   Thomas Brown to un-named person Nov the 24th, 1862. Thomas Brown Collection, Vermont Historical Society.

{8}   T H Brown to "Dear Wife" Dec the 2 1862. Thomas Brown Collection, Vermont Historical Society.

{9}   From "your father" to "Wall my son Horace" Dec 21 1862. Thomas Brown Collection, Vermont Historical Society.

{10}   Thomas Brown to un-named person January the 15, 1863. Thomas Brown Collection, Vermont Historical Society.

{11}   T H Brown to "Wall Horace" Jan the 17, 1863. Thomas Brown Collection, Vermont Historical Society.

{12}   Thomas H Brown to "my wife" Feb the 20th 1863. Thomas Brown Collection, Vermont Historical Society.

{13}   Ibid.

{14}   Ibid.

{15}   Thomas H. Brown to "my son Horace" March the 11 1863. Thomas Brown Collection, Vermont Historical Society.

{16}   Thomas H. Brown to "Dear Wife" April the 10 1863. Thomas Brown Collection, Vermont Historical Society.

{17}   unsigned letter to "Dear Wife" May the 7 1863. Thomas Brown Collection, Vermont Historical Society.

{18}   T H Brown to "my wife" May the 19 1863. Thomas Brown Collection, Vermont Historical Society.

{19}   Father to "Wall Horace" May the 19 1863. Thomas Brown
Collection, Vermont Historical Society.
{20}   Frederick H. Dyer, *A Compendium of the War of the Rebellion -
Two Volumes*. (Dayton, Ohio: National Historical Society. The Press of
Morningside Bookshop. 1979), Volume #2, pp. 1716, 1717.
          "from your father" to un-named June the 18 1863. Thomas
Brown Collection, Vermont Historical Society.
{21}   THB to "Dear Wife" July 6 1863. Thomas Brown Collection,
Vermont Historical Society.
{22}   Frederick H. Dyer, *A Compendium of the War of the Rebellion -
Two Volumes.* (Dayton, Ohio: National Historical Society. The Press of
Morningside Bookshop. 1979), Volume #2, pp. 1716, 1717.
          THB to "Dear Wife" July the 28 1863. Thomas Brown
Collection, Vermont Historical Society.
{23}   T H Brown to un-named August the 17 1863. Thomas Brown
Collection, Vermont Historical Society.
          Thomas Brown to "Wall Horace" September the 15 1863.
Thomas Brown Collection, Vermont Historical Society.
          T Brown to "dare Wife" September the 19 1863.   Thomas
Brown Collection, Vermont Historical Society.
{24}   Thomas Brown to un-named October the 22 1863.   Thomas
Brown Collection, Vermont Historical Society.
{25}   Ibid.
{26}   THB to "Day Wife" November the 19 1863.   Thomas Brown
Collection, Vermont Historical Society.
{27}   T. H. Brown to "my wife" Dec the 5 1863.   Thomas Brown
Collection, Vermont Historical Society.
{28}   Father to "my son Horace" Dec the 12 1863.   Thomas Brown
Collection, Vermont Historical Society.
{29}   Thomas H. Brown to "To My Wife" January 9, 1864. Thomas
Brown Collection, Vermont Historical Society.
{30}   Thomas H. Brown to un-named Jan the 25 1864. Thomas Brown
Collection, Vermont Historical Society.
{31}   T H Brown to "Dear Wife" March the 23 1864. Thomas Brown
Collection, Vermont Historical Society.
{32}   T H B to "Wall Horace" March the 23 1864. Thomas Brown
Collection, Vermont Historical Society.
{33}   unsigned letter to "Dear Wife" April 6 1864. Thomas Brown
Collection, Vermont Historical Society.
          unsigned letter to "Wall Horace" April 8 1864. Thomas Brown
Collection, Vermont Historical Society.
{34}   T H Brown to "dear Wife" April 19 1864. Thomas Brown
Collection, Vermont Historical Society.
{35}   T H Brown to "Dear Wife" April 20 1864. Thomas Brown
Collection, Vermont Historical Society.

{36}   Frederick H. Dyer, *A Compendium of the War of the Rebellion - Two Volumes.* (Dayton, Ohio: National Historical Society. The Press of Morningside Bookshop, 1979), Volume #2, pp. 1716, 1717.

Captain C. A. Stevens, *Berdan's United States Sharpshooters in the Army of the Potomac 1861 - 1865* (Dayton, Ohio: Press of Morningside Bookshop, 1984), pp. 413 - 415.

{37}   Captain C. A. Stevens, *Berdan's United States Sharpshooters in the Army of the Potomac 1861 - 1865* (Dayton, Ohio: Press of Morningside Bookshop, 1984), pp. 415 - 418.

{38}   Captain C. A. Stevens, *Berdan's United States Sharpshooters in the Army of the Potomac 1861 - 1865* (Dayton, Ohio: Press of Morningside Bookshop, 1984), pp. 424 - 431.

{39}   United States War Department. *War of the Rebellion. A Compilation of the Official Records of the Union and Confederate Armies. 128 Vols.* (Washington: 1881 - 1902), Series #1 -- Volume #36 -- May 4 - June 12, 1864 - Campaign from the Rapidan to the James River, Va. No. #158 - Reports of Brig. Gen. Lewis A. Grant, U.S. Army, commanding Second Brigade.

{40}   United States War Department. *War of the Rebellion. A Compilation of the Official Records of the Union and Confederate Armies. 128 Vols.* (Washington: 1881 – 1902), Series #1 -- Volume #36 -- May 4 - June 12, 1864 - Campaign from the Rapidan to the James River, Va. No. #2 - Return of Casualties in the Union forces, commanded by Lieut. Gen. Ulysses S. Grant, from the Rapidan to the James River, May - June, 1864.

Corporal James Raymond
Co. D - 4th Massachusetts Cavalry

XIII
"your loving brother."
Corporal James G. Raymond
Co. D - 4th Massachusetts Cavalry

Eighteen year old James G. Raymond enlisted in Company D of the Fourth Massachusetts Cavalry on January 1, 1864 at Hingham, Massachusetts, a few miles southeast of Boston. James found himself, eight days later being mustered into the service at Readville. He received a bounty of $50.00 for his enlistment and advance pay of $13.00 for his first month of service.[1]

James joined a regiment that was a regiment in name only. Four of the companies in the regiment, (I, K, L and M) were to be designated, for the time, as the First Battalion. These companies left Readville on February 7, bound for Lake City, Florida where they would immediately take part in the Federal disaster at the Battle of Olustee on February 20. From the Florida battlefield they traveled north to Bermuda Hundred and Petersburg, Virginia where they participated in the siege of Petersburg as four semi-independent companies, doing duty as needed until the Confederate Army abandoned that city and headed west, eventually surrendering to General U. S. Grant at Appomattox Court House on April 9, 1865. When General Robert E. Lee and his army left Petersburg these four companies joined the Army of the Potomac in pursuit, even though they were still officially assigned to the District of Florida. Events were happening in those final days of the war faster than orders and regimental transfers could be issued and executed.[2]

The Third battalion (companies E, F, G and H) sailed from Boston Harbor to Hilton Head, South Carolina on April 23, 1864 and moved in a northerly direction until they arrived at Newport News, Virginia on May 1st. The battalion eventually served in the City Point and Bermuda Hundred vicinity until it also, like the First battalion, followed Lee to the west, arriving at Appomattox Court House for Lee's surrender. These eight companies (E, F, G, H, I, J, K, L) remained together but served as two distinctly different organizations until mustered out in November of 1865.[3]

The remaining battalion, the second, was composed of companies A, B, C and D and James G. Raymond served with them. James had been born near Weymouth, Massachusetts, date unknown, into the family of Enos and Mary Jane Pratt Raymond. Enos and Mary Jane had been married on the last day of December, 1840 in Weymouth. At the time of James's birth there were already two children in the family, Margaret, age three and Walter F. age one. By the time of the Civil War this small family had expanded to ten children with the eleventh, a little girl named Mary, born in 1863.[4]

Walter F., the second child of the family, died at the age of four. In August, 1847, another male child was born; this one was named Walter B. He reached adulthood and served with distinction in the 44th Massachusetts Infantry. He also spent considerable time at a prison camp in southwestern Georgia called Andersonville.[5]

James G. Raymond, however, was a member of Company D, Second Battalion, Fourth Massachusetts Cavalry and was promoted to the rank of Corporal on March 1st. The men of this battalion sailed from Boston to Hilton Head, South Carolina on March 20, 1864 and arrived at that city on April 1 where they did extensive picket and guard duty.[6]

On April 4, James wrote a lengthy letter home to his sister Margaret from the city of Beaufort, South Carolina. He informed her that the men in the regiment had been paid and most had "alloted their money to their folks at home but I had no choice. As I being a minor could not draw it anyway." His passage on board the steamer *Western Metropolis* was rough. He continued by saying, "I was not seasick at all on the way, but felt a little squarmish at times to see others heave up."[7]

James explained to Margaret that they had remained at Hilton Head for just a short time before they steamed the ten miles to Beaufort. At Beaufort, the day of their arrival was spent in removing the horses from the steamship by hoists. It was hard work for them but by the end of the day the job was finished and the men had pitched their tents. That same night they "slept under the canvas." James had, at the time, health that had "never been better" and he was enjoying himself "tip top."[8]

Shortly after this letter was written, the men of the Second Brigade of the Fourth Massachusetts Cavalry headed back to Hilton Head. They were, according to a letter to the entire family dated April 16, always expecting orders to go elsewhere. James indicated he expected "to leave here within a short time but can not tell where to."[9]

Inspections were almost a weekly occurrence for the men. They had one "last Sunday" and expected another "next Sunday." Drill was done daily with the horses and, he said, "The more I see of the Cavalry the more I like it. It is fine fun to run and jump our horses over logs." James wrote briefly of his own mount. "I have not got a very good horse. he is a large grey, good looking and looks as if he might make a good cavalry horse. But he is contrary and will not go at all with a curb bit."[10]

As late as the middle of April, not all of the men were armed. Corporal Raymond explained: "We expect to get our Carbines before long. I have already drawn mine. It is a little more than three feet long and is quite heavy. It loads at the breach and shoots seven times." This was a Spencer Carbine and it was often credited to assisting the Federal Cavalry in becoming at least equal if not superior to the Confederate horsemen. James further stated that this weapon "will carry a ball 800 yards." This was true, but accuracy at that range would have been very poor.[11]

Also, in this letter is James's description of the town of Beaufort, South Carolina as it was then.

"Beaufort is not as large a place as I had supposed it was but what there is of it is right in style. It is on an island and the city faces toward Hilton Head. The place is well laid out, being divided into squares, much the same as New Orleans, the roads crossing each other at right angles. There is only one street that is called by any name and that is Main Street which runs along the levee and is the principle street. All the buildings on this street are either two or three stories high, most of them three, and were principally summer houses, but are now used for hospitals and for the Invalid Corps. All the other streets are either numbered or lettered, the streets running one way being one, two etc. and those running the other being A, B, C, etc. Most of the buildings are built in good style, and are very much like buildings found in a northern watering place. There are several churches in the place, but they seem to be used for other purposes than for that for which they were first intended. There are quite a number of Dining Saloons and Grocery stores in the place but they charge very high prices. There is one tailor's shop and two watchmakers in the place. There are no horse cars here and but very few conveyances of any kind. The streets are not paved but most of them are well shaded by a row of shade trees on either side of the street. All the streets have sidewalks. There are plenty of negroes but very few white people, especially women. In the rear of the city and on one side, is a plain suitable for a campground, and is used for such, there being several regiments there at present. Directly in rear of the city is a campground used lately by the 4th Mass. Cavalry and a regular U.S. Battery, and once used by the First Mass. Cavalry. There are plenty shade trees there and it is a very desirable campground. There are very few fruit trees on the island and those few are of little good, bearing, as they do, natural fruit. There are plenty of peanuts around and they are much larger and better than those we get at home. Beaufort was once a beautiful place but is now fast going to decay, as soldiers will spoil any place. All of the land and most of the houses have been sold by the government and most of the buyers are negroes, thus making them feel very self important. Most of the soldiers there now have been there since the place was taken and they are willing to stay there for the remainder of their terms of service. Some of them have got things fixed up so well that they will be a little sorry to leave it, even for home. It would seem strange if some of them did settle down here, if ever this cruel war is over, as the climate is healthier than any other place in the South, but it will probably be some time before the southern people enjoy its advantages, or any advantages they once did.

J.G.R."[12]

On May 1, 1864, James again wrote to his sister, Margaret.

"Hilton Head South Carolina Sunday May 1 1864
My dear sister -

Today being the first day of May I thought that I would write to you in particular as I suppose that you will feel bad if I don't. The first day of May is usually called May day at home from the reason that there are plenty of May flowers to be found on that day but if it usually called May day on account there are no May days out here. Here in a place called Sunny South when there is nothing but sand and swamps a very fine place to raise flowers. If it were not Sunday I might think that you are in the woods gathering those May flowers while I am sitting on the floor of my tent all alone trying to write something that would be of interest to you.

It is a very fine day here today but I hope that it is stormy at home thus keeping you from meeting and giving you plenty of time to write to your brother who is languishing in a Southern clime for want of a letter from home. The duty of the private is pretty hard in the 4th cavalry just now. There is a detail sent out every week on picket at the end of the and _____ it is a relief to go out there. Campbell is out there at present and I intend to go as soon as I get a chance. There is a place there said to be the birthplace of John C. Calhoun (perhaps you have heard of him). I should like to get a picture of the place and perhaps I can draw one. We have rather warm weather here in the daytime but have one advantage over those encamped within the entrenchments. We always have a cool breeze here through out the whole year thus making it quite comfortable in the shade. Our camp guards have had shades built for their comfort. We are camped almost within a stone's throw of three negro regiments and have ample chance to watch their proceedings. There is a great difference between different regiments of negros in respect to color. One regiment is composed principally of big burly fellows and another regiment had several in it that were nearly white. There is always a great difference in their drill, but they all drill pretty well and seem to take more pride in their drill than most white regiments. There is some talk here of taking two sergeants from each company for Lieutenants in Negro regiments in that which case I know of two sergeants in this company who would be glad of the chance. In that case there might be some chance for promotion for your humble servant. But I should laugh to see myself joining a negro regiment. I had rather be a private in Cavalry than a Sergt in Infantry or a Lieut. in a colored regiment. But our regiment is infantry in one sense of the word since we lost our horses. All our drills have been on foot with carbines and looks very much like infantry. Our battalion is now called the first and our Major ranks both the other Majors much to the annoyance of the old veterans who thought that they were some big until we came along. Bradford Hawes is with them, but I have not been able to see him. The third battalion is here but have not yet been ashore or at least I have not yet seen any of them. I should like to see Henry Pratt and Mary's Joe and find out how things were when they left. And that glorious Band. Do you remember it tooting away when you last went to Readville to see me? That band has been assigned to our battalion and will probably be with us. A Band always has great influence in doing away the monotony of Camp life and thus making the time pass much quicker than it does at present. Have you been to Readville since I left? and if so what regiments were there? What has become of the nigger colony? There are not many white women in this place but yesterday I saw three ladies riding out on horseback with three officers. Do you think that you could ride a horse now, if not, you had better learn as I shall want to exercise some when I get home and it is always pleasant to have company. I shave once a week and shave smooth. My health is very good and I like Cavalry, tip top. I don't know but what you have written but I have not received any, and have written 5 (what patience). You must tell others to write, I don't care who, but if any one (especially the women folks)(and more especially the younger ones) will write to me I shall write to them and not before.

No more at present from your brother,

James

A Brother's love 'tis said to fail;
A Mother's smile grow dim and pale:
But naught on earth, avails to move,
The fondness of a Sister's love, Thats so.   Jim"[13]

On May 15, James wrote:

"My dear Sister,

You wrote in your letter something about that $50 that I left with you, wanting to know what to do with it. I think that the best use that I could put it to would be to improvements around Home. But $50 will not go far towards fixing up, but I shall leave it entirely to you, and you may be sure that any arrangements that you make will be satisfactory to me. The house would look much better painted, and I should like very much to come home and find that fence on the line between Father's and Elias', If the family should need it you know then where I want it to go. You can devote a little of it in this manner - There is every reason to suppose that we shall stay here through the summer and I should like very much to have you send me a box. I have considerable time to study and as Mechanic's is a favorite branch of study with me and as I think some of learning a Machinists trade if I ever get home, I should like to have you get me some work on Mechanics if you can without too much trouble, you might also put in some good paper and envelopes and a few cans of condensed milk. That is all that I want sent in particular but I think that you and Mother know how to fill up a box that is to be sent to your loving brother James."[14]

Sometime after James wrote, he became ill. He developed a high fever and an extremely sore throat and was admitted to a hospital for care.

These symptoms, along with a myriad of others, seemed to indicate to the physicians of the time, that the patient was suffering from typhoid fever.

As well as James's symptoms, other indications that typhoid was present were stages of diarrhea followed by constipation and a return to diarrhea. Also there were severe chills, fever peaks, frequent vomiting of dark-green bile, extreme headaches and the tongue becoming large and flabby with a thick coating resembling a brown fur. There were often extensive nose bleeds and heavy sweats which were followed by coma, convulsions and finally death.[15]

These "continued fevers" as opposed to "Intermittent fevers" were treated by a wide variety of medication, depending on what the attending physician had found to be successful in previous cases. Some used a medication called "Blue Mass," which was also used for a wide variety of other maladies, ranging from apoplexy to toothaches and from constipation to worms. It seems to have been a general cure-all for whatever ailed you. The composition of Blue Mass was, according to a study published in the Summer 2001, issue of Perspectives in Biology and Medicine, a mixture of liquorice root, rosewater, honey, sugar and dead rose petals. Added to this seemingly harmless potion was a heavy amount of mercury which would easily result in mercury poisoning the consequence of using this concoction. Other medications used to combat typhoid were grains of quinine, compound of rhubarb, tincture of iron and various other methods thought to have been successful by individual doctors. It was often thought, by the physicians of the time, that there was a close malarial complication with typhoid, but such was not always the condition. Medication, although quite advanced then, was still in its formative stages as compared to the medical knowledge acquired by the twenty-first century.[16]

On May 26, 1864, eighteen year old James G. Raymond succumbed to typhoid fever while a patient at Hospital #4327 at Hilton Head, South Carolina, just 117 days after his enlistment. His effects -- one cap, one blouse, one flannel shirt, one pair of trousers, one pair of socks, a vest and a pair of boots -- were all he had and they were turned over to Captain Morton of the Fourth Massachusetts Cavalry. The following day he was buried in what is now Section #14, grave #12 of the Beaufort, South Carolina National Cemetery located in the city that he once described in a letter to his family as "right in style."[18]

1}   Record Group 94, Office of the Adjutant General, Compiled Service records. Volunteer Soldiers, Raymond, James G. - Pension file & Service Record.

{2}   Frederick H. Dyer, *A Compendium of the War of the Rebellion - Two Volumes*. (Dayton, Ohio: National Historical Society. The Press of Morningside Bookshop. 1979), Volume #2, p. 1240.

{3}   Ibid.

{4}   Ibid.

{5}   Record Group 94, Office of the Adjutant General, Compiled Service records. Volunteer Soldiers, Raymond, Walter B. - Pension file & Service Record.

{6}   Record Group 94, Office of the Adjutant General, Compiled Service records. Volunteer Soldiers, Raymond, James G. - Pension file & Service Record.

Frederick H. Dyer, *A Compendium of the War of the Rebellion - Two Volumes*. (Dayton, Ohio: National Historical Society. The Press of Morningside Bookshop. 1979), Volume #2, p. 1240.

{7}   James to "Dear Sister" Apr 4 [1864], Collection of Shirley Ann Rice Garrepy.

{8}   Ibid.

{9}   James to "Dear Folks at Home" Apr 16th, 64.   Collection of Shirley Ann Rice Garrepy.

{10}   Ibid.

{11}   Ibid.

{12}   Ibid.

{13}   James to "My dear sister" May 1st 1864. Collection of Shirley Ann Rice Garrepy.

{14}   James to "My dear Sister" May 15th [1864].   Collection of Shirley Ann Rice Garrepy.

{15}   Surgeon General Joseph K., Barnes, United States Army – *The Medical And Surgical History Of The War Of The Rebellion. (1861-65)* (Washington Printing Office, 1870), Reprinted by Broadfoot Publishing Company – Wilmington, North Carolina 28405 – 1990 – 15 vols. Vol. #V, pp, 212 – 268, 345 – 360.

{16}   Ibid.

{17}   Record Group 94, Office of the Adjutant General, Compiled Service records. Volunteer Soldiers, Raymond, James G. - Pension file & Service Record

Colonel Matthew Starr
6th Illinois Cavalry

XIV
"Aunt Stacy is not a copperhead."
Colonel Matthew H. Starr
6th Illinois Cavalry

Matthew Henry Starr was the first born and only son of Reverend Thomas and Rebecca Kinney Starr. His birth on October 3, 1839 in Jacksonville, Illinois was followed in subsequent years by the birth of four more children, all daughters. Thomas was a thirty-year-old part time lay minister from Taylor County, North Carolina. He had migrated to Morgan County, Illinois in the early 1830's where he met and married Rebecca on February 4, 1834. Thomas provided a meager living for his family as a farm laborer, but the contributions he received as a Methodist minister assisted his family greatly in providing for the necessities of life.[1]

In 1843 Thomas left Jacksonville, Illinois with his family and traveled to Platte County, Missouri where he had accepted a position as pastor of the Platte City Methodist Church. Thomas also served the Trenton Circuit and the Rockeport Community with his pastoral skills. His faith was strong but not as strong as his dislike of the Federal Government, particularly in regards to governmental policies. Although he was not a supporter of the institution of slavery, he fully supported the concept that a man had the right to own slaves. As tensions escalated in Missouri and Kansas in the late 1850's, Thomas Starr found himself supporting the anti-abolitionist beliefs while his son Matthew had much different views concerning the subject.[2]

In the years 1859 and 1860, Matthew Starr was elected the constable of the township where the family resided. This would, many hoped, serve two purposes. One, to provide the citizens with sound and firm support of the laws of the community as Matthew was highly respected for being a young man of great resolve, regardless his youth Two, the community hoped the added income of a township constable would assist the family. Thomas, although very outspoken regarding his beliefs, was well respected.[3]

On August 20, 1861, Matthew Starr found himself back in Illinois where he had convinced himself that he should offer his services to the Federal Government in putting down the rebellious southern states. According to his sister Margaret, there had been much discussion between Matthew and Thomas regarding this action. Testimony given by John Grierson, indicates that Thomas was known as a radical supporter of southern views. In fact, according to Captain Grierson, Thomas Starr was greatly opposed to Matthew Starr joining the Federal service as a private in Company C of the Sixth Illinois Cavalry on August 20, 1861. The Sixth Cavalry's colonel was none other than Colonel, later General, Benjamin

Grierson, John Grierson's brother. Thomas Starr was so against his son joining the service that he, according to Captain Grierson, insisted Matthew's picture should be returned to his son because he was dressed in blue. Sister Maggie, as Matt called her, failed to do this.[4]

On November 19, 1861, Matthew was mustered into the service of his country at Camp Butler, Springfield, Illinois. He started a military career that would provide him with a wealth of experiences and find him eventually serving as colonel to his regiment.[5]

By May 7, 1862, because Matthew was a good soldier and had shown his officers an inclination toward literacy, he was promoted to second lieutenant. This was the beginning of a series of military promotions, all of which he viewed with great pride. Correspondence to and from his family from this point on was through Margaret who was but twelve years old at the time. She seems to have been his favorite sibling and his contact with her appears to be all that survives. Maggie, in her correspondence with the government offices after the war, suggests that was simply because any correspondence between a Union officer and an adult citizen in western Missouri would have been a very unwise practice. Feelings ran high between Kansas City and St. Joseph. Thomas, she explained, would have been the brunt of animosities had he received mail from his "Blue Belly" son.[6]

When Lieutenant Starr was commissioned in May of 1862, he provided his own horse and equipment which were valued at $120.00. His immediate duties were as acting quartermaster for the regiment and by the end of July he was promoted to first lieutenant with the duties of adjutant for the regiment. This duty was done in superb style and on October 23, he was again promoted. Matthew Starr was captain of Company L due to Captain T. G. S. Herod attaining the rank of major.[7]

In February of 1863, Starr and the rest of the regiment began preparations for a raid through the state of Mississippi which would both baffle the Confederacy and bolster the spirits of many Federal troops. This raid, led by Colonel Grierson, provided a distraction to General John C. Pemberton, the Confederate commander at Vicksburg, the river town on the Mississippi which had become a huge obstacle for General U. S. Grant and his troops.

Grierson's troops would leave the Memphis, Tennessee area and slice through the heart of the state of Mississippi destroying everything in its path to Baton Rouge, Louisiana more than four hundred miles to the south. Along with the destruction of military goods and supplies, more importantly, perhaps, this raid destroyed Confederate morale and created a great amount of Confederate confusion. During the preparation, on April 16, Captain Starr was advanced to the rank of major. The foray, consisting of the Sixth and Seventh Illinois Cavalry and the 2nd Iowa Cavalry, was to depart the following day.[8]

It was at Louisville, Mississippi that Major Starr received his first assignment of military importance. There, on April 22, he was given the task of organizing a sizeable command to picket the town and retain control until the entire column had passed through. This was well done and was mentioned by Colonel Grierson in his lengthy report concerning the expedition.[9]

Two days later, the 24th, the cities of Philadelphia and Decatur, Mississippi, were passed and the column arrived at the small railroad crossing of Newton Station. Two trains were captured with a total of thirty-eight cars loaded with ammunition for both shoulder arms and artillery. Also captured and destroyed was a massive quantity of commissary and quartermaster supplies and almost five hundred small arms which were stored in the village. These, as well as the trains and locomotives were ruined.[10]

Starr was sent on one more special assignment during Grierson's Raid through Mississippi. East of Newton Station, on the Chunky River, was a series of bridges and miles of railroad track that Grierson deemed in need of destruction. The men, under Starr's leadership, completed this task and returned to the column in less than a day.[11]

When the cavalry regiments involved in this daring and exhausting raid through the heart of Mississippi reached their destination, Baton Rouge, Louisiana, on May 2, the men and officers were met with much enthusiasm, awe and admiration. Such a brazen accomplishment would have been labeled as impossible by most. However, to be returned north with laurels of victory was not the object of such a grandiose expedition. In fact, these men were retained in the area and incorporated into the command that was planning the downfall of Port Hudson, the ultimate last bastion on the mighty Mississippi River.[12]

These daring and brave men became involved in the siege and eventual fall of that Confederate stronghold from May 24 until its surrender on July 8. Serving not only as armed soldiers during the siege, they were also invaluable in the delivery of orders from one area on the siege lines to another.[13]

Confederate forces refused to abandon Port Hudson and on May 27 the first assault on Confederate works proved unsuccessful. These undaunted men inside the fortifications were not about to be easily relieved of their stronghold. Further attacks on the Confederate works were of no value to the Federal forces. One assault, on June 14, was considered a near disaster and it was not until July 8, 1863 that General Franklin Gardner C.S.A. surrendered unconditionally to General Nathaniel Banks. As soldier and courier, the men of Grierson's command served well under Banks' command. The Mississippi River now truly flowed unvexed to the sea.

On August 31, 1863, Grierson sent orders to Colonel, later General, Edward Hatch of his Third brigade at Memphis, Tennessee to investigate the facts concerning reports of some twelve hundred

Confederates moving on the Memphis and Charleston Railroad with thoughts of destroying the vital link. Colonel Hatch was specifically instructed to take Major Starr to assist in determining the validity of these rumors. If these reports were true, Hatch was to draw upon the service of whatever cavalry troops were available and prevent the Rebels from reaching their destination.[14]

Starr, on August 4, had been appointed acting-assistant-inspector-general on the staff of the Cavalry Division, Sixteenth Army Corps. The duties of the acting-assistant-inspector-general required extensive travel and travel is exactly what Major Starr did. September 22 found him proceeding up the river from Memphis to inspect the regiments and detachments on duty at Fort Pillow on the Mississippi. That was followed by inspections at Columbus, Missouri, Paducah, Kentucky and then Union City, Tennessee. His travels lasted almost a month.[15]

One of Starr's last duties as a major was to accompany Colonel William H. Morgan of the 25th Indiana Infantry from LaGrange to the small Tennessee village of Lafayette, east of Memphis. Morgan's purpose was to repel the Confederate forces under General Nathan Bedford Forrest. It seems, however, that he was on standing orders to be "in readiness to move at a moment's notice." It took more than two hours for Morgan to depart.

Starr's report to General Grierson was anything but supportive of the colonel's actions. Dated January 1, 1864, it concludes by stating "I would report Col. W. H. Morgan, Twenty fifth Indiana Infantry Volunteers, commanding Third Brigade, Cavalry Division, Sixteenth Army Corps, as inefficient." General Grierson's report was even less complimentary. On January 24, 1864, he stated "If Colonel Morgan had evinced as much enterprise in pursuing and attacking the enemy as he has in making excuses for his tardy movements, success would undoubtedly have attended our efforts."[16]

On January 25, 1864, Matthew Starr was promoted to Lieutenant Colonel of the Sixth Illinois Cavalry. This was a direct result of the advancements that had made him a captain just one year earlier. Lieutenant Colonel Reuben Loomis had been murdered by Major T. G. S. Herod. These were the men whose rise in rank had made the vacancy of captain available in company L. In a fit of anger regarding military protocol, or the lack of it on Colonel Loomis's part, Major Herod shot Loomis, in the presence of Colonel Hatch and customers in the dining room of the Lucken House in Germantown, Tennessee on November 2, 1863.[17]

The conversation between Herod and Loomis, according to Major Charles W. Whitsit, also of the Sixth Illinois Cavalry, was reported as follows:

"Major Herod: 'Colonel Loomis, you said this morning thus and so, in the presence of Colonel Hatch; take it back or I'll kill you.'

Colonel Loomis: "Major Herod, you have got a pistol in your hand, and I am unarmed. If you want to kill me, kill me.'"

Major Herod immediately fired, the first shot knocking Loomis down, the second entering his breast, killing him instantly. He fired three more shots at the prostrate body, none of which took effect. Colonel Loomis was dead. Major Herod certainly would not be promoted thus Major Matthew Starr was next in line for the position.[18]

A lengthy report in the Official Records of the War of the Rebellion by Lieutenant Colonel Starr dated March 1, 1864 explains in full his, as well as the Sixth Cavalry's, part involving the Meridian, Mississippi expedition from Germantown, Tennessee to West Point, Mississippi under the command of Brigadier General William Sooy Smith.

From February 11 to 26, these men traveled more than three hundred miles, built one bridge and destroyed eleven, as well as 500,000 bushels of corn and two hundred bales of fodder. On February 22, the regiment was under enemy fire no less then five separate times. Upon their return to Memphis, Lieutenant Colonel Starr reported the loss of seven men wounded and five men missing.[19]

His report was verified by Lieut. Colonel William P. Hepburn's statement where he cited the success of the Sixth Illinois Cavalry under the command of Starr. He specifically made mention of the bridge built across the Tippah River at Callahan's Mill under the direct supervision of Starr.[20]

On June 1, 1864, Starr wrote the following letter to his young sister, Maggie.

"Memphis   June 1st 1864
Sister
Your letter of May 8th was handed me on my return from the North. I am pleased to hear that the family is enjoying good health. I was not particularly afraid to come home on account of any rumors afloat as I had heard none but the fact of your being without the Federal lines and the bare possibility of trouble occurring made it my duty to refrain from any risk. An Officer has no business outside the lines except with a command.

Han was married Dec 3, 1862 to Mr. Wm C Ferguson of Charleston. I visited while in Illinois   They are well. Aunt Stacy is not a copperhead. We have no copperhead relatives in Kentucky or Ills except the Shearers at Paducah and the Pattons in Sangamon County. The others are as loyal as it is possible to be.

I received a letter today from Joe Stacy. All are well except Mag.

There are so many families here by the name of Young that I can not find father's sister without some more data than you have yet given. Give me the name in full. <u>Where</u> <u>from</u> & when she moved here.

My Regiment is now without horses. I expect to draw arms and perhaps get to Kingston, Ga or near Richmond as Infantry.

My love to Father, Mother and the girls

Your brother
M. H. Starr[21]

Being in the Memphis area, unhorsed and poorly armed, did not last long. Supplies were soon provided and by mid August the men were part of an immense force of Federal soldiers which left LaGrange, Tennessee bound for Oxford, Mississippi more than fifty miles to the south east. The expedition, when completed, was an estimated two hundred miles.[22]

It was not until August 13 that the Illinois troopers came into contact with the enemy. On Hurricane Creek, just north of Oxford, General Nathan Bedford Forrest had taken a strong defensive position behind earthworks on the south side of the creek. Hurricane Creek is a tributary of the Tallahatchie River which flows southwest from Oxford where it joins the Yohnapatapha River and the Cold Water River to form the Yazoo River. It would be Starr's job, with the sixth, to attack these well-fortified men from the left flank, assisted by the men of the Ninth Illinois Cavalry. The responsibility to attack the right flank of the Confederate forces would fall to the men of Colonel Walter Herrick's First Brigade of the First Division. Adding to the strike, from the main road, would be the Second Iowa Cavalry under the command of General Mower.[23]

According to General Hatch, Colonel Starr's troopers skirmished for three or four hours and eventually drove the enemy across the creek and back into the main force and they then finally captured the enemy's earthworks. Starr's losses were six men killed and fourteen wounded. Upon the completion of the expedition, on August 28, General Hatch reported his final losses - twelve men killed and thirty seven wounded. The majority came from the ranks of the Illinois troopers under Colonel Starr's command.[24]

Immediately after the engagement at Hurricane Creek, Colonel Starr and the sixth were sent back to Memphis. But Memphis was not to be a scene of rest and recuperation. On August 21 these seasoned veterans repulsed an assault on the river city by Nathan Bedford Forrest's forces.

Entering the city by way of the Hernando Road, the Confederate troops threw panic and disruption into the Federal forces there. Generals Buckland, Hurlbut and Washburn, all three, barely escaped capture. Having very little or no success in their daring raid into the city, the Confederate troopers withdrew, again using the Hernando Road. Their exit was assisted and encouraged by a small force of men from the Sixth Illinois Cavalry under Colonel Matthew Starr. During this action Starr was wounded in the left thigh. The physician's report indicated "The ball entering one inch inside of the Trochanter Major and taking its range obliquely from without to within leaving the body 1 1/2 inch outside and about one inch above the Symphysis of the Pubis." Colonel Starr had been shot in the groin by a .57 caliber mini ball. It was serious.[25]

After being attended by doctors at Memphis for several days, Captain John Grierson, his close friend, helped place Matthew on a boat taking him north. Starr was to be assisted on the journey north by Hospital Steward Edmond W. Tyler of the regiment. He was headed north, but not to his family in western Missouri. His destination was Jacksonville, Illinois where relatives lived. There, on October 2, 1864, one day short of his twenty-sixth birthday, at the home of his uncle and the man for whom he was named, Mr. Matthew Stacy, Colonel Matthew Starr died. He is buried in the southwest corner of the Jacksonville East City Cemetery in a lot belonging to the Stacy family. There is a well-weathered obelisk marking his final resting place.[26]

{1}   Record Group 94, Office of the Adjutant General, Compiled Service records. Volunteer Soldiers, Starr, Matthew H. - Pension file & Service Record.

{2}   Ibid.

{3}   Ibid.

{4}   Ibid.

{5}   Ibid.

{6}   Ibid.

{7}   Ibid.

       Brigadier General J.N. Reece, *Adjutant General of the State of Illinois* (Springfield, Illinois - 1900), Volume 8, p. 3

{8}   D. Alexander Brown, *Grierson's Raid - A Cavalry Adventure of the Civil War* (Urbana, University of Illinois Press, 1954), p. 3

{9}   Ibid., pp. 87, 88.

       United States War Department. *War of the Rebellion. A Compilation of the Official Records of the Union and Confederate Armies. 128 Vols.* (Washington: 1881 - 1902), Series I - Volume 24 April 17 - May 2, 1863 – Grierson's Raid from LaGrange, Tenn. to Baton Rouge, La. No.3 - Report of Col. Benjamin H. Grierson, Sixth Illinois Cavalry, commanding expedition, p. 524.

{10}   D. Alexander Brown, *Grierson's Raid - A Cavalry Adventure of the Civil War* (Urbana: University of Illinois Press, 1954), pp. 105 - 118

{11}   Ibid., p. 111.

       United States War Department. *War of the Rebellion. A Compilation of the Official Records of the Union and Confederate Armies. 128 Vols.* (Washington: 1881 - 1902), Series I - Volume 24. April 17 - May 2, 1863 – Grierson's Raid from LaGrange, Tenn to Baton Rouge, La. No.3 - Report of Col. Benjamin H. Grierson, Sixth Illinois Cavalry, commanding expedition, p. 524.

{12}   Frederick H. Dyer, *A Compendium of the War of the Rebellion - Two Volumes.* (Dayton, Ohio: National Historical Society. The Press of Morningside Bookshop. 1979), Volume #2, pp. 1024, 1025.

{13}   Ibid.

{14}   United States War Department. *War of the Rebellion. A Compilation of the Official Records of the Union and Confederate Armies. 128 Vols.* (Washington: 1881 - 1902), Series I - Volume 30. Correspondence, orders and returns relating to operations in Kentucky, Southwest Virginia, Tennessee, Mississippi, North Alabama, and North Georgia, from August 11, 1863 to October 19, 1863. - Union correspondence

{15}   United States War Department. *War of the Rebellion. A Compilation of the Official Records of the Union and Confederate Armies. 128 Vols.* (Washington: 1881 - 1902), Series I - Volume 52. Union Correspondence, Orders, and Returns relating to operations in Southwestern Virginia, Kentucky, Tennessee, Mississippi, Alabama, West

Florida, and Northern Georgia, from January 1, 1861, to June 30, 1865. - #13.

Record Group 94, Office of the Adjutant General, Compiled Service records. Volunteer Soldiers, Starr, Matthew H. - Pension file & Service Record.

{16}   United States War Department. *War of the Rebellion. A Compilation of the Official Records of the Union and Confederate Armies. 128 Vols.* (Washington: 1881 - 1902), Series I - Volume 31. December 18 - 31, 1863. - Operations in Northern Mississippi and West Tennessee. No 1. - Report of Brig. Gen. Benjamin H. Grierson, U.S. Army, commanding Cavalry Division, Sixteenth Army Corps.

{17}   United States War Department - Adjutant General's Office, Washington, D.C. February 13, 1865 - General Court Martial Orders No. 76.

{18}   Ibid.

{19}   United States War Department. *War of the Rebellion. A Compilation of the Official Records of the Union and Confederate Armies. 128 Vols.* (Washington: 1881 - 1902), Series I - Volume 32. February 3 - March 6, 1864 - The Meridian Miss., Expedition and cooperating expeditions --- No 47 - Report of Lieut. Col. Matthew H. Starr, Sixth Illinois Cavalry, of operations February 11 - 26.

{20}   United States War Department. *War of the Rebellion. A Compilation of the Official Records of the Union and Confederate Armies. 128 Vols.* (Washington: 1881 - 1902), Series I - Volume 32. February 3 - March 6, 1864 - The Meridian Miss., Expedition and cooperating expeditions --- No 46 -- Report of Lieut. Col. William P. Hepburn, Second Iowa Cavalry, commanding Second Brigade, of operations February 11 - 26.

{21}   Record Group 94, Office of the Adjutant General, Compiled Service records. Volunteer Soldiers, Starr, Matthew H. - Pension file & Service Record.

{22}   Frederick H. Dyer, *A Compendium of the War of the Rebellion - Two Volumes.* (Dayton, Ohio: National Historical Society. The Press of Morningside Bookshop, 1979), Volume #2, pp. 1024, 1025.

{23}   United States War Department. *War of the Rebellion. A Compilation of the Official Records of the Union and Confederate Armies. 128 Vols.* (Washington: 1881 - 1902), Series I - Volume 39 - August 1 - 30, 1864 - Expedition from LaGrange, Tenn. to Oxford, Miss. No - 19 --- Report of Brig. Gen. Edward Hatch, U.S. Army, commanding First Division.

{24}   Ibid.

{25}   United States War Department. *War of the Rebellion. A Compilation of the Official Records of the Union and Confederate Armies. 128 Vols.* (Washington: 1881 - 1902), Series I - Volume 39 August 21, 1864 - Attack on Memphis, Tenn. No 1. Reports of Maj. Gen Cadwallader

C. Washburn, U.S. Army, commanding District of West Tennessee

United States War Department. *War of the Rebellion. A Compilation of the Official Records of the Union and Confederate Armies. 128 Vols.* (Washington: 1881 - 1902), Series I - Volume 39. August 21, 1864 - Attack on Memphis, Tenn. No. 3 - Report of Brig. Gen. Ralph P. Buckland, U.S. Army, commanding District of Memphis.

United States War Department. *War of the Rebellion. A Compilation of the Official Records of the Union and Confederate Armies. 128 Vols.* (Washington: 1881 - 1902), Series I - Volume 39. August 21, 1864 - Attack on Memphis, Tenn. No. 13 - Report of Brig. Gen. Charles W. Dustan, commanding Tennessee Enrolled Militia.

Record Group 94, Office of the Adjutant General, Compiled Service records. Volunteer Soldiers, Starr, Matthew H. - Pension file & Service Record.

{26}   Record Group 94, Office of the Adjutant General, Compiled Service records. Volunteer Soldiers, Starr, Matthew H. - Pension file & Service Record.

Quartermaster Sergeant Edward Boots
101st Pennsylvania Infantry

XV
"I want to hear from you."
Quartermaster Sergeant Edward N. Boots
101st Pennsylvania Infantry

Edward Nicholas Boots was twenty-seven years old when he enlisted in the Beaver Guards on October 4, 1861 with two cousins and several friends. He was born in 1834 to the Reverend John and Sylvia Coleman Boots in Beaver County, Pennsylvania, west of Pittsburgh. The Reverend Boots family eventually increased to five more sons and two daughters and when John passed away in 1853 he left his widow and eight children to work out a living on the small family farm in North Sewickley Township.[1]

The Beaver Guards, when at Camp Curtin in Harrisburg, Pennsylvania, became Company H of the 101st Pennsylvania Infantry. The 101st organized and trained from November, 1861 until February, 1862 and during this time Edward was mustered into the service at the rank of Sergeant. The regiment was moved to Washington, D.C. on February 27, 1862 and continued on into Virginia in mid-March, camping at Manassas Junction on the 15th of the month. After thirteen days in the vicinity of the battlefield of Bull Run, the men, on March 28, were ordered to the Peninsula Campaign, arriving at Yorktown on April 5 to participate in the siege of that city until May 4. While en route, Edward wrote a letter home on April 1, while on board the Steamer *State of Maine*. The Knob School House teacher from Sewickley Township, Beaver County, Pennsylvania wrote that they were at the mouth of the Potomac River where it flowed into the Chesapeake Bay. He told Mrs. Boots that he had visited the Marshall House in Alexandria where the celebrated Colonel Elmer Ellsworth had been shot and that he, Boots, had seen the stairs where Ellsworth fell. This letter, continued on April 2, informed his family that he had actually seen the famous *Monitor*, "which fought the rebel steamer Merrimac so well."[2]

On April 12, Edward again wrote his mother from Camp Keim, named for the division commander General William H. Keim who later died of camp fever or Chickahominy Fever, as it was also called, on the 18th of the month. Edward wrote of an opportunity, or so he felt, for the division artillery on the bank of the James River at Norfolk, Virginia, to fire on the *CSS Merrimac* but they were unable to do so because "two abominable British war vessels lay at anchor just between where the artillery, and the Merrimac lay and there they would stay, I think," he continued, "that our men would have been justifiable in firing on the Merrimac through them if they would not move." Boots felt this inaction

141

of the British war ships solidly confirmed that the "sympathies of England are with the rebels."[3]

On May 5, the men of the 101st participated in the battle of Williamsburg under the commands of General Henry W. Wessels and Erasmus Keyes. A letter on May 20 explained Edward's interpretation of the siege of Yorktown. He simply stated that "our enemy ... would not risk a siege & so he left his forts and fled towards Richmond. " Boots mentioned his great disappointment in not having the opportunity to visit the historic town of Williamsburg as it was recognized, in 1862, as being "the oldest corporate town in Va. its charter dates back to 1735, it is also the seat of William and Mary College, except for Yale, The oldest college in the United States." He mentioned the burial place of the Custis family, which was "fast going to ruin" and that a Custis became the wife of President George Washington. Apparently Boots was well aware of the origins of the nation that he was helping to preserve.[4]

Sergeant Boots and the men of the 101st Pennsylvania contributed little to the overall advance on Richmond by General McClelland's Army of the Potomac but they did play a part in the battles of Fair Oaks and Seven Pines on May 31 and June 1, 1862. In a letter dated June 3, Edward informed his mother of the terrible battle he was in on the previous Saturday afternoon. Within five miles of the city of Richmond, the regiment, in the advance on New Bridge Road, was attacked by twenty-four thousand Confederate soldiers. The division, according to Boots, held its ground until it was "all cut to pieces" and then they withdrew to a position "behind Couche's Division, which shared fully much the same fate as our own." The engagement, Fair Oaks, lasted until evening and the Confederates were driven back even closer to the capitol of the Confederacy, Richmond, Virginia.[5]

The following day, June 1, 1862, at the battle of Seven Pines, the Federal units drove General Joseph E. Johnston's Confederates even further towards Richmond. The Federal losses, according to Sergeant Boots, were fearful. He explained to his mother that he had been ill for the last ten days and had not been actually involved in the combat. He did, however, see "plenty of rebel balls fly over my head & as I was trying to help move back the sick. The rebel cannon balls were flying over my head in a brisk manner, but I escaped through it all and am in quite good health." He then, in June of 1862, made quite a prediction: "I expect that we shall have another big fight," he wrote, "before we get into Richmond, but you may depend, that we will be there some of these days."[6]

The Pennsylvania soldiers did advance to the gates of Richmond, as Edward's next letter, dated June 9, 1862, was written from "Camp on the Chickahominy river on the road to Fort Darling." This particular letter was not mailed but sent home by the person of "esqr J. Wilson, who has come to remove the body of the Col. to Penn." The colonel was Joseph H. Wilson, who had died of disease on May 30.[7]

In this letter, which contained ten dollars for his mother, Boots also tells of witnessing the work of Doctor Thaddeus Lowe. He commented, "the frequent balloon ascensions of Prof. Lowe gives to Gen. McClelland all the necessary information about the whereabouts of the rebel army. We often see the balloon when up, it is generally just before sunset & it looks grand to see it floating in mid air while the tops of the vast pine forest are made glorious by the rays of the setting sun."[8]

The sergeant continued his poetic flourish with his next letter from a camp near White Oak Swamp. He began, "The long hours lengthen into days & the days drag slowly into weeks, & still no letters come from home & I wait & wait until the heart is tired of waiting." Edward Boots was becoming upset regarding his lack of communication with his family so far away. The majority of the day, for the men of the 101st Pennsylvania, seems to be built on the activity of taking down their individual tents and picking up or policing the litter that had accumulated throughout the camp over the days. This activity was performed three of four times over the course of two weeks and Boots believed it all for no good cause as "to - morrow we may be ordered to march ten miles & leave all our work behind us, but such is camp life."[9]

After the battle of Malvern Hill on July 1, 1862, the men spent the next seven weeks at Harrison's Landing. More excitement is recorded in a letter dated July 8 from the landing. After a brief explanation concerning mail arriving, the cutting of timber to create breastworks, digging trenches and receiving pay (which he "can not spend because there is nothing to buy"), Edwin informed his family at home that "Last evening we were reviewed by President Lincoln, who is on a visit to the army. He looks care worn, but the whole expression of his face is one of goodness. He was received with loud cheers."[10]

While still at Harrison's Landing on July 13, Boots found time to write a note to one of his sisters. He described a phenomenon that none of the family at home had witnessed. "This is the first place," he stated, "that I have been enabled to observe the action of the tide & it is worth seeing. For six hours it comes flowing up the creek & then stands still for a short time, then it flows out for six hours & then we are at low water for a short time & then the upward flow begins again..." Boots continued by writing "so it has ebbed & flowed since the dawn of creation & will flow on until the finger of time shall mark the last hour on the dial plate." Edward also explained to his family that their location, Harrison's Landing, was the area President William Henry Harrison was born. He speculated that President Harrison "died without ever dreaming that the country that he so bravely fought for & afterwards, so honestly ruled, would in a few years be divided into two parties, whose chief object is mutual destruction. Happy are they who lived and died while the Union was yet one and undivided."[11]

On August 16, the men of the 101st Pennsylvania moved to Fortress Monroe, Virginia, a huge fortification located on the site of Old

Fort Comfort where the James River flows into Chesapeake Bay. The regiment remained there for a brief eight days and on the 23rd they found themselves at Suffolk, Virginia. While at Suffolk, Sergeant Boots received his promotion to the rank of Commissary Sergeant. Very little mention is made in his letters but the address at the closing of his letters clearly makes note of the new rank. The regiment moved even further south, arriving at New Berne, North Carolina on December 4, 1862. The journey, aboard the Steamer *"Pheonix"* was rather uneventful, the steamer grounding itself in Currituck Sound. The fear of being attacked by Confederate forces while being grounded was never realized and the journey soon continued on with no further incidents. Boots did remark, in his January 6, 1863 note home that the regiment, like so many, had not been paid for at least six months and that he was very much in need of at least a dollar from home.[12]

Boots next wrote home on February 16, 1863 and he thanked his mother for her letter dated the eighth. He had been able to attend church services with regularity in a chapel "... built in the olden style. Pulpit half way up to the ceiling, gallery around three sides, organ & choir in the gallery opposite to the pulpit. The wall," he continued, "is adorned with marble tablets in memory of those who were the first members & founders of the church. I observed," he wrote, "that the dates of the births of some of them were far back in the last century. They have lived & passed away ere the terrible struggle that we are engaged in began, happy are they."[13]

In this same letter Edward requested a box of supplies to be sent from home, giving special instructions as to what he wanted and how to pack it for its long trip south. Among the many items on his "wish list," was a shirt, a handkerchief, "threat," and also "a testament bound in morocco & gilt edged with the Psalms bound with it." Specific instructions regarding the wrapping of each item in such minutia as the number of wraps of paper and the thickness of the cloth were included.[14]

Later, on St Patrick's Day, Boots again wrote his mother concerning his camp life, mail and the express package he had received from home. Almost casually he mentioned that his health was pretty good and that he had left the hospital the previous Friday. He knew his appetite was good but he was not very strong. He found irony in the fact that he could hear "The sound of the death dealing cannon mingled with the sound of the church bell."[15]

Boots became very busy with the responsibilities of his rank during the spring of 1863 and the frequency of his letters posted homeward decreased noticeably. From February to May, he found time to send only two letters to his family. Edward wrote his mother to give her information regarding the war and advice concerning her investment of money that Edward had expressed home. His health was still steadily improving and, with the coming of the fishing season he said he was enjoying military life as well as possible. His diet of fresh herring, shad, perch and trout "formed a great ration for the army." He also mentioned that he thought they would eventually go to Plymouth on the Roanoke River and probably remain there for quite some time. Commissary Boots was, it seemed, adjusting well to his new military life style, one with significant rank.[16]

Boots was correct. By May 29, 1863, the regiment had moved to Plymouth, North Carolina, and at evening of that date he took the time to tell his mother about the trip and request a "good callico shirt ... without a collar ... and with two pockets." He closed his letter by writing, "I send you a rose that I have pressed. There are many & most beautiful varieties of the rose here. They have one variety of a bright green color. If I can get one I will press it and send it to you." This letter, along with the pressed rose that Edward sent to his mother, is on display at the Port - O - Plymouth Museum in Plymouth, North Carolina.[17]

A brief note dated June 21, 1863 from Edward gave his mother assurance that things were well. Edward's health was fine and he was spending much spare time smoking cigars and reading Victor Hugo's classic, "Les Miserables." His next letter home was not until September 8. Life at Plymouth was not uncomfortable or arduous for the young Pennsylvanian but the difficulty seemed to be the tediousness of camp life. Weather, mail, meals and health make up the majority of the next two letters. It was not until March 8, 1864 that there was any military news to be sent home. On that date, in a letter to his brother Horace, Boots explained that his regiment had left Plymouth for New Berne. They had been gone for almost a week and Edward's life in the Plymouth fortifications had been very lonely. Since he was the quartermaster's assistant, it was decided that Boots would remain at Plymouth and the quartermaster would accompany the regiment to its new location at New Berne. This did not make Boots a happy soldier. With the 101st Pennsylvania as well as the Sixteenth Connecticut absent, the Plymouth area was in a "rather defenceless condition" with no more than eight hundred troops actually present. Most of those were North Carolinians and Boots was not positive of their loyalty or ability.[18] Edward also told his brother about the Federal gunboat called *"Bombshell"* and the slim diversion it had suffered in early March. "The gunboat," he wrote, "had a narrow escape last week. She went up the Chowan river & while she was gone the rebels got below her and planted a battery upon the river bank. The rebels thought that they had her safe enough. They sent a flag of truce & demanded her surrender, But Brinkerhoff her commander could not see the propriety of such a proceeding. He refused & kept up the river out of the reach of the rebel guns. The next day the gunboats Southfield & Whitehead went to his assistance. They arrived at the rebel batteries just before dark and were warmly received. A few shots were exchanged, but night coming on both sides quieted down. In the morning the gunboats opened in earnest & the rebels left. The Southfield bursted her hundred pounder & its fragments wounded two men: no other damage was received."[19]

Edward included a Confederate stamp and closed this letter to his brother with a somewhat prophetic comment, "if I ever should be so unfortunate to be taken prisoner you can send me a letter & this stamp will pay the rebel postage."[20]

The regiment made one more expedition, to New Berne and Roanoke Island before returning to Plymouth. On April 17, 1864, Confederate forces commanded by General Robert Hoke placed themselves in siege operations around the Federal garrison at Plymouth. The 2,834 Federal soldiers at Plymouth, under General Henry W. Wessells, were guarded by the gunboats *Southfield* and *Miami*, Commander Charles W. Fleusser on board the *Miami* in authority. Confederate forces, arriving from New Berne, came with the added armament of a new Confederate ship, The *CSS Albemarle*, under Commander James W. Cooke. In this, the first combat seen by the *Albemarle*, the *Southfield* was quickly sunk when rammed by Cooke's ship and fire from the vessel's guns damaged the *Miami* and Commander Fleusser was killed by a ricochet shot. Damaged and without its commander the *Miami* withdrew quickly leaving the infantry regiments totally defenseless and without support. The Federal garrison surrendered to the Confederate forces at 10:00 A.M. on April 20, 1864. The Confederates claimed, in their after action report, five thousand small arms, five hundred horses, twenty eight artillery pieces and two thousand five hundred men captured. Edwin Boots, quartermaster sergeant for the 101st Pennsylvania Infantry, was one of the unfortunate prisoners of war. His next letter home placed him in much different circumstances than he had ever been in before.[21]

"Camp Sumpter
Andersonville Georgia
June 23
Dear Mother
        I wrote to you from Hamilton N.C. just after I was captured. I hope that you received it. I am enjoying pretty good health for which I feel thankful to our Heavenly Father. I want to hear from you. Let me know how you all are, especially let me hear of William. you need not write anything except how you all are. I hope that an exchange will soon take place. My love to all. yours truly
E N Boots
Andersonville Ga.
Via Ft Monroe & Flag of truce boat
Prisoner of war"[22]

        Edwin Boots, along with the other captured enlisted men from his regiment, had been taken to southwest Georgia; Andersonville, prison. The prisoners now referred to as "The Plymouth Pilgrims" found conditions at the prison simply terrible. With no protection from the elements, no sanitation for the prisoners and very little, often no, food for the prisoners, Edwin Boots soon was stricken with scurvy - a deficiency in Vitamin C - resulting in the loss of teeth, the weakening of the gums, the bloating of the lower limbs and the weakening of the skin. If not remedied, it almost always proved to be fatal.

By the time of the Civil War, reports in the military, regarding scurvy, were diminishing, thanks to the work done by Surgeon Charles S. Tripler, USA, while he was on duty at various remote frontier forts. According to Surgeon Tripler's studies, an absence of fresh meat and vegetables was the primary cause of the many symptoms of scurvy, or scorbutus, as it was known. The many and varied symptoms do not always appear in every individual that has contracted the disease. Beginning with a simple depression of spirit, soon a loss of strength appears which is then followed by an affection of the gums and a sallow appearance. Also, livid, liver-colored patches may appear on the skin as well as ulcerations on the extremities and a loosening of the teeth. Other possible conditions such as blistering on the feet, ankles and toes or an excessive salivation may also present themselves. Most patients will develop an extreme diarrhea, a stiffening of the joints, fetid breath or a swollen stomach.[23]

Scurvy was very prominent in reports of the medical personel at Andersonville. For prisoners at Andersonville, when the legs of the prisoner became swollen like a churn turned upside down, it was commonly understood that death was soon to follow. There were 5,662 cases of the disease reported there and of that number, 3,614, or 68.4 percent died.[24]

Four and one half months after entering Andersonville, Edward Boots, on September 12, 1864, died of scurvy and, like the 12,911 other prisoners of war who died there, was buried by his fellow prisoners in a common grave, his place marked by a simple numbered stake driven into the soft earth at his head. That spot was later marked more permanently by Miss Clara Barton and her work detail which was sent to the site after the war had ended in 1865.[25]

Edwin Boot's grave site, at the Andersonville National Cemetery, is number #8606.

{1}   Record Group 94, Office of the Adjutant General, Compiled Service records. Volunteer Soldiers, Boots, Edward N. - Pension file & Service Record.

{2}   Ibid.

Frederick H. Dyer, *A Compendium of the War of the Rebellion - Two Volumes*. (Dayton, Ohio: National Historical Society. The Press of Morningside Bookshop. 1979), Volume #2, pp. 1607, 1608.

E. N. Boots to "Dear Mother" April 1st on board the Steamer State of Maine. Collection of Ed Boots.

{3}   E. N. Boots to "Dear Mother", April 12, 1862. Collection of Ed Boots.

{4}   Frederick H. Dyer, *A Compendium of the War of the Rebellion - Two Volumes*. (Dayton, Ohio National Historical Society. The Press of Morningside Bookshop. 1979), Volume #2, pp. 1607, 1608.

E. N. Boots to "Dear Mother" May 20th, 1862. Collection of Ed Boots.

{5}   Frederick H. Dyer, *A Compendium of the War of the Rebellion - Two Volumes*. (Dayton, Ohio: National Historical Society. The Press of Morningside Bookshop. 1979), Volume #2, pp. 1607, 1608.

E. N. Boots to "Dear Mother" June 3rd, 1862. Collection of Ed Boots.

{6}   E. N. Boots to "Dear Mother" June 3rd, 1862. Collection of Ed Boots.

{7}   E. N. Boots to "Dear Mother" June 15th. 1862. Collection of Ed Boots.

{8}   Ibid.

{9}   Ibid.

{10}   Frederick H. Dyer, *A Compendium of the War of the Rebellion - Two Volumes*. (Dayton, Ohio: National Historical Society. The Press of Morningside Bookshop. 1979), Volume #2, pp. 1607, 1608.

E. N. Boots to "Dear Mother" July 8th, 1862. Collection of Ed Boots.

{11}   E. N. Boots to "Dear sister" July 13th, 1862. Collection of Ed Boots.

{12}   Frederick H. Dyer, *A Compendium of the War of the Rebellion - Two Volumes*. (Dayton, Ohio: National Historical Society. The Press of Morningside Bookshop. 1979), Volume #2, pp. 1607, 1608.

Record Group 94, Office of the Adjutant General, Compiled Service records. Volunteer Soldiers, Boots, Edward N. - Pension file & Service Record.

E. N. Boots to "Dear Mother" Jan 6th 1863. Collection of Ed Boots.

{13}   E. N. Boots to "Dear Mother" Feb 16th 1863. Collection of Ed Boots.

{14}   Ibid.

{15}   E. N. Boots to "Dearest Mother" March 17th, 1863. Collection of Ed Boots.

{16}   E. N. Boots to "Dear Mother" April 28, 1863. Collection of Ed Boots.

{17}   E. N. Boots to "Dear Mother" May 29th, 1863. Collection of Ed Boots.

{18}   E. N. Boots to "Dear Mother" June 21st, 1863. Collection of Ed Boots.

         E. N. Boots to "Dear Mother" Sept 8th, 1863. Collection of Ed Boots.

         E. N. Boots to "Dear Brother" March 8th, 1864. Collection of Ed Boots.

{19}   E. N. Boots to "Dear Brother" March 8th, 1864. Collection of Ed Boots.

{20}   Ibid.

{21}   Frederick H. Dyer, *A Compendium of the War of the Rebellion - Two Volumes.* (Dayton, Ohio: National Historical Society. The Press of Morningside Bookshop. 1979), Volume #2, pp. 1607, 1608.

         Peter M. Chaitin, and The Editors of Time-Life Books – *The Coastal War - Chesapeake Bay to the Rio Grand* (Alexandria, Virginia: Time Life Books 1984), pp. 84 - 97.

{22}   E. N. Boots to "Dear Mother" June 23 [1864]. Collection of Ed Boots.

{23}   Surgeon General Joseph K. Barnes, United States Army – *The Medical And Surgical History Of The War Of The Rebellion. (1861-65)* (Washington Printing Office, 1870), Reprinted by Broadfoot Publishing Company – Wilmington, North Carolina 28405 – 1990 – 15 vols. Vol. VI, pp. 683 – 715.

{24}   Surgeon General Joseph K. Barnes, United States Army – *The Medical And Surgical History Of The War Of The Rebellion. (1861-65)* (Washington Printing Office, 1870), Reprinted by Broadfoot Publishing Company – Wilmington, North Carolina 28405 – 1990 – 15 vols. Vol. V, pp. 34 – 37.

{25}   Record Group 94, Office of the Adjutant General, Compiled Service records. Volunteer Soldiers, Boots, Edward N. - Pension file & Service Record

Private Thomas Morrison
Co. D - 22nd Wisconsin Infantry
Marietta, Georgia, National Cemetery

XVI
"but the childrens is the Prettyest"
Private Thomas Morrison
Co. D - 22nd Wisconsin Infantry

The Twenty-second Wisconsin Infantry, mustered into Federal service at the small city of Racine, a few miles to the south of Milwaukee, and began its military service in a most inauspicious manner. After the men had mustered and the regiment formed on September 2, 1862, these Wisconsin soldiers spent the next two weeks training, and they were then transported to Cincinnati, Ohio, and across the Ohio River to Covington, Kentucky, where they were attached to the Department of the Ohio, Army of Kentucky. The men left Covington in early October, for Nicholasville. In mid December, the men again left their encampment and this time went to Danville, where they served until late January of 1863 doing basic garrison duty.[1]

By January 26, these men were sent to Louisville, Kentucky; by February 7, they were in the Tennessee capital, Nashville, Within two weeks they were relocated to the small city of Franklin, about forty-five miles to the south. During a reconnaissance to Thompson's Station, in March, over two hundred of the men found themselves in the dubious situation of being classified as prisoners of war, having been captured there by General Earl Van Dorn's Confederate Cavalry, part of General Braxton Bragg's Army of Tennessee.[2]

The remainder of the regiment, in early March, was still in Tennessee at Brentwood Station on the Little Harpeth River, and, on March 25, 1863, they met a similar fate, surrounded and captured by troops commanded by Confederate General Nathan Bedford Forrest. The reputation of the Twenty-second Wisconsin was not one of great admiration. At best these men would be considered a hard luck regiment.[3]

The Twenty-second was exchanged, en masse on May 5, 1863, and spent the next five weeks reorganizing in St. Louis, Missouri. After the reorganization, the regiment served garrison duty at Nashville, Tennessee for ten days, Franklin, Tennessee for ten days and then Murfreesboro.[4]

While the Twenty-second Wisconsin was on garrison duty in Murfreesboro, efforts were being made in the state of Wisconsin to recruit enough men to make the regiment a combat ready organization. Part of that recruiting effort centered in the village of Delavan, Wisconsin and one of the new recruits was Thomas T. Morrison.

Morrison's background is, at best, rather vague. It is not known, for certain, whether he was born in Canada, Connecticut or in Schoharie County, New York, but it is understood, from a family Bible, that he was born on June 4, 1830, making him, at the time of his enlistment on December 21, 1863, one of the older recruits, thirty-three years of age. Thomas was the father of two young daughters, Clarissa, born in the fall of 1853, and Elsie, the spring of 1859.[5]

In February, 1853, Morrison had taken seventeen year old Elen P. Sweet as his wife at the home of the Justice of the Peace of Jefferson, Jefferson County, Wisconsin. Within two weeks of this marriage, Thomas was headed west to the gold fields of California leaving his young and pregnant bride, living with her older, bachelor brother, Giles Sweet.[6]

After five years in California looking for gold and also working as a clerk in a general store, Morrison abandoned his quest for riches and returned to Elen and his daughter Clarissa, who was almost five years old. Upon his return he pursued the occupation of farming with his brother-in-law, Giles. By December of 1863, the wanderlust had grasped Thomas again. The attraction of military life had lured him and he succumbed to the temptation. On December 21, he enrolled in Company D of the Twenty-second Wisconsin Infantry which was making efforts to rebuild itself after its disastrous beginning. Thomas collected a $60 state bounty which was offered at the time.[7]

After his enrollment, Morrison returned to his home in Delavan and waited almost two weeks before the men reported to the recruitment office in Milwaukee. His first letter home, to Elen, was posted in Milwaukee and it simply informed her that he and the other recruits would be leaving for the state capitol, Madison, the following morning, January 12, 1864, at 10:00. In a postscript, he informed her that it would not be the next morning that they left but the next night. This bit of minutia was important to Thomas as he continued making such corrections in several of the eighty-two letters he wrote to Elen in the next seven months.[8]

In a great majority of the letters Thomas wrote to his wife, now twenty-seven and with two young daughters, he took it upon himself to serve as a community reporter, indicating the status and situations of many of the men in his company. He told Elen that he would be seeing Captain Alphonso G. Kellam as soon as he arrived at Madison to "asertain whether I can get a furlow to come home again or not." He also instructed his wife to send everything that Thomas had forgotten, with a friend, Ed Goodwin, another of the twenty-three recruits that joined Company D in December of 1863 and January of 1864.[9]

This first letter, from Camp Randall, the training facility which is now the site of The University of Wisconsin's football stadium, contained words seldom seen in any soldier's messages home. After two short pages Morrison ended his letter with the unique postscript, "You Need Not Write at Present."[10]

Elen did not heed her husband's suggestion as in almost every letter Thomas sent home, he would mention her most recent letter, often receiving two in a single day. In her few letters available, Elen exhibited an innate ability to promote loneliness in her absent husband. She made no effort to hide her wishes for his presence. On January 14, she wrote to Thomas, "If there is any chance I want you to be sure and get a furlow to come home without fail." Her closing, perhaps not intended to evoke loneliness, must certainly have done so. She simply said, "Elsey looks for you every time the Cars come in." These were hard and difficult words, surely, for a father away from home.[11]

These thoughts never seem to vanish in the five letters available from Elen to Thomas that January of 1864. Her letter, dated January 18, 1864 began by telling Thomas "I am so full of trouble that I am almost crazy how much I would give to have you back with your family it seems as if I never could get reconciled to your being gone it is so lonesome here that I dont know what to do with myself." A few lines later she reminded Thomas, "I dont want you to go south before I see you ... it is hard to part with a Husband ... it may be forever for war is uncertain business ... dont fail to write and let me know soon enough if you can come home or not for I must see you once more before you leave the state ...Oh Thomas how I wish I could see you to night ... it seems as if you had been gone a month ... I never knew what it was to have trouble before ... I will try to make the best of it and wish for your safe return ... it will be the happiest time of my life when you are once more free and come home to stay." To add to Thomas's problems, Elen revealed "Elsey misses you and calls for you every night when the cars come in ... she says there comes my pa."[12]

These expressions of loneliness did not stop. On January 20, just two days later, Ellen told Thomas about her loneliness in yet another way. "We have looked for you every time the cars come from the west but all in vain. I would come home," she said, "if I was in your place before I went south ... I dont think they can have much feelings for the soldiers or they would not serve them as they do." On the 22nd, her desire was, "I want you to be sure and come home before you go south ... Elsey," she remarked, "is looking for you home every day and she says when you do come she will not let you go again for she is so Lonesome here without you." Again she remarked, "I dont think them officers can have much feelings for the soldiers or they would let them have the privledge to come home and see their friends."[13]

In Elen's last surviving letter she wrote, "it seems as if my heart would break to part with you." This letter, dated January 27, 1864, is brought to a close with "the children is both well and want to see you but I am afraid it will be a long time before they do." Adding further anxiety to Thomas, she then commented, "this from your affectionate wife Elen P. Morrison" and placed two large Xs at the end.[14]

Throughout his correspondence, Thomas continually assured Elen that the war was, for all practical purposes, over. He mentioned this first in his January 19th letter and he continued to express these feelings. On the

22nd he commented, "the Battles hear after will be few and scarce." Again in the letter of the 23rd he reassured her, "as for the fighting Part I don't think we Shal Ever be in a Battle while we are gone."[15]

By January 28th, Thomas had left Madison. "We arrived" he wrote, "in chicago about ten oclock   left about 1 or 2 arrived Michigan City Between 5 and 6   left at 9 oclock A.M. got into Lafayette Indiana on Tuesday Night at 1 oclock   about 11 o'clock two of the Back cars got off the track and we ware Detained Some little time   arrived in Indianapolis at 1 A.M.   left at 10 A.M.   arrived in Jeffersonville Wednesday about 7 o'clock P.M.   crossed the Ohio River to Louisville Kentucky and Staid to the Soldiers home for the night."   Elen must have been mystified, confused, hurt and greatly disappointed that Thomas had not been able to visit her one more time before he went south.[16]

At Louisville, Morrison got his first view of the enemy. "I have had the Pleasure of Seeing some Hundred Hungry Raged Ill Begotten Rebels on their way North" he wrote. "they ware locked up in the cars with a heavy guard over them." Thomas Morrison would see more Rebels in his remaining months of service and they would not be "locked up with a heavy guard over them."[17]

A brief letter dated January 31st, 1864 indicated Thomas had reached Nashville, Tennessee and was hopeful he would join his regiment within a few days. His description of the city of Nashville and the pleasant weather he had enjoyed filled the majority of his rambling. He followed this note with another, dated February 3, which was posted at Murfreesboro, Tennessee. Thomas Morrison had reached his regiment.[18]

Men that Elen knew were there to greet Thomas. John McClain of Delavan was there as well as Charles Menzie "that Little Dutch Barber." George Coburn was in a Nashville hospital. Coburn succumbed to disease March 10, 1864 and was buried in what is now the Nashville National Cemetery. "Osker Conick", Second Lieutenant Oscar Conrick - later promoted to Adjutant for the regiment, was, according to Morrison, "glad to see him." Also delighted to see Morrison was his good friend and constant companion, Ed Goodwin. Even First Lieutenant Charles Dudley was pleased when Thomas arrived.[19]

On February 7, Morrison told of an unfortunate incident which he witnessed. "Their was a Man Shot through the Leg last Night for Running the Guard ... he had to have his leg taken off this morning ... his time would of Ben out in 3 Months." Also, Bill Brabazon of Delavan blamed the Delavan postmaster, Charles Smith, for the soldier not receiving his mail from home. Brabazon was positive the letters had been written and posted but they were not sent to him by the postmaster. Imagination running rampant within a soldier's mind was a very common occurrence.[20]

Morrison informed Elen in a letter dated February 11 that many men in the regiment were enjoying the past times of soldiers. "They are washing their laundry, mending their clothing, writing letters and playing ball. Thomas enjoyed the mending and writing more than the other past times. He was, "as happy as a clam in high water" because he said, "their is a grate Many Men in the Regiment that are having trouble with their Wifes at home in reguard to their leaving with other Men But I have No fears in that way." He also said, in the same letter, "their is Men that has gone home for the Purpose of killing the Persons that Seduced their woman." Perhaps this was included in Thomas's letter because Elen had told him, in an earlier letter, that "there has been some excitement in town this week ... Mirandy Berdine and the black barber was catched together in an improper way ... it has made an awful fuss besides a great deal of talk ... I think they both ought to be punished for it is a disgrace to the town."[21]

Perhaps the most interesting part of Thomas's letter to Elen the next day, February 12, was his post script. Almost as an afterthought he told her, "I was told this morning that Huntley did hug and Squeased John Willis Wife and felt of her Bubbies and Besides all that their was other things More disgraceful than all of that." Who Huntley and John Willis were remains unknown. Neither were members of Company D of the Twenty-second Wisconsin Infantry.[22]

The next three letters were rather dull following the one written on the 12th of February. However, one dated the 17th included a bit of military gossip involving his good friend Ed Goodwin. "I Rather guess that Ed has got him Self in Trouble ... the last time he went home according to what the Recruites Said when they got hear if they serve him as they did others he will loos about thirty Dollars and be shut in the Bull Pen until the Next Squad comes down and if that is So it will be Rather bad But I hope it is Not So you Need Not Say Enything about this to her."[23]

Receiving pay was a constant problem for the Federal soldier. On February 20, Thomas explained the pay situation, or the lack thereof, to his wife back in Delavan, Wisconsin. "The Pay Master is around and the Boys will get their Pay in a few days But the New Recruits will have to wait Next Pay day So you will have to be a little careful until Next Pay day." This would have been true if everything would have run like the well oiled machine was designed to do. More often, however, it did not.[24]

As February of 1864 was drawing to a close, Morrison and the Twenty-second Wisconsin found themselves spending a very uneventful and boring tenure in Nashville, Tennessee. On the 26th, Thomas wrote his tenth letter of the month. He did not "think from the actions of things that we Shal Ever go to the Front." He mentioned correspondence he had received from her and the usual reasons or excuses every soldier must give for his lack of correspondence home. He had been busy moving from Murfreesboro to Nashville on the 23rd. This move had consumed three full days and his company had been assigned to garrison duty at Fortress Rosecrans, which was located just north of Murfreesboro. Thomas simply had "not the time at Present" and there was "No Place to write onley a Shelter tent to write in."[25]

March of 1864 was a far better month for correspondence for the Morrison couple as Thomas found the time and the place to write sixteen rather long letters home. On the 4th, he explained the duties of a "Train Guard". Since that had been his assignment for a few days as he told her "their is Eight men and two Corperals Detailed from a company each day to Guard the Passanger train that is to keep off all Citizens and Soldiers with out Papers...their is a Military conductor to read the Papers ... they are the ones to let on and No others." Duty as a train guard found Thomas riding the rails from Nashville to Chattanooga and back. This trip began on Monday afternoon and the ten men did not return until Friday morning.[26]

In yet another letter, also dated the 4th, Elen is told that Marcus Becker, a Delavan man in Company D had "ben Sick about two weeks Not so but what he is about but is weak and is getting Poor every day ... he does Not appear to have eny Energy ... Just Mopes about ... Some of the Boys Seems to think that he is a Playing off But his looks Shows that he is sick." The cause, Thomas believed, was that Becker's wife had passed away a few weeks earlier. News of a loved one's death at home was often a discouraging situation that lonely men frequently found they had to deal with.[27]

Thomas Morrison found a way to overcome camp loneliness and illnesses. He had, himself, "Ben on hand to do my duty all the while. When I had Nothing else to do I would walk about and see the Different Redoubts and fortifycations and got a Pleanty of Exercise But I am Pretty careful what I eat and how much." He also mentioned that "Young Peck," Page P. Peck from Delavan, "is well ... you can't kill him Eny how ... he is the hardiest Nut we have in the Regment."[28]

On March 6th Thomas again found time to dash off another short note to Elen. He again chose to report on the friends in the company. Charles Crandle, a recruit from Big Foot, Wisconsin, had just arrived from the north but Jim Foster was still being detained in Madison because of the riot there. Ed Goodwin was serving picket duty again having replaced Jacob Weisher, the Dutch Barber from Delavan. Henry Hunt, William Tinker and Ed Goodwin were still tent mates of Morrison and Hunt and Tinker were "Raising the old Hairy So that I can't hard ly think what I want to write but what I forget this time I will write Next time." Camp life for Morrison in middle Tennessee was not unbearable.[29]

A short two page letter of rambling, dated March 7, was followed by a four page letter on the eleventh. A new diversion was mentioned for the first time. Thomas told his wife that "I did Not have time to write Before I had to go out on Picket ... when I got in from Picket Supper was Ready and as Soon as Supper was over the Brass Band commenced to Play and they Play Most Butyful you had better believe. I suppose it is the Best Band in the Country at least they have the Name ... Eny how by the time they got through the String Band commenced ... it Made Me feel very queer to think how we have Spent a meny Pleasant hour in the Preasants of Such a Band ... it makes me feel Home Sick in one Sence of the word to think of the Past comforts we have taken togather and Now we Must be Parted."[30]

On the thirteenth Thomas informed Elen that he had sent, with John Coburn, shell bracelets that he had made for his daughters, Clarissa and Elsie. These bracelets, hand made by Thomas and tent-mate William Tinker, were the subject of several letters over the next few months and seemed to always break just as they were close to being finished. The shells, from the now famous Stones River at Murfreesboro, were to serve as a sort of souvenir of the recent battle of Stones River or Murfreesboro on December 31, 1863 and January 2, 1864. The frustration of the shells continuously breaking must have been great but not as great as the boredom of camp life. Thomas continued to work on the projects while he remained at Nashville.[31]

Two letters later, in his eight-page, March 16th letter to Elen, Morrison told in great detail about a southern plantation located near the capital city of Nashville. The huge home with its wings and porticoes at the front, carriage lanterns at the entrances with special windows of yellow and pink colored glass were, to the Wisconsin soldier, awesome to see. The splendid yard surrounding the home was filled with evergreens, southern and northern shade trees lined the walkways and roads. There were copper and stone statues and monuments scattered around and one that truly amazed Thomas was "A Niger and Wench a Dancin the Polka ... they look as natural as life." There were flowers "of all sorts" and Plants of all Description." The soldier was impressed with this particular southerner's affluence and he took great effort to offer Elen his best possible description of the entire plantation.[32]

The remaining seven March letters all followed the same basic mind set of a lonesome and bored soldier who would far rather be with his wife and daughters in Wisconsin than with his regiment in Nashville, Tennessee. He was sorry to hear of Elsie's illness. He discussed the March 10th illness and death of George Coburn and the continuing absence of Jim Foster, still in Madison, Wisconsin. Weather was discussed as well as rumors of all types and their possibilities of being fact, and, of course, his continued belief that the Twenty-second would never get closer to the fighting than they were at present. These letters were long, they were repetitious and they were full of information that only a lonely man would feel important enough to write to his equally lonesome wife.[33]

However, in his last March letter, dated the 31st, Morrison gives a graphic description of an area at Murfreesboro "whare the grate Battle was Fought ... the tenth Wisconsin helped to fight that Battle. I have bin on the Battle ground whare the tops of the Trees limbs that ware cut off by canon Balls and their is a Small Space of ground on the rice of the hill whare the heaft of the men fell ... they are Buered on the Spot whare they fell ... they

156

have Built a Stone Wall of Mason work Some Six or Seven feet high Eighteen or twenty inches wide then in the centure of this Place they have a large Monument the No of the Regmt State officers in command Besides other things that I have forgotten." This depiction described the memorial at the battle of Stones River located in what was referred to as "Hell's Half Acre." Within the fenced area are located the graves of many of the men who lost their lives in combat there.[34]

Morrison wrote twelve letters in April. The first eight, all from Nashville, continue his experiences he and the other men of the regiment had in camp. Thomas was also concerned about the November elections but for a different reason than most. He indicated, "this Fighting Business will be wound up Just as Soon as Old abe is reelectted ... you will see that the thing will Dry up if Not before." Morrison's heart was full of hope but facts would prove him mistaken. Lincoln was re-elected but the war did not come to a quick conclusion.[35]

He was correct in regard to the upcoming grand strategy of the Federal Armies and the future of the coordination of the troop movements which were being designed to promote the future outcome of the war. "they aint a going to commence their Spring Campaign until they are all Ready from the Potomac to the Cumberland So they can opperate together." This was great insight for a private.[36]

He related an experience seldom seen in his letter of April 11. Dick Williams "went to town got his Discharge Papers ... got his commission for Second Lieutenant. Reenlisted for three years or Sooner Discharged came back to camp all wright ... Invited Co. D to go to the Sutlers and Drink Beer on his Expense and we did So then we give him three cheers ... the thing Passed off very Nicely."[37]

Thomas's size became the subject of his April 16th letter. He felt his health had never been better and just a few days before he had weighed himself. He was "one hundred and seventy without my overcoat" and a few weeks previously he had had himself weighed while at a grinding mill. Then, with his overcoat he had weighed only "one hundred and fifty Seven and a half So according to that I have gained about twenty one and a half Pounds ... I am agoing to weigh two hundred (when) I come home and Maybe More."[38]

Thomas had much concern for fellow soldier, Charles Crandle from Walworth, Wisconsin. He wrote "there is one that can get his Discharge if he is a Mind to Make application for it for he haves fitts Some two a week he was downtown the other day and in Coming in to camp he was alone he got along whare their was Some Mud and he was going around it when he See he was agoing to have a fit and he got down as Soon as he could when he got over it he was Scarceley able to get to camp I suppose he would Not like to have his folks No it for a good deal. I think I should hate to have fitts ... he wants to go with the Regiment. I feel Sorry for him But he will have to Stay hear to Nashville in Some Hospittle and that is Disagreeable to be Tyed up in a Hospittle." Crandle was discharged in October for his disability.[39]

Two days later another soldier in the company was the subject of discussion. Jack McClain had returned to camp from Chicago and a furlough and had failed to bring Thomas any tobacco. "It costs a great deal hear and I was in hopes that he would Bring Me down Some their is not Much dependence to be Put in him Eny way he thinks of Nobody But him Self ... he was in chicago two Nights and I guess he and Norm ware on a Regular Bum ... Jacks Mother haves But a very little idea how he carrys sail on when he is gone from home and it is not Best She Should for I think She would worry worse than She does Now I could tell Some Pretty hard yarns about him." Morrison then cautions his wife regarding discreetness. "what I write to you about the Boys I want you Should keep to your self Because it would be the Means of Making bad Friends down hear." He then assures her, "there is Not eny of the Boys can Say Enything in Regard to My Bumming arround Town or Eny whare else."[40]

Thomas also gossiped about Norman Perry, a sergeant of Company D and, in October of 1864, a first lieutenant in Company F of the 44th Wisconsin Infantry. "But I suppose Norm has got two or three Nigar Babys at Murfreesboro at least the wenches say and the Boys Says he owes Some fifty or Sixty Dollars for beer in Murfreesboro and I suppose he intends to cheat them out of it," he wrote. In an undated April letter, also from Nashville, he seemed to have reached the ultimate regarding his trepidation for his friends within the company.[41]

Regarding his friend, Ed Goodwin, Thomas wrote, "... Sorry that I enlisted for he Proves to be Different than what I thought he was ... he has Proved to be dirty and Filthy ... he dos Not Seem to have eny Energy ... just as Soon as he Eats his meals insted of helping to wash the Dishes or sweeping out or Bringing a Pail of water he will go to Some other tent and Play cards until Rool call and then he will Poke his head out of the door and Answer to his name then Back he goes to his Jeneral work and when he is in the Tent he is hawking and Spiting and Blowing his Snot all over the floor and throwing his Tobacco cuds in the Dried Apples that was stewing over the fire and Never Said a word about it until after Hank had given them to little Peck By accident Hank happened to see him when he took the cud out of the two quart Pail that we had the apples cooking in and he is full of all such tricks ... the other Boys are all getting down on him in the tent ... they Blackarde him all the time." It is probably a wonder that Mr. Goodwin was not the victim of serious physical reprimand from his tent mates.[42]

In finishing this letter, Morrison tells Elen "I heard by the way of the Boys the other Night that the Wenches in Murfreesboro ware making grate Enquiry for Norm Perry for he has right smart of women coming in down their and they want something for his children to Eat and ware and they say he owes about fifty Dollars in Murfreesboro for beer and I expect it is all so." As a final comment, Thomas requests that Elen "keep this all to your Self" and "Burn this as soon as you Read it." She did not.[43]

A letter written on the 22nd while the regiment was camped near Fosterville, Tennessee indicates that the regiment was on the move. From Overall Creek to Fosterville on the 22nd, Morrison's only complaint was that his feet were sore after the one day march of the twelve miles. "Now it is No town at all for the Soldiers have tore down the Buildings and are a Burning them for fire wood ...to morrow we Shal go to Shelbyville distance 14 or 16 Miles ... I will write a letter every Night and then when we get to a Post office I can Drop it in." The same letter, dated from Shelbyville, gives a partial explanation of how and why the violence in the war seemed to be escalating. Shelbyville was a Union town according to Thomas. The men of the 85th Indiana, brigaded with the Twenty-second Wisconsin, "gut a man yester day that helped to kill their Captain and a Private about a year ago. A Union Man Reported him and they went and gut him. I think they will shoot or hang him in a day or two ... the 85th are a hard lot of Boys   they dont have much sympathy for such men or bushwackers."[44]

This three day letter was finished eight miles from Tullahoma and much was said regarding the weather and rough rocky roads as "worse than old Connecticut for rocks or Else I have forgotten." These rough roads and the wet weather were playing havoc with the "twenty five Hundred Men and the 43 wagons and eleven Ambulance wagons" that were accompanying the regiment.[45]

Before his next letter was sent, the regiment had crossed the Cumberland Mountains where the men had to "carry our Napsakes, haver sacks, canteen and forty Rounds of catrages in all makeing about fifty Pounds and it made quite a Load." This was a distance of five or six miles and he expected the regiment's destination would be Bridgeport, Alabama. He received Elen's letter of the 23rd while there. Three or four more days of marching were anticipated before the men reached their final destination, Chattanooga, Tennessee. According to his calculations, the total march was in excess of 150 miles. Other than the first day's complaint of sore feet, Thomas said he had withstood the march quite well.[46]

April and its spring days gave way to May and its warm, often hot, and humid days. Thomas was at Chattanooga preparing to embark on the Atlanta Campaign under the command of General William T. Sherman. While making these preparations, Morrison continued his lengthy letters to Elen. He wrote, on May 2nd, from Lookout Valley, "their is More or Less Deserters coming in every day ... the trees and Shrubry is a getting So much more Leaved out and that gives them a good chance to Desert and their will be a grate deal of it done ... we are a going to Shove them into the Gulf this summer if they dont Surrender." He also predicted that the entire south would soon "cave in a Short time with the Exception of Gurily and

159

Bushwacking." He acknowledged that now they were in "an Enemes country" where the mail would not be carried with as much safety as before. It was probable that neither of them would be receiving mail with the regularity to which they had become accustomed.[47]

While at Tunnel Hill Ridge, Georgia, on May 8th, Morrison predicted the Rebels would make their first stand "when we get them Back to Atlanta." He was "most afraid that the fun will Be over Before we are permitted to get their." He estimated the federal forces in this area at "about one hundred and twenty thousand men."[48]

On the 12th the men in the regiment moved to Dugout Valley. "we have got [them] surrounded with about two hundred and fifty thousand and we Expect a considerable more force Besides a cavilry force from the Potomac." He was concerned, however. "What gives me the Most at Present is Tobacco. Our Sutler was not alowed to come with us." The realities and horrors of war had not had an effect on Morrison as yet. That would change.[49]

The men of the Twenty-second Wisconsin were heavily engaged at the battle of Resaca on May 14th and 15th. It was not until the 20th of the month that Thomas had the time to write home again. A different tone and a far different subject matter was evident. "we have faught the Enemy Nine days But the 22nd was only in the fight one half day ... our company had But very few wounded and None killed. Bill Brabazo was Slightly wounded acrost the for head, Jack Edwards in the arm Slightly, Julius Smith in the arm." Morrison realized the regiment and the company was very fortunate in their first battle of this campaign. He was afraid. "The Bullets flew around my head about as thick as I wanted them to ... the musketry Sounded like Giles Poping corn ... Every now and then they would come in a Shell and burst among us and that wernt quite So Nice." The Twenty-second Wisconsin had seen the elephant, as many men referred to their first experience of combat. The elephant was far more then Thomas Morrison had expected.[50]

A letter written on the 22nd mentioned some of the many rumors circulating within camp. One such rumor said the Twenty-second was to go to Knoxville, Tennessee. Another declared they were to be sent to Bull's Gap, Tennessee. The men listened to every possible rumor and then repeated them to others as fact.[51]

What was fact, however, was the amount of foraging being done by federal soldiers. Food was never scarce, according to Thomas. "We keep," he wrote, "quite a little drove of cattle and sheep on hand all of the time and we have Pleanty of hard tack Sugar coffee Rations of good Salt Pork ... the other Rations of Meat is fresh Beef and while we are in this Part of the country their will be No trouble but what we will get a Plenty of Tobacco." Prisoners of war were saying "that if they only knew how they ware treated when they get in our lines that their would be about half that would Desert But their officers tell them if they get in our hands that we will kill them."[52]

As the days moved on, so did the soldiers. By the 27th, they were near Dallas and New Hope Church, southwest of Dalton. He was not certain as to where he was located and simply gave his location as "Georgy." He was much more concerned about his welfare and related to Elen, "Night Before Last we had one man killed ... he lived about 12 hours after he was Shot ... he was our comisary in the company ... he was liked by all the Boys in the company." This soldier was Corporal Thomas P. Kavanaugh of Delavan, Wisconsin, the only man killed in Company D at the Battle of New Hope Church.[53]

There were shirkers in camp and Morrison believed his acquaintance William Norman Perry was one. Norm had "Pretended to be very sick when we come in the fight and some of the other Boys Sliped out Behind in the same way." Thomas had an attitude also. "Our corps dos not have much fighting to do only to hold some Particular Point while the other Corps dos the fighting and that does Me for I dont feel like Rushing the thing as I have Seen Some others do ... I am not so corragus as all." Thomas seemed to have been a quick learner when combat was the teacher.[54]

Yet a new location, "Altona Ridge" was Thomas's location on the 28th of the month. They had been fighting, he told Elen, for five days in a row but the regiment still had not been placed in heavy action since they had been placed on the extreme right of the battle line. They were, he said, behind a very heavy breast works and had been ordered not to advance but to hold the position. However brave most of the men in any regiment were a few feared combat greatly. Wartroop Owens, of Sugar Creek, Wisconsin, seemed to Morrison to have served as Company D's bad example. "Wort owens is Subject to a Court Marshall ... he is a coward and had Proved him Self to be ... So far he has fell out of the Ranks at Both Battles and our Regiment has Not to do any fighting yet." Owens was not censured officially for his actions, mustering out of the regiment on July 12, 1865, with the regiment.[55]

Thomas Morrison had opinions as to why his particular regiment had not seen much heavy action. "We are under general Hooker and he is an Eastern General and our Western Generals do Not intend that he Shal have Much Prais in Regard to winning battles." This fact did not cause Morrison anxiety. He was perfectly willing to accept this fate.[56]

Thomas's letter on the 29th of May states they were near Kingston, Georgia, where Confederate prisoners of war were being handled by the hundreds. Provisions were plentiful and "we made a Rade on about 25 hundred Pounds of Plug Tobacco ... so we are all right on that scale." By June 2, near Allatoona, conditions within the camp were as usual. Soldiers were lamenting illnesses in families back home and both officers and enlisted men were constantly on the lookout for "gray backs" or Body lice and most of the men, Ed Goodwin in particular, were doing very well. Thomas closed by mentioning in a post script, "I Should like to See you all this Morning But I will be home Next winter then we will have a gay old time Christmas and New Years. T. M."[57]

Almost a week later the Twenty-second was still located on "Alatona Ridge" and things were still progressing well. To a man they were sure the war was about over and they would make it through the war safely. At this time the men were involved in the flanking operations involved with the battles fought around New Hope Church, Dallas and Allatoona Hills. They would soon move south for operations around Pine Mountain, Lost Mountain and Kennesaw Mountain. One more letter, dated the following day, was sent reassuring Elen that Thomas was indeed safe.[58]

By the 11th, the men were camped near Acworth and more southern enlisted men were "giving them Selves up as out prisoners." "Atlanta," these prisoners of war said, "had been evacuated and the only thing they are fighting for Now is Pride." It was curious that the men "stopped in a house the other day to See what we could See and the old lady told us that we did not fight fair for if their Folks Made a Stand eny whare our folks would up and Flink them then they were oblidged to Evacuate and that was the way we Drove them."[59]

Humor was not often one of Thomas's attributes but he did find the following imaginative attempt to amuse is wife. He wrote, "Grey Backs are very anoying to us at Present ... More So than the Green Back but I dont think will be in this Shape a grate while for I want to get rid of the Grey Backs and get the Green Backs and it wont Be a grate time Before we have that Privlage and then I shal feel Better for I want to Send it home." It seems Thomas felt the only battles the men would see would be the battles with the body lice.[60]

Four letters later a skirmish with the enemy on June 22nd near the Kolb Farm, located close to Kennesaw Mountain gave the men a slight taste of their future, according to Thomas. While trying to re-establish a line of breast works the regiment was attacked. One man, "Johnny Congden was killed almost Instantly ... he was shot through the Neck ... Gibson Hunt was wounded Slightly ... the ball that Struck Gib Hunt passed through Put Gragery's Hat pulling his hair from that into his knappSack Making forty holes through his tent his Rubbers through his Port folio then it struck Gib ... Silas Rowley was wounded in the Shoulder a flesh wound ... Nothing serious." Morrison may not have considered Rowley's wound as anything serious but, without a doubt, Silas Rowley did.[61]

Morrison wrote to Elen on the 29th, two days after the regiment's involvement on the Confederate trenches at Kennesaw Mountain. "I was out on the Skirmish line for the last 24 hours ... we had a considerable fun with the Rebs we asked them all Sorts of questions and they did the Same to us. We ware about 20 rods apart. Both Sides ware in Rifle Pits and occationaly we would Pour in a volley of musketry which would Make them Drop their heads in a Hurry. the Rifle Pits are about 4 rods apart and four Men in a Pit So it makes quite a Strong Picket line then their is a Reserve that lays in the Rear in case of Necesity and as a Releaf." He also informed her that "in addition to our Breast works we have a dich of about Eight feet wide and four feet Deep and covering it over Slightly with Brush and leaves and in advance of that about ten rods we have another obstruction in the way of Small Trees cut down with the limbs left on the Body But trimed out and Sharpend and laid clost togather with the top toward the Enemy." He felt he was extremely safe in such protection but there was no mention of preferential treatment or the withholding or denying of possible honors simply because the men were under the command of Eastern General Joseph Hooker. Thomas was in combat.[62]

Personal reports involving men in the regiment were included. Lyman Perry had not yet reported back to the regiment and no one had heard from him. Lieutenant Dudley had returned from Chattanooga where he had seen both Norman Perry and Charles Menzie, the Dutch barber. Charles did not look well. He had been wounded at Resaca and still had the ball in his leg. Morrison was positive that it would have to be removed before his condition would improve. "Wort" Owens had been seen in Chattanooga and Dudley had said he looked as well as anyone. Thomas assumed that Bill Brabazon and Jack Edwards would soon be returning, both men having been slightly wounded, merely drawing blood enough to have been sent to the rear.[63]

Another rumor was sent home by Thomas. It brought hope to him as he wrote, "the Report now is that Johnson has sent word to Lee that if he would surrender he would the fourth of July." As history proves, General Joe Johnston did not surrender on July 4, 1864, but on July 17 he was relieved of his command by President Jefferson Davis and General John B. Hood was placed in command of the Army of Tennessee.[64]

On July 4, Thomas wrote home the longest letter of his seven month military career. He was between "Mary Etta and Atlanta" but in actuality still at Ruff's Station. He reported that hundreds of southern soldiers were deserting and wondered how long the southern army could survive with so many men leaving. No doubt the southern officers were having the same thoughts and concerns. He mentioned the importance of the Union troops getting across "the river" referring to the Chattahoochee. The crossing of that river would be considered a fine morale booster for the Federal men and no doubt, a huge morale destroyer for the southerners. Spirits and health had never been better. The Fourth of July was celebrated in Dixie by much martial music and singing in all of the camps; all but the southern camps.[65]

An offer was made at this time to send Elen's older brother, Giles Sweet, at whose home she and the children were living, a fine gift. "if he had a Pair of these Grey Backs he would think they ware all rady tamed. I have a good Notion to Send him a Pair in this letter ... if I thought they would be alive when they got home I would send them." It was a generous offer from a man that must have had a wealth of these creatures available for the purpose.[66]

One statement in this typical mundane letter stood out. After he had written of more southern prisoners of war, the sureness of Old Abe being re-elected to see the finish of the war and the never ending shortage of tobacco, Thomas indicated he had "just heard that the Rebs have crossed the River last night So we Shal Probably move again to day or to morrow ... the River is about Seven or Eight Miles from Atlanta ... I expect the Rebs will make a Stand a Short Distance the other side of the River." This same prediction was prevalent in his next letter dated July 10. "I suppose they Mean to Make quite a Stand on the other Side of the River," he wrote.[67]

Again this prediction proved to be correct. The Twenty-second Wisconsin was camped on the Chattahoochee River when he wrote again on July 12. He mentioned a situation that had happened just the previous day that must have made Elen wonder about the strangeness of war. "Yester our Pickets and the Reb Pickets ware in Swimming to gather ... Our boys was over on their side and them over on ourn a Treding coffee for Tobacco and was like old acquaintance togather a Laughing and talking and Joking ... the Boys said they ware Mostly Irish that was on Picket yester day and they admit when we get after them we make them Skedaddle and they cant help themselves."[68]

In his July 14th letter, Thomas explained how the men built their sleeping area. "My Self, Ed and Jimey Foster went a Distance of about one and a half Miles got some Bords and Backed them into camp Built us a Stage about eighteen inches high from the Ground Just the width we wanted to occupy then we went about a Mile and cut Some long grass about three feet long for our Feather Bed and while doing all this we arranged it so as to Put up our tent in case of a Rain Storm." The weather however, Thomas mentioned, was still very hot and dry.[69]

Picket duty, he explained, was continually not taken with a great amount of concern but a lot of co-mingling among the soldiers, northern and southern. "It is No worse on Picket then it is hear in camp Because our men or the Rebs do Not Shoot a gun ... they have made a comp romise ... the Set around on the Bank of the River and talk and Laugh together and have all Sorts of fun Togather and that is more agreeable in My way of thinking." War was a strange and unexplainable activity.[70]

In an extension of his letter of the 14th, Thomas spoke of the blackberry picking with Jimmy Foster, Henry Hall and Wendel Fuhr and continued his disgust with his friend Ed Goodwin's card playing habits as well as his belief that the postal clerk at Delavan, Charles Smith, was greatly overcharging certain individuals for the expense of sending tobacco products to the soldiers. Two pounds of tobacco had cost a friend's wife a total of $2.28 to mail. "I think," he mused, "Charley Smith Intends to Make Money out of the soldiers." His closing was typical of what so many had been before. "From your True and Effectionate Husband Thomas Morrison."[71]

While still located on the Chattahoochee, on the 16th, Thomas wrote another lengthy letter of which the first three pages allowed him the opportunity to express his total displeasure with the much discussed William Norman Perry. Now that Perry was away from the regiment he was telling everyone that would listen back in southeastern Wisconsin of his individual heroics in battle and of the overall shameful behavior of the rest of the Twenty-second Wisconsin. He was making every effort to become an officer in one of the new one year regiments being formed in the state at the time. Thomas wrote Elen of Perry's cowardice as well as his many enemies in Company D. He mentioned that letters from various men would be appearing in the Delavan papers. These letters, if published, did not have any effect regarding Perry receiving a commission. On October 5, 1864, Perry became first lieutenant of Company F of the 44th Wisconsin Infantry which saw action at the battle of Nashville, Tennessee on December 15 and 16, 1864.[72]

Three days later, Thomas wrote:

"East Side of Atlanta Georgia   July the 19th 1864
Dear Wife
        I have a few minutes Liesure time to Inform you of the Recept of your kind letter which came to hand yesterday and was glad to hear that you were all well and Improving   we Left from where I wrote to you last we are laying Back in the Rear   we are Not much Nearer Atlanta than we ware when I wrote to you Before But Some of our Forces are   the Rebs are falling Back gradually   I have But little News to write this time But must write in answer to you Letter and let you know that I am in the Best of Health and Spirits But feel mad to hear of their stink that has got Home tell the Storys that they in Regar to the hard times they have Seen and where they ware wounded   John Robiliard told me this Morning that his Wife wrote to him that Bill Brabazan was telling around that he was wounded in the Hip   I was Not ten feet from him when he was wounded and he had a Slight wound acrost the Fore Head   it just started the Blood   it Probably Hurt him a considerable at the time on account of Being So clost to the Brain   Bill has Made his Brags to Many time Publicly that he would Soon Play out and he commenced at Nashville to get eny Simpathy from eny of the Boys   I Suppose he would like to get his Discriptive Role But he will be there a grate while Before he gets it But Still I dont Senshure only as far as I know and what I have heard him Say   I Believe he is Plaing off and I think if he is Sick it is a Judgement on him for trying to Play off   their is So Meny Playing off now that those that have Ben in the Habbit of Playing

off dont get eny Simpathy when they are actualy Sick and have to fall Back in the Rear   I under Stood a few Minutes ago that Norm was Reduce to the Ranks and that Clark Scranton was Promoted to Second Sargent and while writing thes few Sentences it has Ben confirmed and as Soon as the company can get the Blanks all the Men will be ordered to their Respective company   I bet that will make Some of them squarm But they are No Better than the Rest of us   I have Some Little Particulars to write to you in Regard to Norms career in the last year   Some Fucher Time I wonder how Norm will feel when he reads the co. Letter in the Republican and hears that he has ben Reduced to the Ranks   the Boys all feel well over his Being Reduced   they have got him Started down hill and they will all give him a kick   I dont see how he will get around all of this But I Suppose he feels as though he was willing to get out of it Most eny way But his Being Reduced to the Rank will Just about kill him   you must Excuse me for this time and I will try and do Better next time   as for the Specimens of your Dresses I think it is very Nice But the childrens is the Prettyest   it is reported to day that Atlanta was in our Possession But I guess it is what we call grape vine Not So   yours Truly From your Most True and Effectionate Husband Thos Morrison

we got official Report that Peter Burgh was taken

To Mrs Elen P. Morrison   Delavan"[73]

       Three days later, after crossing a small but very steep banked stream called Peach Tree Creek, Morrison and his fellow soldiers were attacked by Confederate soldiers under the commands of Generals Alexander Stewart and William Hardee. These two corps were involved in the first assault by the Confederacy in the Atlanta Campaign.   The Confederate Army of Tennessee had a new commander.

       On July 17, General Joseph E. Johnston had been relieved of his command and General John B. Hood had replaced him.   With the command, Hood was charged with the responsibility of turning back the invading Union Army under the command of General William T. Sherman. This involved the saving of the city of Atlanta and Hood's first action was to attack. After some consultation with Johnston, Hood decided to follow his predecessor's basic plan which had been formulated. Therefore, on July 20th, Johnston's and Hood's plan became reality. Generals Stewart's and Hardee's corps attacked the federal forces at what was believed to be the federal armies' weakest link, the troops on the south side of the Chattahoochee River, more specifically, those on the south side of Peach Tree Creek. These men, the object of this assault included the Twenty-second Wisconsin in the Second Brigade of the Third Division of the Twentieth Army Corps.

       The attack commenced with firing on the skirmish line close to 1:00 o'clock P.M. In that skirmish line was Company D of the Twenty-second and with the Twenty-second was Thomas Morrison. After almost three hours of skirmishing, the grand assault was made. After 4:00 p.m. General Hardee ordered his troops forward and after 6:00 p.m. the battle was over. The Confederate assault failed miserably. In the attack over 2,500 Confederate soldiers fell defending Atlanta for their beloved south. Almost as many Federal soldiers, over 2,000, dropped trying to take the city. There were three men from Company D killed during this assault; Peter Weiskoff of Darien, Wisconsin, Wendel Fuhr, Thomas's blackberry picking friend, and Thomas. As the assault began on the federal lines, the skirmish lines began falling back to their battle lines. As they withdrew, Thomas was struck by a ball, the projectile entering his face through his left eye. His death was instantaneous.[74]

Elen received letters from Thomas's friends, John C. Corbin and Edwin Goodwin, the ill-kempt, thoughtless tobacco chomper, the hacker and spitter, the shirker of camp cleanup and a man that thought very highly of Thomas Morrison. Ed Goodwin, late that night, went back on the field of battle to find the remains of his friend. He finally found the lifeless body after midnight. He dug a final resting place for his friend, wrapped his lifeless form in a blanket, and covered it with dirt. The next day he found someone to carve a headboard for his friend so the remains would be identifiable at a later date. Ed Goodwin must have been heartbroken at his friend's death.[75]

Ed also sent many of Thomas's belongings back to Elen and the children. Among these items was a letter that had arrived for Thomas the day of his death. It was sent from a friend, J. A. Morrison of Palmyra, Wisconsin. This Morrison wrote, "Well Tomas I thought that I would Answer your Letter Since it Took you So Long to Wright. Well wea are all well at Present and Hope these few Lines Will find you the Same But you must Dodge the Bullets or you Will Get Hit With Some of them ..."[76]

Thomas Morrison's remains were removed from the battlefield at Peach Tree Creek and placed in grave #30 at the Marietta National Cemetery, Marietta, Georgia. Due to modern re-numbering, that grave site is now in lot G, grave #6630. His surviving widow, Elen, and two children, Clarissa and Elsie, never knew where their husband and father was buried.

{1}   Frederick H. Dyer, *A Compendium of the War of the Rebellion - Two Volumes.* (Dayton, Ohio: National Historical Society. The Press of Morningside Bookshop. 1979), Volume #2, pp. 1682, 1683.

{2}   Ibid.

        Frank L. Bayne, *The View from Headquarters - Civil War Letters of Harvey Reid* (Madison, Wisconsin: The State Historical Society of Wisconsin - MCMLXV), pp. 29 - 40.

{3}   Ibid., pp. 44 - 47.

{4}   Frederick H. Dyer, *A Compendium of the War of the Rebellion - Two Volumes.* (Dayton, Ohio: National Historical Society. The Press of Morningside Bookshop. 1979), Volume #2, pp. 1682, 1683.

{5}   Record Group 94, Office of the Adjutant General, Compiled Service records. Volunteer Soldiers, Morrison, Thomas H. - Pension file & Service Record.

{6}   Ibid.

{7}   Ibid.

{8}   T.M. to "Dear Wife" Jan 11, 1864.   Collection of Arthur Lillibridge.

{9}   Ibid.

{10}   Ibid.

{11}   E. P. Morrison to "My Dear Husband" Jan the 14 - 1864. Collection of Arthur Lillibridge.

{12}   E. P. Morrison to "Dear Husband" Jan the 18 1864. Collection of Arthur Lillibridge.

{13}   E. P. Morrison to "Dear Husband" Jan the 20 1864. Collection of Arthur Lillibridge.

        E. P. Morrison to "Dear Husband" Jan the 22 1864. Collection of Arthur Lillibridge.

{14}   Elen P. Morrison to "Dear Husband" Jan the 27 1864. Collection of Arthur Lillibridge.

{15}   Thos Morrison to "Dear Wife" Jan 19/64. Collection of Arthur Lillibridge.

        Thos. Morrison to "Dear Wife" Jan 22/64. Collection of Arthur Lillibridge.

        Unsigned to "Dear Wife" Jan 23/64. Collection of Arthur Lillibridge.

{16}   Thos Morrison to "Dear Wife" Jan 28/64. Collection of Arthur Lillibridge.

{17}   Ibid.

{18}   Thos Morrison to "Dear Wife" Jan the 31st 1864. Collection of Arthur Lillibridge.

        Thos Morrison to "Dear Wife" Feb the 3d 1864. Collection of Arthur Lillibridge.

{19}   Ibid.

{20}   T. Morrison to "Dear Wife" Feb the 7th/64. Collection of Arthur

Lillibridge.

{21} Thos Morrison to "Dear Wife" Feb the 11th 1864. Collection of Arthur Lillibridge.

E. P. Morrison to "Dear Husband" Jan the 22 1864. Collection of Arthur Lillibridge.

{22} Thos Morrison to "Dear Wife" Feb the 12th 64. Collection of Arthur Lillibridge.

{23} Thos Morrison to "Dear Wife" Feb the 17th 1864. Collection of Arthur Lillibridge.

{24} Thos Morrison to "Dear Wife" Feb the 20th 64. Collection of Arthur Lillibridge.

{25} Thos Morrison to "Dear Wife" Feb the 26th 64. Collection of Arthur Lillibridge

Frederick H. Dyer, *A Compendium of the War of the Rebellion - Two Volumes.* (Dayton, Ohio: National Historical Society. The Press of Morningside Bookshop. 1979), Volume #2, pp. 1682, 1683.

Frank L. Bayne, *The View from Headquarters - Civil War Letters of Harvey Reid* (Madison, Wisconsin: The State Historical Society of Wisconsin - MCMLXV), p. 120.

{26} T.M. to "Dear Wife" March the 4th 1864. Collection of Arthur Lillibridge.

{27} Thos Morrison to "Dear Wife" March the 4th 1864. Collection of Arthur Lillibridge.

{28} Ibid.

{29} T. Morrison to "Dear Wife" March the 6th 1864. Collection of Arthur Lillibridge.

{30} Thos Morrison to "Dear Wife" March the 11th/64. Collection of Arthur Lillibridge.

{31} Thos Morrison to "Dear Wife" March 13/64. Collection of Arthur Lillibridge.

{32} T. Morrison to "Dear Wife" Mar the 16th/64. Collection of Arthur Lillibridge.

{33} Thos Morrison to "Dear Wife" March the 18th 64. Collection of Arthur Lillibridge

T.M. to "Dear Wife" March the 20th/64. Collection of Arthur Lillibridge.

T. M. to "Dear Wife" Mar the 24th/64. Collection of Arthur Lillibridge.

Thos Morrison to "Dear Wife" Mar the 25th/64. Collection of Arthur Lillibridge.

Thos Morrison to "Dear Wife" March the 26th 1864. Collection of Arthur Lillibridge.

Thos Morrison to "Dear Wife" Mar the 28th 1864. Collection of Arthur Lillibridge.

T.M. to "Dear Wife" Mar the 30th/64. Collection of Arthur

Lillibridge.

{34}   Thos Morrison to "Dear Wife" March the 31st 1864. Collection of Arthur Lillibridge.

{35}   Thos Morrison to "Dear Wife" April the 3d 1864. Collection of Arthur Lillibridge.

{36}   Ibid.

{37}   T.M. to "Dear Wife" Apr the 11th/64. Collection of Arthur Lillibridge.

{38}   T.M. to "Dear Wife" April the 16th 1864. Collection of Arthur Lillibridge

{39}   Ibid.

Record Group 94, Office of the Adjutant General, Compiled Service records. Volunteer Soldiers, Crandle, Charles - Pension file & Service Record.

{40}   T.M. to "Dear Wife" April the 18 1864. Collection of Arthur Lillibridge.

{41}   Ibid.

{42}   Ibid.

{43}   Ibid.

{44}   T. M. to "Dear Wife" Apr the 22nd 1864. Collection of Arthur Lillibridge.

{45}   Ibid.

{46}   Thos Morrison to "Dear Wife" Apr the 28th/64. Collection of Arthur Lillibridge.

{47}   Thos Morrison to "Dear Wife" May 2st 1864. Collection of Arthur Lillibridge.

{48}   Thos Morrison to "Dear Wife" May the 8th 1864. Collection of Arthur Lillibridge.

{49}   Thos Morrison to "Dear Wife" May the 12th 1864. Collection of Arthur Lillibridge.

{50}   T Morrison to "Dear Wife" May 20/64. Collection of Arthur Lillibridge.

{51}   Thos Morrison to "Dear Wife" May Georgia 22nd 64. Collection of Arthur Lillibridge.

{52}   Ibid.

{53}   Thos Morrison to "Dear Wife" May the 27th 1864. Collection of Arthur Lillibridge.

{54}   Ibid.

{55}   Thomas Morrison to "Dear Wife" May the 28th 1864. Collection of Arthur Lillibridge.

{56}   Ibid.

{57}   Thomas Morrison to "Dear Wife" May 29/64. Collection of Arthur Lillibridge.

Thos Morrison to "Dear Wife" June the 2st 64. Collection of Arthur Lillibridge.

{58}   Thos Morrison to "Dear Wife" June the 7th 1864. Collection of
Arthur Lillibridge.
         Thos Morrison to "Dear Wife" June 8th 1864. Collection of
Arthur Lillibridge.
{59}   T. Morrison to "Dear Wife" June Georgia the 11th 64. Collection
of Arthur Lillibridge.
{60}   Thos Morrison to "Dear Wife" June 18th 64. Collection of Arthur
Lillibridge.
{61}   Thos Morrison to "Dear Wife" June the 24th 64. Collection of
Arthur Lillibridge.
{62}   Thos Morrison to "Dear Wife" June 29th 64. Collection of Arthur
Lillibridge.
{63}   Ibid.
{64}   Ibid.
{65}   Thos Morrison to "Dear Wife" July the 4th 1864. Collection of
Arthur Lillibridge.
{66}   Ibid.
{67}   Ibid.
         Thos Morrison to "Dear Wife" July the 10th 64. Collection of
Arthur Lillibridge.
{68}   Thos Morrison to "Dear Wife" July the 12th 64. Collection of
Arthur Lillibridge.
{69}   Thomas Morrison to "Dear Wife" July the 14th 1864. Collection
of Arthur Lillibridge.
{70}   Ibid.
{71}   Ibid.
{72}   Thos Morrison to "Dear Wife" July the 16th 1864. Collection of
Arthur Lillibridge.
         Record Group 94, Office of the Adjutant General, Compiled
Service records. Volunteer Soldiers, Perry, William - Pension file &
Service Record.
{73}   Thos Morrison to "Dear Wife" July the 19th 1864. Collection of
Arthur Lillibridge.
{74}   John Coburn to "Mrs. Morrison" July 21th 1864. Collection of
Arthur Lillibridge.
{75}   Edwin Goodwin to "Mrs Morison" July the 21. Collection of
Arthur Lillibridge.
{76}   Edwin Goodwin to "Dear friend" July the 23 1864. Collection of
Arthur Lillibridge.
         J. A. Morrison to "Well Tomas" July 14 '64. Collection of Arthur
Lillibridge.

2nd Lieutenant Rufus Ricksecker
Co. G - 126th Ohio Infantry

XVII
"We are ready to go but would much rather stay."
First Lieutenant Rufus Ricksecker
Co. G - 126th Ohio Infantry

Present day Dover, Ohio, twenty miles south of Canton, was known as Canal Dover at the time of the Civil War. Canal Dover, located on the Stillwater River, was a flourishing community in 1860, boasting a good school system, peaceful living and, among its many businesses, a fine jewelry store owned and operated by Israel Ricksecker and his oldest son, Rufus. Rufus, a slight but handsome dark-haired nineteen-year-old had finished his schooling, become accomplished in the social qualities of voice and instrument and taken up his father's work, becoming adept in the field of engraving. All was going well within the community but the rest of the country was in great political unrest.[1]

Slavery, state's rights, tariff control and geographical expansion were all subjects of heated conversation and public debate throughout the nation. In early 1861 these conversations and debates had become volatile. This political attitude soon reached Canal Dover and in early 1861 the "Dover Light Guard" home company was formed. The young Ricksecker, born April 19, 1842, served as Orderly Sergeant for the guard. When Southern forces fired on Federal troops at Fort Sumter, in Charleston, South Carolina, the nation found itself at war. Many young men from the Canal Dover area rushed to the recruitment offices to offer themselves to the nation in its time of need. However Rufus was not among the early volunteers. He chose to remain at home assisting his father and being a big brother to sister Adelaide and brothers, Theodore, Julius and Eugene. The close relationship of these siblings is noted in almost every letter that Rufus sent home during the war. There was much correspondence with "Addie" and mention of "Thedie," "Julie" and "Genie" filled his letters.[2]

It was in June of 1862 that young Ricksecker enlisted as a private in Company G of the 126th Ohio Volunteer Infantry. He felt it was his "duty to go and help what I can to squelch this rebellion."[3]

The 126th Ohio mustered into the nation's service at Camp Steubenville, located at Steubenville, Ohio, on September 4, 1862, and twelve days later moved to Parkersburg, Virginia, now within the boundaries of West Virginia. Before leaving for the east, Rufus was assigned the position of Commissary Sergeant for the regiment. This appointment served the young engraver well and he retained it until June of 1864.[4]

As a Commissary Sergeant, Rufus found himself in a far different capacity than that of a regular infantryman. Ricksecker's excellent penmanship and his accounting ability made his appointment one of great

172

advantage to the regiment. Because of this fact, it served Ricksecker well also. The hardships of company and regimental drill were not part of his military life. Instead, his chief responsibility was to see that the men in the regiment received their rations in a timely manner. When three days rations for marching were ordered, it was Rufus Ricksecker who was responsible to see that the rations were both available and distributed. He also was responsible for the immense book-keeping task that was required.

In the many letters that Rufus sent to his family back in Ohio he mentioned the constant chore of filling and filing reports for his work. He also mentioned his several opportunities to participate in the various religious services offered wherever he was located. He never abandoned his religious upbringing, attending services regularly and participating in both Presbyterian and Episcopal ritual as often as possible.[5]

Early in his military career this young man found it convenient to share philosophical advice with his sister, Addie, regarding her correspondence with brother Theodore as well as to himself. He commented, "You ought not to write (especially to a soldier boy who has troubles & trials that no other business brings forth) in the strain you did some time ago; true it did not make me home sick but still I felt as any true brother would, that if I were home I could do a good deal to enliven you. Home sickness I think is caused in the army (to a great extent) by the kind of letter the soldier's friends write to him; I know several cases when men's wives are always calling on them to come home, that they are lonesome, &c and some even urging their husbands to desert if they can't get home another way; my opinion of such writing is that it does more harm than good."[6]

This is profound insight for a twenty-one year old soldier with no psychological schooling or training well over one hundred and fifty years ago. With all of Ricksecker's other character traits, it appears his greatest was common sense.

While with his regiment in both Cumberland, Maryland and Martinsburg, Virginia in the fall and winter of 1862 - 1863, Ricksecker suffered very poor health. In Cumberland he was severely incapacitated with a long spell of lung fever and at Martinsburg, later in the season, he was hospitalized for six weeks with typhoid fever. These facts, however, were not mentioned in any of his surviving letters to his family. Perhaps Rufus was simply following his own philosophical advice regarding what information was acceptable to include in his mail back home. If they could do nothing to aid him, he at least would not give them cause to worry.[7]

As early as April, 1863, from Martinsburg, Virginia, this insightful young soldier observed and recognized the problems the war caused the Confederacy. He described. a Virginia lady who came into town, past Confederate pickets and was astounded by the huge supplies in the stores of the city. She had seen nothing like it in two years. She wanted to purchase shoes and was amazed when she was told the pair she wanted cost $2.50. A pair, not as good, in a southern city were seen for sale for $15.00 and the pair the lady was wearing, homemade and of common split leather, had cost her $9.00. For Ricksecker, the Confederacy was giving the appearance of a doomed project.[8]

Rufus also mentioned a strange turn of events which he, as Commissary Officer, had witnessed. He had received a note questioning if he might have an extra pair of pants to spare for someone to join the army. It seems a man had been taken prisoner by Confederate forces and his capture needed to be avenged. The person wanting the pants, wanting to do the avenging, was the missing soldier's wife.[9]

By June of 1863, after one year in the army Rufus was serving the post of commissary clerk for the regiment with an office located in the Odd Fellows Hall on the second floor of a large stone building located in the town of Martinsburg. Again his time was taken by filling and filing reports and checking supplies which was very tedious work.[10]

On the 14th of the month the regiment was involved at the Battle of Martinsburg but as Rufus was out of harm's way, maintaining his commissary duties nothing was said of the battle in any letter to his family. A careless accident that took the lives of eight men while they had been at Maryland Heights near Harper's Ferry was reported in his letter home. Several boxes of percussion shells had been detonated by a man who had foolishly attempted to open one with an ax. Not only were there fatalities, but "fifteen or twenty" men were wounded or badly burned by the explosion and fire. Shortly after this action, however, the regiment and Rufus found themselves at Boonsboro, Maryland.[11]

Sarcasm, on occasion, served as an informative tool for Rufus. On July 28, 1863, from "camp in the woods writing in a wagon", he explained the situation regarding Robert E. Lee's retreat from Gettysburg, Pennsylvania. The 126th Ohio Infantry had just that month been assigned to the famous Army of the Potomac now under the command of General George G. Meade. They had not been involved in the horrendous battle of Gettysburg but had become involved in the pursuit of Lee. Ricksecker stated, "From then (Boonsboro, Maryland) we went to Sharpsburg stopping on the roads and letting Gen. Lee & his army get away, when I think that he was more than half whipped already." He continued by stating, "… it was quite a disappointment to the troops; it looks as if "somebody" did not care about having this war finished very soon."[12]

From a wagon in the woods on July 28th, Rufus and the regiment were in a much different situation on August 26, 1863, when he wrote to his "Folks at Home" from New York City. As Rufus related to his family the men "left Bealton Station, Va." August 16 with no concept of their destination. Such places as Charleston and Mobile were bandied about but all was conjecture. That evening, however, they arrived at Alexandria, Virginia. On the morning of the 19th Rufus was ordered to provide five days rations to the soldiers and that evening they continued their journey.

First marching to the Potomac River, the men boarded a ship named *"The Merrimac"* although not the *"Merrimac"* of Hampton Roads fame. This was a new ship, well equipped and built for sea travel. On the morning of the 20th they departed, experiencing a pleasant voyage past Mount Vernon and the fortifications along the river. It was after they were aboard that the men were told that their destination was New York City. That evening, still on the Potomac, Rufus slept on the deck of the boat and the next morning awoke on the Atlantic Ocean. Rufus was a "land lubber." The ship was rolling and tossing and he, along with many others, "got pretty sick; vomited twice." By the 22nd they finally saw land and soon entered New York harbor. His entrance to the city by way of the Atlantic Ocean was one he said he would never forget.[13]

The Ohio regiment, camped at Battery Park, did very little in dealing with the civilian draft riots that had torn the city apart. Their mission may well have been more of a peace keeping effort. There was sufficient time for Rufus to socialize with young brother Theodore who had moved to New York City to work for a family member and he eventually became a noted manufacturer of perfume. Several visits with "Theddie" and other acquaintances plus a visit to an envelope factory were the highlights of his stay in the city. Rufus was fascinated with the mechanical aspect of the process of making envelopes.[14]

By September 10, 1863, the men were back at Alexandria, Virginia and once again Rufus was concerned with the work of the commissary department. The 22nd of the month found them at Culpepper, Virginia. Passing over the land that had been the site of the First and Second battles of Bull Run, brought home the atrocities of war. They saw "some awful sights; for example human skulls, - one of which one of the boys got a bullet out of - graves with parts of bodies sticking out of them, lots of shell and ball & & ." War was becoming more of a reality to the young sergeant.[15]

On October 14, 1863, the men took part in the battle of Bristoe Station. Again Ricksecker was in little danger, not being under immediate fire. He did get close enough, however, to see the smoke and hear the reports of the artillery. After the battle the commissary department began issuing individual rations to the men of the 126th Ohio because they were scattered on picket duty. Colonel Benjamin Franklin Smith allowed his personal horses and wagon to be used to distribute those rations and by 11 p.m. all of the men had been fed. As Ricksecker commented in a letter home, "I do not think there are many Brig. Gen's or Acting Brig Gen's who would have had their head quarter baggage thrown in the mud & wagon bloodied up to give the troops their beef."[16]

On November 7, 1863, the men of the regiment engaged in battle at Kelly's Ford, Virginia. Again Ricksecker did not participate but occupied himself distributing rations the following day. Many of the men were as far away from the commissary camp as eight miles but the task was finished by late evening. Each man received his ration.[17]

One month later the men were still near Brandy Station and Rufus wrote his family on December 9. His concise description of the commissary and supplies must have been of great interest to them. "Saturday morning: got orders to go to the front & issue Beef: the whole batch (120 beeves) for the corps started about 10 A M. Crossed the River on Pontoons. Saw some of the gold mines, a good many boys picked up stones full of gold (they thought), but I guess it was about the kind they used to find around home."[18]

A brief passage in the same letter must have given the Ricksecker family cause for concern. "Before I go on I will say I saw a sickening picture. In the woods we came across a dead man – "Union" - there was a small fire near him. We afterwards learned that there were so many wounded in the fight that all the sick were thrown out of the ambulances & it was thought this man was among the number & had built a fire & laid down & died." Rufus seemed to have changed his mind concerning causing concern to his family at home. "War" had worn away his strength to bear such psychological burdens alone.[19]

The winter of 1863 - 64 was not an exciting time for the men of the Army of the Potomac. After the Mine Run Campaign ended in early December there was little activity. Ricksecker's Christmas letter, written December 27, 1863 was from the Third Brigade, Third Division headquarters near Brandy Station. He reminisced about home cooking, specifically the cakes, apples and peaches. The holidays, he hoped, had been pleasant and he mentioned the brigade's Christmas dinner. The men partook in such items as turkeys, chickens, ducks and all kinds of cakes, jellies and candies. It was hardly the meal of a suffering soldier. A short demonstration on the Rapidan River in early February was the extent of the military activity until the movement from the Rapidan to the James River began in early May.[20]

In this same letter, Rufus expressed his insight regarding the stalemate at Charleston, South Carolina under the Federal command of General Quincy Gilmore. He explained that by remaining at Charleston Gilmore could "keep a large force there to watch him & by that means keep the Rebels from using those troops elsewhere."[21]

Two letters and almost a month later the young commissary sergeant was still at Brandy Station issuing rations. By now Rufus had been a soldier eighteen months and his only military action was observing the smoke and noise of battle. The regiment was beginning to suffer a bit from illness as several men were mentioned as having died in camp, but Rufus appeared to be rather well, himself. He had a cold for a couple of weeks but felt he was about over it. He expressed his support of President Lincoln in the coming election but gave no reason for his backing.[22]

The war ground on. The battle of The Wilderness was fought May 5 to 7, 1864. Spotsylvania was fought from the 8th to the 12th and

176

the men of the 126th participated in the slaughter at the Salient or "Bloody Angle" on the 12th. Spotsylvania Court House followed from the 13th to the 21st. From May 26th to the 28th the regiment was on line along the Pamunkey River and then moved to the Totopotomoy River until the end of the month. The bloody operations at Cold Harbor, Virginia took place from June 1 until 12 and this was followed by the siege of Petersburg on June 18. The men of the 126th remained in the siege lines until July 6 and while all of this was transpiring Rufus had the tedious task of supplying rations to the men. Tedious it was. Tiring it was. Difficult it was, but dangerous, in comparison to regular infantry soldiers, it was not. It was a daily grind of acquiring the supplies, checking them and distributing them. It was, in short, a bookkeeper's nightmare. Often supplies were issued before they had been properly accounted for on the proper forms. A constant check, double check and triple check, was followed by yet another check, according to Rufus, to see if the first checks had all been made properly.[23]

In his several letters home during this five month period in 1864, Rufus commented on his activity and its difficulty. He was constantly busy and witnessed the ravages of war often. He felt very much an observer of war and made comments regarding its progress and conduct.

April 3, from Brandy Station, he wrote to his family: "I heard it said that the Army of the Potomac is filled with 300,000 men; if that is done I think Richmond will be taken this summer, (if at all) but the killed will be counted by the thousands."[24]

April 17, still at Brandy Station: "The symptoms of a move have been increased materially; first all ladies have been ordered to leave, any found within the lines of the army after the 12th subjecting the officer protecting them to arrest, Second the Sutlers have to leave before the 16th (yesterday) or if found inside the lines will have their goods confiscated, & and themselves presented with proper implements to work on entrenchments."[25]

June 9, near Richmond, Virginia: "It is generally represented now that we are besieging the Rebels & Richmond; there is almost a continuous fire kept up along the lines. Four days ago the Rebels charged our lines in front of the 2nd A.C. about 7 P.M. and were repulsed with heavy loss. From our Park, which is about 4 miles from the front, we could see the flash of every gun & hear the muskets very plain."[26]

June 21, Camped near Petersburg, Virginia: "Heard Col. Smith say we were to support a charging column when I concluded & did go back as I thought I was exposing myself when I could do no good. I saw Lt. Gen. Grant & Abe Lincoln this evening."[27]

On June 27 1864, Commissary Sergeant Rufus Ricksecker was returned to his regiment from the duties of that rank and promoted to first lieutenant and would serve as Company G's commanding officer. On July 6, 1864, the men of the 126th Ohio were ordered to Baltimore, Maryland where they were placed, briefly, under the command of General Lewis "Lew" Wallace. Wallace's job was to defend Washington, D.C. from a raid by a Confederate force under the command of General Jubal Early.[28]

Shortly after, on July 9, these men took part in the battle of Monocacy. The 126th was only slightly hurt in the attacks by the Confederate forces and it was in rather good condition when the battle was over. The battle here provided a much needed delaying action which allowed time for the rest of the Sixth Corps to enter Washington, D.C. and fortify the many forts surrounding the city. This small engagement, costing the Federal army over 1800 casualties, may certainly be claimed as the one single engagement that saved the Nation's Capitol from the invading Confederate Army.[29]

On August 7, the 126th was re-assigned and became part of the command of General Phil Sheridan, and on the 18th of September, Rufus penned the following note to his family.[30]

"Hhd. Qrs. Co. "G" 126th O.V.I.
Sept. 18th 1864
My Dear Folks at Home,
I will this morning write a few lines before the trains go back to the Ferry.

I was very much surprised & shocked on opening your letter to hear of the sudden death of our dear Ma. I was not at all prepared for such a change in the family circle; I had just received the letter of Father the day before & although he spoke of the severity of the disease, still it hardly seemed possible that the next mail would again leave me a motherless boy. Poor Charlie, what a blow to him it must be.

I suppose he could not get home to see her; I will try and write to him oftener as he will need all the sympathy we can give him. I was very, very glad to learn that you my dear Sister, had the helping heart and hands of dear Lottie, to minister to the wants of ma.

I hope and pray that the probable sickness of Father which Addie spoke of, has not been verified, & that he may be spared to us all for a long time.

How do you intend to manage house-keeping? If Auntie could only be with you; but she needs rest herself & is getting old. Is Lattice still with you?

It is useless for me to offer any more of my poor expressions of feeling so we will drop the very painful subject hoping that we may realize that 'it is all for the best.'

I'm in very good health. We yesterday moved camp about 300 yards in order to get more room, as the Regiment has increased very much within the last 3 weeks. We now have a very fine camp & will have it in very good order if we do not have to leave this place; which, by the way, we are at present very much afraid of as it is said Lt. Gen. Grant has come up to visit this department. We are ready to go but would rather stay. I don't think there are many who would like to be started towards Petersburg. The Rebel statements that they have been whipping the 6th A.C. every few days are altogether untrue as we have not had even a skirmish with them since we have been at this camp. They pitch in on the 8th & 19th A.C. once in a while, but they have been very careful to stay away from us, so far at least.

Well I hear the wagons rattling so I must close in a hurry. Hoping you are all well & will write as often as you can to
Your Son and Brother
Rufus."[31]

At the first battle of Sheridan's Shenandoah Valley Campaign, Rufus Ricksecker led the men of Company G into battle for the first time. With 35,000 infantrymen, the forces crossed Opequon Creek near Winchester, Virginia just before daylight on September 19. This Federal advance, through a two mile long, narrow and heavily wooded Berryville Canyon, slowed to a snail's pace. The entire force was finally through in four hours.[32]

Confederate troops under Generals John B. Gordon and Robert E. Rodes were placed in a strong defensive line. At mid-day, these two armies collided. When the battle was over and the greatly outnumbered, but not outfought Confederate forces had withdrawn from the field, men of the 126th Ohio Infantry lay scattered across the landscape. Also lying on the field was First Lieutenant Rufus Ricksecker, shot three times while leading his men for the first time into battle. One wound, in a hand, was superficial but the other two were potentially fatal. One was through the abdomen and the other through his neck. As the soldiers of Company G began a brief withdrawal Rufus pleaded to not be left behind. An effort was made to remove his wounded form from the battle field but he realized it was to no avail. "Its no use boys," he said, "I'm going to die. Save yourselves." Friends removed two rings from his hands, a breastpin was taken as well as his sword and a blood soaked pocket book to be returned to his family. He was covered with a blanket and left to die.[33]

After the battle of Opequon or, as it is also known, Third Winchester, Ricksecker was buried where he had died, in a small unmarked grave. After the war, if his remains were found, they would have been removed to the National Cemetery at Winchester, Virginia where they would now remain as the grave of an unknown soldier.

{1}   Record Group 94, Office of the Adjutant General, Compiled Service records. Volunteer Soldiers, Ricksecker, Rufus - Pension file & Service Record.

{2}   Ibid.

{3}   Ibid.

{4}   Frederick H. Dyer, *A Compendium of the War of the Rebellion - Two Volumes*. (Dayton, Ohio: National Historical Society. The Press of Morningside Bookshop. 1979), Volume #2, p. 1549.

{5}   Rufus to "My Dear Sister" October 12th, 1862. Letters of First Lieutenant Rufus Ricksecker. The Rare Books Library, Ohio State University, Columbus, Ohio.

{6}   Rufus to "My dear Sister" May 11th, 1863. Letters of First Lieutenant Rufus Ricksecker. The Rare Books Library, Ohio State University, Columbus, Ohio.

{7}   Record Group 94, Office of the Adjutant General, Compiled Service records. Volunteer Soldiers, Ricksecker, Rufus - Pension file & Service Record.

{8}   Rufus to "My dear Folks at Home" April 9, 1863. Letters of First Lieutenant Rufus Ricksecker. The Rare Books Library, Ohio State University, Columbus, Ohio.

{9}   Ibid.

{10}   Rufus to "Dear Folks at Home" June 4th, 1863. Letters of First Lieutenant Rufus Ricksecker. The Rare Books Library, Ohio State University, Columbus, Ohio.

{11}   Rufus to "My dear Folks at Home" July 11, 1863. Letters of First Lieutenant Rufus Ricksecker. The Rare Books Library, Ohio State University, Columbus, Ohio.

{12}   Rufus to "Dear Folks at Home" July 28, 1863. Letters of First Lieutenant Rufus Ricksecker. The Rare Books Library, Ohio State University, Columbus, Ohio.

{13}   Rufus to "Dear Folks at Home" August 26, 1863. Letters of First Lieutenant Rufus Ricksecker. The Rare Books Library, Ohio State University, Columbus, Ohio.

{14}   Rufus to "Dear Folks at Home" August 27th, 1863. Letters of First Lieutenant Rufus Ricksecker. The Rare Books Library, Ohio State University, Columbus, Ohio.

{15}   Rufus to "Dear Folks at Home" Sept 10, 1863. Letters of First Lieutenant Rufus Ricksecker. The Rare Books Library, Ohio State University, Columbus, Ohio.

        Rufus to "Dear Folks at Home" Sept 22nd, 1863. Letters of First Lieutenant Rufus Ricksecker. The Rare Books Library, Ohio State University, Columbus, Ohio.

{16}   Rufus to "Dear Folks at Home & Cousin" Nov 1st, 1863. Letters of First Lieutenant Rufus Ricksecker. The Rare Books Library, Ohio State University, Columbus, Ohio.

{17}   Frederick H. Dyer, *A Compendium of the War of the Rebellion - Two Volumes*. (Dayton, Ohio: National Historical Society. The Press of Morningside Bookshop. 1979) Volume #2, p. 1549.

         Rufus to "Dear Folks at Home" Nov 15th, 1863. Letters of First Lieutenant Rufus Ricksecker. The Rare Books Library, Ohio State University, Columbus, Ohio.

{18}   Rufus to "Dear Folks" Dec 9th 1863. Letters of First Lieutenant Rufus Ricksecker. The Rare Books Library, Ohio State University, Columbus, Ohio.

{19}   Ibid.

{20}   Rufus to "Dear Folks at Home" Dec 27, 1863. Letters of First Lieutenant Rufus Ricksecker. The Rare Books Library, Ohio State University, Columbus, Ohio.

{21}   Ibid.

{22}   Rufus to "Dear Folks at Home" Jan 12, 1864. Letters of First Lieutenant Rufus Ricksecker. The Rare Books Library, Ohio State University, Columbus, Ohio.

{23}   Frederick H. Dyer, *A Compendium of the War of the Rebellion - Two Volumes*. (Dayton, Ohio: National Historical Society. The Press of Morningside Bookshop. 1979), Volume #2, p. 1549.

         Rufus to "Dear Sister" Feb. 14, 1864. Letters of First Lieutenant Rufus Ricksecker. The Rare Books Library, Ohio State University, Columbus, Ohio.

{24}   Rufus to "Dear Folks at Home" April 3rd, 1864. Letters of First Lieutenant Rufus Ricksecker. The Rare Books Library, Ohio State University, Columbus, Ohio.

{25}   Rufus to "Dear Folks at Home" April 17, 1864. Letters of First Lieutenant Rufus Ricksecker. The Rare Books Library, Ohio State University, Columbus, Ohio.

{26}   Rufus to "My dear Sister and Brother". June 9, 1864. Letters of First Lieutenant Rufus Ricksecker. The Rare Books Library, Ohio State University, Columbus, Ohio.

{27}   Rufus to "Dear Brother and Sister" June 21st 1864. Letters of First Lieutenant Rufus Ricksecker. The Rare Books Library, Ohio State University, Columbus, Ohio.

{28}   Record Group 94, Office of the Adjutant General, Compiled Service records. Volunteer Soldiers, Ricksecker, Rufus - Pension file & Service Record.

         Frederick H. Dyer, *A Compendium of the War of the Rebellion - Two Volumes*. (Dayton, Ohio: National Historical Society. The Press of Morningside Bookshop. 1979), Volume #2, p. 1549.

{29}   Ibid.

{30}   Ibid.

{31}   Rufus to "Dear Folks at Home" Sept 18 1864. Letters of First Lieutenant Rufus Ricksecker. The Rare Books Library, Ohio State

University, Columbus, Ohio.

{32}   Thomas A. Lewis, and The Editors of Time-Life Books, - *The Shenandoah in Flames - The Valley Campaign of 1864.* (Alexandria, Virginia: Time Life Books, 1987), pp. 112 - 121.

{33}   Ibid.

J.H. Gilson, *Concise History of the One Hundred and Twenty-Sixth Regiment, Ohio Volunteer Infantry.* (Salem, Ohio: Walton, Steam Job and Label Printer, 1883)

Private Lynn S. Brown
Co. F - 55th Massachusetts Infantry

XVIII
"So mother I Dide The Best that I could."
Private Lyne S. Brown
Co. F - 55th Massachusetts Infantry

Twenty-two year old Lyne Sterling Brown had been assisting his elderly mother at their home since his father, Allen Brown, had passed away on December 11, 1851 when Lyne was but ten years old. It was May, 1863, and the young man, born in Columbus, Ohio and raised in Delaware, Ohio, considered the advantages and disadvantages of leaving his sixty-three year old widowed mother to enlist for three years in a Federal regiment. His mother, Lavina Brown, who was able to only make her mark when signing papers, was unable to contribute much at all to the income needed to support herself and Lyne, a young man who was just becoming established in their community as a plasterer and stone mason. Both endeavors were labor intensive for the 5' 7", Ohio native; however they were not so intense that his toil was becoming difficult. What was difficult was finding enough work to provide the meager income needed to support the two.[1]

In the spring of 1863 Governor John A. Andrew of Massachusetts issued his call for volunteers to fill two regiments of black soldiers. Lyne Brown seriously considered his options. He could remain in Delaware, Ohio, and seek work on almost a daily basis to provide for his mother and himself or he could travel over seven hundred miles east to Readville, Massachusetts and have guaranteed employment by joining one of the two army regiments being formed there. This permanency would allow him to send much needed money to his mother back in Ohio. Brown, born July 12, 1841, chose the second of the two options, headed east and on May 25, 1863, enlisted for three years in company D of the 55th Regiment of Massachusetts Infantry. His muster, as a private at Camp Meigs, Readville, was on May 31, 1863. The 55th Massachusetts had been created by the immense overflow of men that had gathered to become members of the 54th Massachusetts Infantry, the first of the two black regiments of that state.[2]

After four weeks of training at Camp Meigs, the men of the 55th Massachusetts Infantry, men from many northern states as well as southern states, free men as well as runaway slaves, men of education as well as illiterates, left Camp Meigs on an expedition to North Carolina on July 21, 1863. They arrived there on July 25, only to travel further to Folly Island, South Carolina just five days later. It was here that the 55th became attached to Brigadier General Edward A. Wild's African Brigade which was part of the Tenth Army Corps, Department of the South.[3]

The men, Brown included, did fatigue duty for four weeks. It was four weeks of digging, cutting, hauling and, for diversion, trench duty. The following six weeks, until October 28, 1863, found the men on Morris Island, South Carolina doing, basically, the same duty in front of Batteries Wagner and Gregg, part of the Confederate defenses of Charleston, South Carolina. Their duty was the labor involved in the taking of the overall objective of Fort Sumter and the city of Charleston. That work included such chores as simply digging ditches, many of them to be used as latrines, digging bomb proofs for protection against Confederate artillery and digging gun emplacements for the Federal artillery to return fire on the Confederate fortifications.[4]

Not only were these duties performed by Lyne Brown and the other members of the 55th, there were other jobs as well. He and his fellow soldiers created approaches and trenches for the troops, built service magazines for all type of ammunition, and devised gabions, which were large baskets of soil used to protect men and equipment in areas where permanent fortifications were not practicable. They also made fascines, large bundles of long brush branches or stakes, used to fill in ditches and depressions on roads or bridges. These items had to be constructed and moved into place where needed. Because of the seaside location the men of the 55th also built docks and wharves. This exhausting work had to be done to complete the overall plan of the siege of the fortifications, and it was usually the regiments such as the 54th or 55th Massachusetts, the Second North Carolina and the First South Carolina, also black regiments, that drew these assignments. For Brown, this was far more labor intensive than his pre-service occupation.[5]

By the end of October, 1863, the regiment left Morris Island and returned to Folly Island, a few miles to the south. The winter months, from November until early February, were simply a continuation of the fatigue duty the men had done on Morris Island. In February, the regiment embarked again and found themselves at Jacksonville, Florida on February 16, 1864. At this time, the regiment was separated; Company F served garrison duty at Fort or Redoubt Fribley at Jacksonville and Companies B and I at Yellow Bluff. The remainder of the regiment, including Company D and Lyne Brown, went to Baldwin, Florida, ten miles inland from Jacksonville. There they remained, doing fatigue duty and hard labor until March 11, 1864.[6]

On that date the regiment was consolidated and ordered to Palatka, Florida, sixty miles south on the St. Johns River. The men remained here doing guard and picket duty until April 17 when they were returned to Jacksonville and then, by boat, returned to Folly Island, South Carolina. During these days, in fact, for all of his time spent in the military, Lyne Brown remained concerned about his elderly mother in Ohio. Often he would send parcels of his money to her.[7]

On May 21 and 22 the men began to feel like they were indeed soldiers in the Federal Army. On those dates the regiment made an armed demonstration to James Island, to the north, facing a Confederate foe for the first time. Although there was no actual combat on this expedition, the soldiers of the 55th Massachusetts, for the first time, realized the fear of such a possibility. It was just after this journey that Private Lyne S. Brown was promoted to the rank of corporal. On June 30, these same soldiers left Folly Island one more time, marching back to James Island and on July 2, the men "saw the elephant." They were exposed to combat and, to a man, it was reported, they all held their own against the much feared Rebel Army. They returned to their camp on Folly Island, their heads possibly a little higher, their chests possibly a little larger and continued with the everyday doldrums of military life throughout the long hot summer.[8]

In early October Lyne wrote the following letter to his mother.

"Folly Island
55 Reg't Mass vol   October the 5   1864
Dear mother
              I am Ever happy to Day yow a few Lines to Let yow know that I am Well   I hope that a few Lines will find the Same   Mother I Will Sende yow Som money wich to the a mount of $125 Dollars wich Was as much as I could Send at the present under the Sircumstances and Mother I Want yow to use This as you plese   I Resived $169 90   now you know how much I cepe for my Self   I Should of Sent more but from all probility Wee Wont Be Paid of verey Soon A gain   So mother I Dide The Best that I could   Mother When yow get this Write With out De Lay for I Shall Be Eager to from home concerning this money   They Paide use off to Day from The Date of in Listment all The Back Pay
No more at present But I Still Remaned your Soon
              L S Brown   to L. Brown"[9]

In his pension papers, his mother mentioned getting money from Lyne in the amounts of $40.00 and $160.00. The men of the 55th were never paid until October 7, 1864 because they, like the men of the 54th Massachusetts, had refused pay until their pay was equal to the pay of the white regiments. On October 20, Corporal Brown lost his single light blue stripe on the sleeve of his dark blue sack coat because he had lost his canteen as well as his haversack. His pay was withheld by the military to the sum of $0.41 for the canteen and $0.71 for the haversack as well as the reduction in rank for the young Ohioan.[10]

On November 29, 1864, the men of the 55th joined General John P. Hatch's expedition up the Broad River to an area known as Boyd's Neck a few miles south of the settlement of Coosawhatchie. Under the command of General John Gray Foster, the men set off very early the next morning on a long trek to the west of the Broad River toward the community of Grahamville to destroy a portion of the Savannah & Charleston Railroad which was instrumental in providing supplies to the besieged city of Charleston. The maps that had been provided were less than useless and the guides were no better. Twice the men were misdirected before they found themselves on the proper road.[11]

The Second Brigade, which included the 55th Massachusetts, performed its duties with great enthusiasm but the men and officers were surprised by a well placed artillery battery perfectly located at a bend in the narrow road. Four pieces opened fire on the advancing Federal troops as they turned at bend. This position, on a small but significant rise in the terrain, became the sight of the battle which took its name from the elevation where the artillery placement was located. The battle of Honey Hill commenced.[12]

Two or possibly three frontal assaults were thrown at the artillery battery by the men of the First and Second Brigades. However, the battery was well supported by several regiments of South Carolina militia and each offensive was repulsed. These attacks were over ground quite "open, with isolated large trees and low brush; the soil was boggy, with standing water about ten to eighteen inches deep" according to Colonel William Gurney of the 122nd New York Infantry. After several hours of combat the Federal forces withdrew to a strong position back at Boyd's Neck on the Broad River.[13]

Among the wounded was twenty-eight year old Colonel Alfred Stedman Hartwell, an 1858 graduate of Harvard University. Hartwell had been wounded three times -- in the hand by a musket ball, in the side by a spent grape shot and finally in the back by yet another musket ball. He also had been badly burned on the ankle by a fragment of artillery shot and had his horse killed from under him. His performance at Honey Hill battlefield brought a brevet promotion to the rank of Brigadier-General, recommended by General John Foster. Colonel Hartwell survived the war, graduated in 1867 from the Harvard Law School and eventually became Chief Justice of the Supreme Court of Hawaii.[14]

Another of the six hundred thirty-one wounded was Lyne S. Brown, Company D of the 55th Massachusetts. He had been wounded twice, both times by .57 caliber musket balls which penetrated deeply into his abdomen.[15]

Wounds to the abdomen were high risk situations. Such wounds, whether puncture or gunshot, were of grave concern to both patient and physician. When the wound had produced no known damage to the viscera, inner organs, there was a 34% possibility of mortality of the patient. In cases determined not to have caused visceral damage, there was a mortality rate of 92%. The exact organ damaged, when there was known damage, created a wide range of mortality rates. A gunshot wound which knowingly penetrated the liver had the lowest determined death rate, 63%. This was followed with a 66% death rate for men with known kidney wounds. Other organs, when damaged, caused even higher mortality rates. A stomach wound produced a mortality factor very close to 76% while pancreatic and intestinal wounds had an 80% rate of death. A soldier so unfortunate to have been wounded through the spleen had but a 7% chance of living. The overall survival rate for soldiers receiving such wounds, referred to as "gut shot," was a meager 13%.

Very common in abdominal injury such as this was vomiting and a marked retention of urine, but this was not true in all cases. There was a comparatively small amount of pain involved before death. Treatment was usually some form of mercurial preparations and calomel was administrated in many incidents. In all cases, it was reported that opium was the main source of relief during the development of peritonitis. Food and drink were to be forbidden at first and, if signs of recovery became evident, small amounts of ice or cold water could eventually be followed with small amounts of milk.[16]

By December 2, both soldiers had been admitted to the General Hospital at Beaufort, South Carolina. On December 6, Colonel Hartwell wrote and submitted his after action report concerning the Battle of Honey Hill from that hospital. On December 8, 1864, Private Lyne Sterling Brown died in that same hospital of wounds received at the battle of Honey Hill.[17]

Lyne S. Brown, twenty-three years old at the time of his death, is buried in Lot #23, grave #807 in the Beaufort, South Carolina National Cemetery.

{1}   Record Group 94, Office of the Adjutant General, Compiled Service records. Volunteer Soldiers, Brown, Lyne S. - Pension file & Service Record.

{2}   Ibid.

Luis F. Emilio, *A Brave Black Regiment - History of the Fifty-Fourth Regiment of Massachusetts Volunteer Infantry 1863 - 1865.* (Salem, New Hampshire: Ayer Company Publishers, Inc. 1990), p. 24.

{3}   Frederick H. Dyer, *A Compendium of the War of the Rebellion - Two Volumes.* (Dayton, Ohio: National Historical Society. The Press of Morningside Bookshop. 1979), Volume #2, p. 1266.

{4}   Ibid.

{5}   Ibid.

{6}   Ibid.

{7}   Ibid.

Record Group 94, Office of the Adjutant General, Compiled Service records. Volunteer Soldiers, Brown, Lyne S. - Pension file & Service Record.

{8}   Frederick H. Dyer, *A Compendium of the War of the Rebellion - Two Volumes.* (Dayton, Ohio: National Historical Society. The Press of Morningside Bookshop. 1979), Volume #2, p. 1266.

{9}   Record Group 94, Office of the Adjutant General, Compiled Service records. Volunteer Soldiers, Brown, Lyne S. - Pension file & Service Record.

{10}   Ibid.

{11}   William R. Scaife, *"Sherman's March to the Sea"* (Blue & Gray Magazine, December 1989), pp. 30 - 32.

{12}   Ibid.

{13}   Ibid.

{14}   United States War Department. *War of the Rebellion. A Compilation of the Official Records of the Union and Confederate Armies. 128 Vols.* (Washington: 1881 - 1902) Series 1 -- Volume 47. Union Correspondence, Orders, and Returns relating to Operations in North Carolina (from February 10, South Carolina, Southern Georgia and East Florida, from January 1, 1865 to March 23, 1865.

Roger D. Hunt, & Jack R. Brown, *Brevet Brigadier Generals in Blue* (Gaithersburg, Maryland: Olde Soldiers Book, Inc. 1990), p. 268.

William R. Scaife, *"Sherman's March to the Sea"* (Blue & Gray Magazine, December 1989), pp. 30 - 32.

{15}   Record Group 94, Office of the Adjutant General, Compiled Service records. Volunteer Soldiers, Brown, Lyne S. - Pension file & Service Record.

{16}   Surgeon General Joseph K. Barnes, United States Army, *The Medical And Surgical History Of The War Of The Rebellion. (1861-65)* (Washington Printing Office, 1870), Reprinted by Broadfoot Publishing

Company – Wilmington, North Carolina 28405 – 1990 – 15 vols. Vol. IX, pp.202 - 208

{17}   Ibid.

United States War Department. *War of the Rebellion. A Compilation of the Official Records of the Union and Confederate Armies. 128 Vols.* (Washington: 1881 - 1902), Series 1 -- Volume 44. November 30, 1864 - Engagement at Honey Hill, near Grahamville, S.C. No. 6 -- Report of Col. Alfred S. Hartwell, Fifty - fifth Massachusetts Infantry, commanding Second Brigade

XIX

"Surely it cannot be long before I can return to home and those I love most dear."
Sergeant Richard J. Foley
Co. B - 6th Kentucky Cavalry

Camp Fisk was to be the first stop before home for thousands of men who had served time as prisoners of war in the southern states. Sergeant Richard Jordan Foley of the Sixth Kentucky Cavalry was one.

Camp Fisk, a prisoner exchange camp, was located just four miles east of the city of Vicksburg, Mississippi and west of the Big Black River. The location had been a campground for several regiments during and after the siege of that city, in the spring and summer of 1863. While soldiers from various southern prisons passed through Camp Fisk, the large majority of the men had been incarcerated at either Andersonville or Cahaba prisons. Sergeant Richard Jordan Foley of the Sixth Kentucky Cavalry likely was confined in one of these; records simply were not well kept during the last months of the war.

Andersonville, or Camp Sumter as it was officially named, was located near a tiny hamlet in southwest Georgia named Anderson. It had opened in late February of 1864 and in fourteen months had become the scourge of Confederate prisons. Simply a stockade located not far from the railroad depot, Andersonville housed, at one time or another, almost 45,000 prisoners.[1]

Cahaba, also known as Castle Morgan was a prison located in the equally small community of Cahaba, Alabama, was a few miles southwest of Selma. Cahaba had, at one time, been the capitol of the state of Alabama but its unfavorable location, due to the countless flooding conditions at the confluence of the Cahaba and Alabama Rivers, had made it unfit for social life. At the time of the Civil War, it had almost ceased to exist. However, a cotton/corn shed situated at the location was determined to be suitable for Yankee prisoners. Thus, over three thousand unfortunate Federal soldiers were housed there until the end of the war.[2]

Richard Foley was but twenty-two years old when he enlisted for three years or the duration of the war into Captain Stephen's Mounted Infantry Battalion. This designation, however, was soon to become known as Munday's First Battalion Cavalry. A Fayette County, Kentucky native, this six-foot tall, young man declared himself a farmer when he enlisted and was quickly voted the rank of sergeant. His fair complexion, blue eyes and dark brown hair must have certainly turned the head of many fair maidens in the Lexington area before the war. Surely his departure to the defense of the Union caused anxiety for many.[3]

On December 23, 1861, hundreds of men from several central

Kentucky counties assembled at Camp Irwin just outside of Louisville and mustered into the service of their country. They immediately were attached to The Army of the Ohio and placed in the 12th Brigade. However, in February of 1862, the unit would be transferred to the Seventh Division of the army. As such, their service would not be long. Their service would be difficult but honorable. They spent time in Lebanon, Kentucky before being transferred to London, in the same state. From London an expedition to the Cumberland River, made in early February, was followed by another to Flat Lick Ford on that same river in March. From there, the men occupied the Cumberland Gap from mid June until mid September when they retreated to the Ohio River. The organization, now seasoned veterans, was then assigned to the Sixth Kentucky Cavalry and became the first five companies of the regiment.

It was in late August of 1862 that young Foley was designated as missing in action. In reality he had been captured at the battle of Richmond, Kentucky on the 17th of the month and paroled immediately to Camp Chase, Ohio. A total of 61 men of the regiment along with one officer were captured and one soldier had been killed. Time at Camp Chase, Columbus, Ohio, was spent awaiting orders regarding their exchange. These finally arrived and Richard was sent to his old company in the new regiment. He joined them in January of 1863 either at Nashville, Tennessee or Franklin, some forty miles south of Nashville.[4]

After their duty at Franklin in the spring, the men moved to an area near the small town of Triune, between Franklin and Murfreesboro to the east. Arriving there June 4th, the men participated in General William T. Rosecrans' Middle Tennessee or Tullahoma Campaign from June 23rd to July 7th. Young Foley was not able to withstand the rigors of this action and in mid July was reported absent, "sick from his regiment."[5]

From the middle of July, 1863 until March of 1864, Foley was at his home in central Kentucky recuperating from his illness described as Camp Fever and diarrhea. Although home, his health probably prevented his enjoying the holiday festivities of Christmas. It is certainly probable, however, that his mother, Mary Jane Wymore Foley, his sister Kate as well as his brother, Charles Preston, were anxious when he had regained sufficient health to return to his regiment in March.

March of 1864 found these Kentucky men near the city of Chattanooga, Tennessee and there they would remain until May. Many of the members of the regiment had "veteranized" or re-enlisted for the duration of the war and they had also returned to their homes on veteran furlough. The returning enlistees converged on Chattanooga, furloughs over, at the same time Richard arrived. The Sixth Kentucky Cavalry was about to embark on The Atlanta Campaign and a summer of hardship that they would not have believed had they had prior knowledge.

From May 5th to June 18th, the Sixth Kentucky Cavalry was at Wauhatchie, Tennessee. From there they traveled to Lafayette, Georgia on

June 18th and, in a severe action near Lafayette on June 24th, 1864, Richard Foley again became a prisoner of war. This time, however, he was not paroled. He was sent either to Andersonville, Georgia or Cahaba, Alabama. Records of his imprisonment are vague and since no pension was applied for by any of Richard's family after the war it is impossible to verify at which site Foley was held.

The fall of that year, Richard spent either suffering under the dehydrating hot Georgia sun at Andersonville or the muggy sweltering Alabama sun at Cahaba fighting mosquitoes. Neither could have been pleasant. Poor rations at both were the norm and the winter in southwest Georgia in 1864 was one of the coldest on record. Although west of Andersonville, Cahaba is also north of Andersonville. The temperature and climate there could have been even more unpleasant than Andersonville. Each location was, for all the men, a proverbial Hell on earth.

By late March into early April of 1865, the men at both prisons were being transferred for return to their beloved homeland. Many of the men at Andersonville were taken east for parole, eventually finding themselves at Camp Parole near Annapolis, Maryland. Several of the Andersonville men were shipped by train south to Jacksonville, Florida and others were taken west by rail, past Cahaba where they were joined by men restrained there. The journey then resumed westward to Jackson, Mississippi. From there they marched forty miles further west to Vicksburg and into Camp Fisk. One of the men that arrived, after ten months confined to one of these two hell holes, was Sergeant Richard J. Foley of the Sixth Kentucky Cavalry.

After his arrival at Camp Fisk, Richard felt well enough to correspond with his family. He wrote:

"Camp Fisk, near Vicksburg, Mississippi
April 8, 1865
Dear Sister,

My anxiety to hear from home increases daily because of having to wait so long, yet time and patience I hope will bring forth good news from home . . . that dear place is always uppermost in my thoughts.

Indeed, Kate, it has been so long since I have been home, I have seen and gone through so much it is but natural I should be anxious to hear from and be with those loved ones at home, and it is not possible for me to get home just at this time, and make no delays, but let me hear from you as early and as often as possible. My fears will get the better of me sometimes when I think maybe affairs are going wrong at home, which, God forbid. I shall rely on the good judgement and careful management of Brother Press and sincerely hope all goes well.

He ever has my best wishes for his future success in cares, trials, and troubles of this world from past experiences I would advise him to always be satisfied with well enough and let do better alone.

I would like the best in the world to be with him to second him in his manly efforts to maintain mother's family, not doubting his ability to do so, but I know he has a young family of his own to care for and moreover, I feel it to be my duty to take my share of the responsibility as well as he, it is really chafing to my impetuous nature to lie idly here when if I was only exchanged and could be at home assuming that responsibility.

If what I hear is true, laboring hands must be scarce in consequence of negroes being in the army.

It has been a theme of speculation to me often and over whether Thomas and George had left your service to join the army, but generally came to the conclusion they had not unless forced to do so by the military authorities. Maybe you can inform me if my conclusions were correct. If they have left you, brother must be put to some straight to obtain help on the farm, for if they are gone, others will be equally as scarce.

Would like you to write me a synopsis of affairs at and around home. It would be some satisfaction to know what relations, old neighbors and friends generally are getting along around my old Kentucky home. What is the general feeling around you regarding slavery? My conviction is the same now as it was one year ago . . . The complete abolishment of slavery throughout the South.

War news is most cheering. The most prevailing is the evacuation of Richmond and capture of some fifteen thousand prisoners of [by] Grants troops. One hundred guns were fired here two days ago, in honor of the occasion and great joy was manifested by the prisoners here. We have news of a severe battle between Joe Johnson and Sherman's forces at Bentonville, North Carolina which resulted in a victory to the Union arms.

I hope the end of the rebellion is not far hence. The weather here clear and extremely cool at night. With the exception of water, we could not be living better, yet a great many are complaining. I am healthy, hearty, fat and saucy; always able to consume my rations, have nothing to do but eat, drink and sleep. Have no idea when I can start home.

My regards to all inquiring relatives and friends; my best love to yourself and the family. Tell 'Brother & Josie' to take precious care of that little niece; I forget her name.

My love to Mother in particular whose heart has had many a sad aching for the absent one. Give my love to Maggie and tell her I would write if I knew whether she was at Lexington or not. Do this and oblige your Dear Brother Dick.

> Address: Sergt. Richard J. Foley
> Co. B   3rd Battalion
> Prisoners of War, Camp Fisk, Vicksburg, Miss"[6]

A few days later, Richard wrote another letter to his family.

"Camp Fisk, Vicksburg, Mississippi
April 13th, 1865
Dear Sister,

Still my letters remain unanswered, whether it is your own negligence or irregularity of the mails remains a mystery to me. You know not, nor can you imagine the yearnings of my heart to hear from or see the loved ones at home.

At eve when all around are free from the care and toils of the day in the calm repose of sleep, my thoughts wander far away to that dear place I call home, to 'Mother, Sisters and Brothers dear.'

Many are the wild fancies I create at times concerning you. It is hardly to be wondered at, if you knew the many told me concerning the existing state of affairs in Kentucky. Guerilla bands are said to be roaming at will through many parts of the State.

Sergt. Hobbs has been commissioned Captain of Company "A" and William Neal is now acting orderly. Also that Sergt Nord was killed near Hopkinsville last winter while in pursuit of Gen. Lyon's rebel command, that his commission as captain arrived a few days thereafter.

It must be a severe blow to his family. I am told old Robert Anderson was killed in Louisville the night he was to leave for home. No doubt it was for his money. Capt. Cook I am told, lost the use of his hand from the wound he received at Lafayette. He and his brother are farming on a grand scale.

Sergt. Brock and Thomas Gano were left at Jackson, Miss. and fear they are dead. Three days a go Capt. Ed Parrish, Company "C" Lieut. James Surbreigh Company "G" with thirty five of the regiment captured near Tuscalossa, Alabama arrived here. Louis Bean and Robert McKinney of Company "A" are among the number. Sergt. Root of Company "C." I guess these are all you know. It was by this means I learned my news from their accounts. Many are the sad changes taken place around the city of Lexington.

They were captured 1st of April in the rear guard of the Brigade. They did not meet with but little opposition in their march through Alabama. Selma was captured with six thousand of Forrest's command and a large amount of artillery with other trophies. Montgomery and all important cities on the Alabama River have fallen an easy prey to our victorious troopers. Today Mobile is said to have fallen. The most glorious news of all is the fall of Richmond and the old flag waves triumphant there. It floats over Charleston, Savannah, Wilmington, 'and long may it wave over the land of the free and home of the brave.'

While I write the sound of artillery is reverberating through the air and great joy prevails over the news of the entire capture of General Lee and his army on the 9th, of this month. He surrendered on the same terms as Pemberton at Vicksburg. Surely the day cannot be far distant when peace will reign supreme throughout the length and breadth of the land. Surely it cannot be long before I can return to home and those I love most dear.

It is rumored that we are to leave here shortly as exchanged; how true, time will surely disclose. The weather here is still changeable, cold rains and uncomfortable cold nights. All nature is clothed in the loveliest green. I am in the very best of health and today feel proud to say I am a Union Soldier. I am in hopes now the war may close before my discharge from the army; that I may have it to say, 'I served during the war'. What do some of our rebel sympathizers think of the phase of affairs now? Doubtless they are like the little boy, 'haven't a word to say'.

Tell Uncle Henry I long to grasp him by the hand once more. I don't think I would ever get through telling him what I know. Give my kindest regards to him, and all his family, also to all inquiring relations and friends.

From what I can learn, you are all doing well, which I am glad to hear, and hoping you may all be in good health. I will draw my letter to a close. Do not fail to give my love to Maggie, for I cannot write, not knowing where to address her letter. Tell mother I may surprise her one of these days when she little thinks of it. I am expecting better success with this letter and expect an immediate answer without fail.

Kate, do not forget what I requested in this and my last letter in reference to Maggie, and I will still be your kind
Brother Dick
Address: Sergt Richard J. Foley
Co B. 3rd Battalion
Prisoner of War, Camp Fisk, Vicksburg, Miss."[7]

On April 16th, a steamboat left Memphis, Tennessee headed south to New Orleans, Louisiana with an agreement to transport men north from Camp Fisk when it returned up-river from the Crescent City. The boat functioned well on its down stream journey and after being relieved of its cargo, it steamed back up river to Vicksburg on April 23rd with a 400,000 pound cargo of sugar. Repairs were done on one of the four boilers that had spring a leak, but they were done hurriedly and they were done miserably. Other boats at the Vicksburg wharf were headed north, but these vessels left with no passengers or, in one possible case, with less then 100 former prisoners on board.[8]

J. Cass Mason of St. Louis, Missouri, captain of the steamer, was not about to let this financial windfall escape to another ship line. Just a week previous, he had been given a promise that he could carry these men north at $5.00 per person and, by taking all 2,400 passengers, he would realize some $12,000 profit. There was no concern that the boat would be crowded with over six times the number of passengers it was legally allowed to carry. After all, they were simply ex-prisoners of war that had been fighting for the preservation of their country for the past four years. [9]

Almost all of April 24th was spent loading all of the remaining men from Camp Fisk onto the boat, 260 feet long and three decks high, which was equipped to carry no more than 376 passengers. Three train loads of ex-prisoners of war were crowded onto this steamer, one of which was Richard Foley. He was going home. His sister Kate, his brother Charles Preston and his mother would have been foremost on his mind. He was going home.[10]

The steamboat pulled away from Vicksburg, late in the evening of the 25th of April, loaded with its human cargo as well as livestock. When it docked at Memphis, Tennessee the cargo of sugar was unloaded. Late the following night, just after midnight the morning of the 27th of April, the vessel resumed its long trip north. Scarcely seven miles north of Memphis, around two o'clock in the morning, in an area known as the "Hen and Chick Islands," on the Mississippi River, the poorly patched boilers exploded. The *SULTANA* became an inferno. It burned and floated some five miles down river to Hen Island then sank. It is the largest maritime disaster in the history of the United States. Over 1,800 of the more than 2,400 passengers on board were lost, either to the explosion, the fire or drowning.[11]

Sergeant Richard Jordan Foley of the Sixth Kentucky Cavalry was one.

{1}   Ovid L. Futch, *A History of Andersonville Prison* (University of Florida Press, 1968), p. 44

{2}   Lonnie R. Speers, *Portals To Hell - Military Prisons of the Civil War* (Stackpole Books - 1997) p. 332

{3}   Record Group 94, Office of the Adjutant General, Compiled Service records. Volunteer Soldiers, Foley, Richard J. - Pension file & Service Record.

{4}   Ibid.

{5}   Ibid.

{6}   Richard J. Foley to "Dear Sister" April 8, 1865 - Private Collection

{7}   Richard J. Foley to "Dear Sister" April 13, 1865 - Private Collection

{8}   Gene Eric Salecker, *Disaster on the Mississippi* (Annapolis, Maryland: Naval Institute Press, 1996), pp. 28, 35, 37, 64 - 80.
        Frank R. Levstik, Civil War Times Illustrated, January, 1974. *"The Sultana Disaster"*, pp. 18 - 25

{9}   Ibid.

{10}   Ibid.

{11}   Ibid.

XX
"I remain your affectionate brother until death."
Private Spencer Harrison Williams
Co. C - 3rd Tennessee Cavalry – USA

Much has been written about the bravery and resolve of the many soldiers from Kentucky that found reason within their hearts to offer their service and, too often, their lives to the Confederate States of America. The famous Orphan Brigade from that state has had volumes written glorifying their feats and daring. However, the same praise should be afforded the men from Tennessee, a state which seceded from the Union yet contained many men that were not supporters of the Confederate Cause or secession. These individuals, loyal to their country, had their own cause - preserving their nation. Union men from the state of Tennessee formed fourteen cavalry regiments, eight mounted infantry regiments, eight artillery batteries and nine infantry regiments. Added to this were three artillery batteries and two infantry units of colored troops. One of these courageous cavalrymen was Spencer H. Williams.[1]

Nathan, Spencer's older brother, became the first Williams to cast his fate with the Federal government, enlisting in Co. C, Sixth Tennessee Infantry on April 18, 1862; brother Jason, living in Missouri, joined the Eighth Missouri Cavalry, Company M, that same fall. Spencer Harrison Williams enrolled in the Third Tennessee Cavalry at Covington, Kentucky in January, 1863, and he mustered into the service with that unit at Murfreesboro, Tennessee as a corporal.[2]

Earlier, in November of 1861, events took place that fanned the political embers into a raging fire in Tennessee. Senator William C. Pickens and several other faithful American citizens from Sevier and Hamilton counties had been arrested as a result of encouraging a rebellion of loyal citizens from the Confederacy. Colonel W. B. Wood, C.S.A., the arresting officer was in favor of applying the gallows to all of those arrested but realized the futility involved in creating martyrs within the area. He requested of Judah P. Benjamin, Secretary of War for the Confederacy, that these men be retained as prisoners of war, "if not as traitors."[3]

Benjamin's reply was terse and to the point. If any of those arrested could be identified as bridge burners, they should be "tried by a drum head court-martial and if found guilty, executed on the spot by hanging." All others were to be treated as prisoners of war and incarcerated in Tuscaloosa, Alabama. He added as a post script to his message: "Judge Patterson," Andrew Johnson's son-in-law, "and Colonel Pickens should be sent at once to Tuscaloosa as prisoners of war."[4]

Situations such as this became a determining factor in the minds and actions of Tennessee men, and all southern men, that would feel compelled to join a Federal military unit. They, like the soldiers that would later belong to the United States Colored Troops, realized their membership in a Federal unit was different than a soldier from Illinois or Ohio. They, to a Southern soldier, were considered to be traitors to the cause. These men must, therefore, conduct themselves with more resolve. There is no doubt twenty-two year old Spencer Williams had this resolve.

Shortly after mustering into his regiment Williams and his fellow Tennesseeans began their service as cavalrymen. From January 31 to mid November, 1863, they were on expedition to Franklin, Tennessee, forty-five miles to the west, then back to Murfreesboro. That was followed by several journeys to Nashville. However, from May 6 until late March, Williams served as a courier carrying dispatches to and from Federal Headquarters at Camp Spear, near Nashville, and General William Starke Rosecrans' headquarters in Murfreesboro. There were numerous trips between the two cities, each carrying messages regarding the upcoming Tullahoma Campaign.[5]

On November 14, 1863, Harrison sent a letter to his sister-in-law, Malinda, Jason's wife, in Missouri. His health, he told her, was much better than when he had been home. Army life was very disagreeable in regards to exposure and although his accommodations were satisfactory, eight men and a stove to a tent, he seemed very concerned regarding the men - the "welfare of there owen soles." There were drunks as well as much "swaring" and even men who were "calling there Makers name in vain." But Williams assured Malinda that he was a good Christian, stating "May the Lord Thy God be with them and turn them away from such wicked ways before it is two late with them." He prayed for them every morning and "evaning." His prayers also included the hoped for "destruction of this wicked rebellion and the rebuilding of the Old Federal Union and Constitution." Finally he told Malinda that he realized she was destitute and he included $50.00 for her assistance. He promised to send another $35.00 in the near future. These funds were from a man making only $13.00 per month as a soldier in the Federal army.[6]

Everything he wrote showed his unshakable faith in mankind and his belief in eternal hope. Within two weeks a letter left Nashville to his family in Tennessee. Addressed to "Mother, brothers and sisters" he assured them that he was well and enjoying life as a Christian. It became obvious that Federal soldiers in Tennessee had not been kind to the Williams family. "I thought," he wrote "that you would be all right with the yankees. You told me how the yankees had treated you in respect of your turkees, chickens and fence. This I know was very bad, but only remember that we have mean men in our army as well as any other, and never let such things trouble your mind in the least. Only keep in mind the value of all . . . taken or destroyed by the yankees and unkle Sam will satisfy you in greenbacks for all."[7]

Harrison even accepted the fact that his mule at home had died but he was somewhat disheartened to know it had been killed by a yankee soldier. He suggested they sell his horse for money to assist the family. He said, "if the rebbels has took him on this last rade, I will take one from them in his place, or if the yankees want him let them have him and I will get pay for him." He ended his letter by saying that he still had his Bible and a splendid prayer book and that he made good use of it daily. He told his sister, Mary, that he had received the nice socks and that he had sent money to Malinda in Missouri. He was fine but small pox had taken ten or twelve men of the regiment.[8]

From December 27, 1863, Harrison was away from his regiment on detached duty until the first of March. What that special assignment was he never mentioned to his parents and it is not explained in his military papers at the National Archives in Washington, D.C. In yet another letter to his family, dated March 20, 1864, his concern for the family's safety is mentioned again. If Williams had these concerns for his family, it is not beyond reason to believe that a majority of the Tennessee men in Federal uniform had them also. He stated that he found "that a great deal of meanness is done by those who profess to be our friends. I am vext when I think that we have left our homes, our friends and all that is near and dear to us, and fighting for the destruction of this wicked rebellion. And forst to remain back here while we could fill the place of thoise of our own kind (in principal) of men who are now trodding our own soil, and robbing you all of every mite you possess while there fameleys are feasting highly. I doubt not, but what our soldiers had hard times, and was run short of rations there, Tho I will know that you would all devided allmost every mouthful of victuals you had with them, without them taking many other small articles that was of no value to them and a great deal to you. Tho I beg you all to not be out of heart for when what you have gives out, the Government is bound to support you."[9]

In this same letter, the young Tennesseean proceeded to inform his family in great detail of the raid he participated in from Collierville, Tennessee through Holly Springs, Pontatock and Okalona, Mississippi to West Point, near the Alabama state line and his return to Collierville. This raid, from February 11 to 26, was typical of cavalry raids within the southern states. Much hard riding, a few fierce skirmishes, when "the little blind ball's sed zip zip zip in a hurry over our heads" and it seemed that "the good man above would not low them to enter our flesh." He estimated losses for the raid at 250 men killed, wounded or missing. "There loss was three times as grate as ours besides 200 prisoners we had of them."[10]

In a June, 1864 letter, Williams was sure that Lincoln would be re-elected president and that Richmond, Virginia and "Atlanty" Georgia would fall by the Fourth of July. An August note found him at Camp Decatur in Alabama after another extensive raid, this one from Decatur to Moulton, Alabama. The following day, August 22, the men departed for Huntsville.[11]

As in his prediction of Richmond's fall, Williams was partially incorrect regarding this move. Many of the men did indeed depart for Huntsville, but Williams and the men of the Third Tennessee Cavalry went north to Athens, Alabama to serve as guards on the Nashville and Decatur Railroad. All four hundred of the men in the Third Tennessee Cavalry were placed at blockhouses near the Sulphur River Trestle. With them were the men of the Ninth Indiana Cavalry and the 111th United States Colored Infantry.[12]

On September 24, these blockhouses came under attack by the men of General Nathan Bedford Forrest. After severe fighting, General Forrest sent a flag of truce to the colonel in command of the blockhouses. Forrest asked for the surrender of the outnumbered Federal soldiers. The colonel in command refused the request and the courier returned to the Confederate lines. Forrest then sent another courier under a white flag to the colonel requesting an interview. This was granted and General Forrest invited the colonel to inspect the Confederate forces and determine firsthand their ability to capture the garrison. As a result of this inspection the blockhouses were surrendered and Spencer Harrison Williams of Company E, Third Tennessee Cavalry was a prisoner of war.[13]

The family back in Knox County, Tennessee heard nothing more from Harrison until they received a short note from him dated "Feb. 11, 1865, Castle Morgan, C.S.A. Prison in Cahaba, Alabama." Harrison was yet "numbered among the living" and "enjoying some prisoners life." He requested they tell the Peter Rule family that their "two sons and son-in-law are all alive and well."[14]

Five weeks later another letter arrived at the Williams home.

"Exchange camps
March 19th/65
Dear Mother,

With pleasure I again take my pen in hand to drop you a few lines, that you may know that I am yet No among the living, and once moor releaced from the endless foe. 800 of us had the pleasure of landing at these camps on the 16th ins. for exchange. we may be exchanged, and furlowed, soon or we may remain here untill the 1st of May Tho we are where we can be fed and clothed by our Government, and the Sanitary Commission are already supplying us with all small artickles that we desire, of which we have long since been deprived of. There is many things that I would like to tell you, but time and paper will not admit at present. Our treatment while prisners was as good I expect as the

Confedercy could afford, as Cahaba prison was sed to be the best prison in the South, Tho we sufferd at times for grub. We was guarded principaly by the OLD ISHUE I mean men from 45 to 75 to 100 years of age if they had one sound eye, and able to carry there gun and cane. These men comonly had feelings for us, and many of our ouwn sentiment but fourst to do the duty. There was a few mean debridations commited ----- ----- ---- - ----- feelings as some of our boys was ----- ----- and one of our regt so bad that ----- ----- ----- one was shot for I might say nothin ----- ----- - ---- died, but Capt Heenderson Com'd the prison immeteatly relieved him from his post and sent him front where he could find armed yanks to content with. We left the prison on the 6 inst. and left it in a miserable condition as there had been heavy rains and the Alabam river had rose untill it had overflowed the whole town, and was also half leg deep all over the prison and had been for 5 days, it was bad tho amayzing to see the yanks (no 2200) climbing from bunk to bunk and building our fires on skillet leds to do our cooking. The wether was very comfortable all winter. There was no snow only at one time and it but little. One of our greate plagues while thare was small animals sometimes called Graybacks which created a considerable scratching and clost skirmishing each day to keep them whiped out. I must close soon. You must delay no time in answering this letter as I have not heard from home since I was captured. Direct your letter to me, company, regt and to Exchange camps near Vicksburg Miss.

These few lines leaves me enjoying fine health and hope that they may come to hand in due time finding you all enjoying like blessings. May our daily trust and actions be close with God that we may be numbered with the blest. Give my best love and respects to inquiring friends. I remain your obedient son untill death.

S. H. Williams"[15]

This letter, so full of hope and expectation was followed by another, the following month.

"Parole Camps near Vicksburg Miss.
April 17th/65
Dear brother.

With much pleasure I availe the opportunety of droping you a few lines, as a reply to yours and mothers, of the 3rd inst. which come to hand yesterday, finding me enjoying good health. you have no idea what pleasure, and satisfaction, the parusal of your letters gave me. as being the 1st that I had received from either of you since I was captured and also the 1st time that I had heard from any of you. With the exception of a letter that I received the other day from Jason. he stated in his that he had received a letter from you (at Knox) and all of the connection was well. I was sorry to hear that you had suffered so severe for a while by the effects of the gangreen taken place in your side, Tho proud to learn that you recovered from your severe spell as soon as you did, and had the pleasure of spending the winter at or near home. While myself and others was deprived of such happy privleges, tho reaping the contents of a prisners life. You stated in your letter that you would be sorry to acknolledge had you not remembered us daily in your prayers since we was captured. I will say to you, mother, and to all others, that I am more than a thousand times obliged to all for each prayer that you delivered up in my behalf, as I believe they was answered from the most high, as I bore the trip with much patience, and moor satisfaction than might be supposed as my mind was troubled not but what all was doing well at home. We are yet here on parole of home. Tho they commensed on yesterday to paroleing and sending the North and are going to continue until we are all gon from here, tho to what parole camps or where a bouts they may send us I cannot tell. I hope that, we will all soon get furlows home. I also prohisy that we will have no more fighting to do. That the so called Confederacy has about played, and peace will soon be made, and we as soldiers of our country soon be mustered out and return to our happy homes again. ----- Grizzle, J. F. Wolfe, ----- -----, Martin King, Wm Keyhill, G. R. Ford, Jacob _____, Wiley Payn. Wm. Love and Wm Hood are all at the hospitals sick and Wm. Ford aught to be thare, some of the here, some at Vicksburg, and some others left on the boat to what hospitals I cannot tell. Tho some are getting most stout again. Monroe Winkle died at Cahaba hospital. Kus Nickles was left on the way (at Demopalas Ala) very bad off. and have no doubt died since as we have not heard from him since he was left. W. A. Heart send ----- and the boys generly sends ther best love to you, M. V. May also sends his best love and respects to you and says that he would like to see you, and wants you to pick out some nice young girl for him against he comes. I will tell you the good luck I met up with since I came here, the day after I came hear I was rambling around hunting some greens and found 4 half dollars in silver that had been lost out of an old satchel that by near or no doubt from the pocketts of some brave and true soldier that had lost his life on the battle ground in defence of his country. I have been offered 5 times the amount for it but refused to take it. as I am desirous of keeping it as a rememberance of the battle ground of Vicksburg. I took to chewing tobacco while in the prison. believing it to be good for my helth, my helth has also proved good ever since with the exception of a few slight spells of the Diore. and have not been troubled with the tooth-ache any whatever. We was all proud to heare that W.H.H. Cruze and Joshua Hines, had got to there homes again. we supposed them to be dead from what we could learn. These few lines leaves me well. (& the boys say I look fleachery [fleshier] than I have since I have been in service) and hope they may come to hand in due time finding you all enjoying the blessings. Give my respects to all inquiring, friends May the love of god be with you all boath know and forever.

I remain your affectionate brother until death.
S. H. Williams"[16]

On April 24, 1865, Spencer Harrison Williams, along with thirty-one other men from Company E of the Third Tennessee Cavalry, 397 men from the Third Tennessee Cavalry, 463 fellow Tennessee Federal soldiers, and yet another 1,600 more ex-prisoners of war from Alabama, Illinois, Indiana, Iowa, Kentucky, Michigan, Ohio and even Nebraska and Pennsylvania climbed on board the steamboat *SULTANA*, headed north on the Mississippi River to their homes. Well more than 2,100 ex-prisoners of war were going home.[17]

On April 27, 1865, a few miles north of Memphis, Tennessee, the *SULTANA* exploded and burned. More than 1,800 of these passengers died as a result of the blast, fire and drowning. More than 240 of these men were patriotic Union soldiers from the state of Tennessee. Over 210 were members of the Third Tennessee Cavalry and seventeen members of Company E perished, the number included Spencer Harrison Williams.[18]

{1}   Frederick H. Dyer, *A Compendium of the War of the Rebellion -
Two Volumes.* (Dayton, Ohio: National Historical Society. The Press of
Morningside Bookshop. 1979), Volume #2, pp. 1636 - 1647.

{2}   Record Group 94, Office of the Adjutant General, Compiled
Service records. Volunteer Soldiers, Williams, Spencer H. - Pension file &
Service Record.

{3}   United States War Department. *War of the Rebellion. A
Compilation of the Official Records of the Union and Confederate Armies.
128 Vols.* (Washington: 1881 - 1902), Series 1, Volume 4, Chapter 12.
November 8 – 18, Revolt of the Unionists in East Tennessee.

{4}   United States War Department. *War of the Rebellion. A
Compilation of the Official Records of the Union and Confederate Armies.
128 Vols.* (Washington: 1881 - 1902), Series 1, Volume 7.
Correspondence, Orders, and Returns relating to operations in Kentucky,
Tennessee, Northern Alabama, and Southwest Virginia from November
19, 1862 to March 4, 1862. Confederate Correspondence, etc - 1.

{5}   Frederick H. Dyer, *A Compendium of the War of the Rebellion -
Two Volumes.* (Dayton, Ohio: National Historical Society. The Press of
Morningside Bookshop, 1979), Volume #2, p. 1638.

{6}   S. H. Williams to "Dear Sister". Nov 14th / 63. Collection of
James Joplin.

{7}   S. H. Williams to "Mother, brothers, and sisters" Nov 27th/63.
Collection of James Joplin.

{8}   Ibid.

{9}   Record Group 94, Office of the Adjutant General, Compiled
Service records. Volunteer Soldiers, Williams, Spencer H. - Pension file &
Service Record.
        Unsigned letter to "Dear Mother, brothers, & sisters". March 20th
/ 64. Collection of James Joplin.

{10}   unsigned letter to "Dear Mother, brothers, & sisters". March 20th
/ 64. Collection of James Joplin.

{11}   S. H. Williams to "Dear Mother" June 15th/64. Collection of
James Joplin.
        S. H. Williams to "Dear Mother" Aug 21st/64. Collection of
James Joplin.

{12}   Civil War Centennial Commission of Tennessee, *Tennesseans in
the Civil War* Volume #1 - 1964.

{13}   Ibid.

{14}   S. H. Williams to "Dear mother" Feb. 11th' 65. Collection of
James Joplin.

{15}   S. H. Williams to "Dear Mother" March 19th/65. Collection of
James Joplin.

{16}   S. H. Williams to "Dear Mother" April 17th/65. Collection of
James Joplin.

{17}   Gene Eric Salecker, *Disaster on the Mississippi* (Annapolis, Maryland: Naval Institute Press, 1996), pp. 28, 35, 37, 64 - 80.
{18}   Ibid.

XXI
"it wasn't the smell wee wass after."
Private Thomas W. Horan
Co. H - 65th Indiana Infantry

At Evansville, Indiana, twenty-two year old Thomas W. Horan enlisted for three years on August 1, 1862, and was assigned to Company H of the 65th Indiana Volunteers which was being organized at that time at Princeton, Indiana, thirty miles to the north. This new regiment of Hoosiers mustered into the service at Camp Lewis, located near Evansville, on August 18 with a complement of only nine companies.[1]

Two days later the new recruits left Evansville headed for Henderson, Kentucky, just across the river and on August 25, 1862, the men were engaged in a skirmish at Madisonville almost forty miles to the south. This brief but violent exposure to combat made guard duty on the Louisville & Nashville Railroad seem much more agreeable. They were joined by Company K at Madisonville and the regiment was completed on September 10. Two days later, on the 12th, the men saw combat again, this time at Vanderburg and then again at Henderson, both in Kentucky. The rather raw recruits were well on their way to becoming seasoned veterans in this first month of duty.[2]

The regiment became a mounted infantry unit in April of 1863, just after Thomas had served for several weeks as a nurse at the post hospital. The New York born farmer was certainly experiencing a different life than he had previously known. Thomas was the son of English born Hugh and Hannah Smith Horan and had two younger sisters, one named Ellen and the other Rebecca. When his father passed away June 5, 1859 he and sister Ellen assisted the widowed "Anna" by hiring out. Ellen worked as a hired girl in the area and Thomas as a farm laborer to whomever needed the help around McCutchenville in Vanderburgh County, Indiana. Young Rebecca was sent to live with relatives nearby.[3]

On July 20, 1863, the 65th Indiana participated in a skirmish near Cheshire, Ohio in the Federal Army's pursuit of General John Hunt Morgan's Confederate Raiders. At Cheshire, about sixteen miles north of Gallipolis on the Ohio River, over 1,000 Confederate soldiers were captured by General James M. Shackelford's Northern troops. The men of the 65th Indiana were instrumental in relieving the citizens of Ohio of their fear of Confederate Raiders plundering the country side of Southern Ohio.[4]

From mid August to mid October the men participated in General Ambrose Burnside's East Tennessee Campaign, occupying Knoxville on September 2, 1863 and then seeing action at Greenville on the 11th and occupying the towns of Kingsport, Bristol and Zollicoffer from the 18th to the 21st. During the Knoxville, Tennessee Campaign, which lasted from early November to late December, 1863, Thomas was a courier for the officers of the regiment, running messages and reports from headquarters to various places in the vicinity. Places such as Mulberry Gap, Walker's Ford on the Clinch River, Maynardsville and Bean's Station became familiar destinations for the young rider. It was just after the skirmish at Bean Station that Thomas and other couriers left their regiment and began the journey into their unknown future.[5]

On March 27, 1865, some fifteen months later, at Camp Fisk near Vicksburg, Mississippi, Thomas informed his family in Indiana just what that future had been.

"March 27, 1865

A Sketch of my 15 months in the C.S.A. Prison. Some three days or more after the fight at Bean's Station not far from the month of December Myself and five more of the same Co. being detailed as couriers started the same night in charge of our Captain Carrieo in order to establish our line that same night. After riding some 10 miles wee arrive at one William Scaggs, a suitable place for our post. Here wee took our station for post No. 2. Here we remained some 5 weeks finding considerable duty to perform without much alarm with the exception of a few scouting parties of the Enemy. Here wee done well untill our Forces being compelled to fall back from Blanes Cross Roads which left our line exposed to the enemy But wee still held our position until the eavening of January the 27 when Post No. 1 became allarmed at the Enemy being in that neighborhood wass compelled to abandon their post and fall back to our post No.2. Wee then thought it best to Saddle our Horses and fall back to Maynardsville and Report to Lieut. Admire which wee did without delay There wee remained that night. The next morning before daylight the Lieut. thought best to fall back to Clinch R which wee did taken Post No 3 and 4 with us. Here wee remained until the evening when wee received orders from Capt Carrieo to establish the line at all hazards. Wee then moved the line over on the Jacksonborough Road leading from Knoxville to Tazewell. Riding most of the night and the next day wee esstablished our line without much difficulty. Wee arrived at our post on the evening of the 23 at one McClouds, apparently a very fine Union man, but wee had not the opportunity of testing their goodness long for on the Evening of the 24 a scouting party of the Texas Rangers being 20 in number charged in on us by surprise and captured us after stripping us of everything in our possession, nearly leaving us naked they marched us that night and the next day in the evening wee arrived in Newmarket as hungry as wolvs for they gave us nothing to eat on the march. Here wee remained in prison until the morning of the 28th when wee were taken out and marched to Morristown. There wee were drove in to a pen like hogs. There wee were kept until the 2nd of Feb. when wee were taken out and marched to Russelville where wee remained until the 8th on the Evening of the 8th wee took the cars for Bristol, V.A. and arrived there that night. I will give you a slight Idea of our Rations on this trip when wee arrived at Bull's Gap, Tenn. They turned us out to help ourselves to beef which wass in great quantity but not quality but wee skinned and eat quite hearty of the Beef Heads that our Forces left after butchering some three weeks before. It had no nice smell I assure you but it wasn't the smell wee wass after. Well wee remained in Bristol until the 10 when wee took the cars for Lintchburg, V.A. and arrived there the next evening. There wee changed cars for Grand Junction and arrived there the next day at 12 o'clock. There wee changed cars for Richmond and arrived there on the evening of the 11. There wee remained in prison until the 13 when wee were taken out and marched through the principle streets of the city to feast the eyes of the Southern Ladies on Yanks. When this wass well performed wee marched across the James River to Bell Island. Here wee find a Retchard place Men die more or less every day with cold and hunger our Rations per day are two spoon full of beans and a little piece of corn bread equal to a half pint of meal. Here wee were turned on the island destitute of blankets or shelter with but two sticks of cordwood to 20 men for 24 hours. I have had to take my shirt wrap around my feet to keep them from freezing   men freeze to death every night. On the 4. of March our spirits were revived by the removal of several 100 being taken off for exchange but I wass not in the lucky squad. On the 6 of Mar one of the Boys killed a Dog belonging to a Reb. Lieut. which is not incomman in this place. I could relish a piece of dog or cat and be glad to get it. Well, when this was done our Rations was stoped untill we had to take the poor fellow out that killed the dog   it was a hard task but had to be done. When they got him they hung him up by his thumbs for one Hour then let him down and made him eat one quarter of the dog raw but that part wass no great task to perform. I could doe that myself and be glad of the chance. Well here wee remained in this condition untill the 10 of Mar when wee were marched to the city and there put in prison untill the morning of the 12. between the hours of 3 & 4 o'clock when wee were taken out and put on the cars and told wee were going for exchange   Oh.   no one can imagine the feelings of the poor starved yank when he think he is a going from starvation to the land of plenty   well the first place wee found ourselves was in Petersburgh   here wee changed cars for Gaston on the Roanoke River   here wee changed cars for Raleigh. N.C. and a rived there on 14   here wee changed cars for Charlott   here wee remained untill the 16 then took the cars for Columbus S.C.   there took the cars for Brantchville   here wee took the cars for Andersonville G.A.   here wee arrived on the 18 of March and if ever there was a Hell on Earth its one.   here I wass turned in the Stockade without a Blanket or a shoe to my foot and the skies above for my shelter.   here I remained in this condition untill the 13 of Sept   During this time I saw sights and went through hardships to numerous to mention all at this time I have run several narrow escapes in trying to make my escape   I have worked a many a night in tunnelling under the stockade. During my stay in this place from the 18 of March untill the 13 of September the number of deths are Thirteen Thousand and 800 poor fellows their bones are lying in the sands of G.A. I have beheld some awfull sights in this retched place. I have saw men lying not able to help themselves with Maggots working in their eyes and nose and them alive. Well I saw a hard time here untill the 13 of Sept when wee started as wee were told for our lines but I could not believe it so of wee starts for Savannah so Bob Wheeler of the 4th Ind Cav and I Resolved to jump of the cars and try our luck wich is no foll of a job to risk being killed with the cars or shot by the guards wich many a one is any how wee thought wee would try it. Bob said he would go first if I would follow so over Bord he went and he was hardly out of the door untill I took the ground a welt wich skinned my nose and forehead rather more than I liked wether the guards shot or not I cant say for it a shot had been fired I could of heard it any how I felt no Bullet but I have never saw Bob from that time to this Well I will tell you a little of my tramp through the swamps about one 100 miles I cannot give all the particulars now I wass out some two weeks I could travel only by night some times up to may waste in water all alone a living on raw sweet potatoes and Peanuts. Well I tramped a long untill with in six miles of our lines when I came a crost two Rebs Diserters from the first and fifth Georgia cav -- they treated me so kind that I made up my mind to stay with them two or three days wish I did to my own sorrow for one eavening after eating a harty supper of corn Bread and Beans wee were lying under a tree and the first thing I knew wass you G.D. suns of Bitches dont you run or I will blow you to Hell. looking around saw two doublebarrel shot guns cocked within 20 ft of our heads well there was no time for running then so off they marched us to Savannah there they put me in a stockade but I wass not there long before I turned groundhog and dug out - a half canteen and a wooden paddle wass our tools to dig with so off wee started myself and a little Frenchman for our Gunboats wich were some 30 miles distance wee sicceeded in geting to the Coast and a queer time wee had in geting there, not being aquainted with the raising and falling of the tide wee were some time a wadeing and some time a swimming. the Frenchman lost his boots, pants and hat in the opperation for wee would put our clothes on a log and shove them a head of us in the water. my feet were so badly cut with the oister shells and stones that I could hardly walk. wee swam out on an Island to get in sight of our Boats but wee could not get them to send in for us they threw several shells over us but would not come to our assistance they have been decoyed so often by the Enemy. here wee remained in this place thru day without food or fresh water wich compelled us to retrace our steps in search of food and water. but we had not gone far before wee found our selfs surrounded by 7 big Buck negrous an one white man who compelled us to march back to the old Bullpen as we term it. wee wass not there long untill wee tried the same old trick but was not successfull in geting out   wee had the tunnell completed and my head out of the hole just in the set of crawling out when the Balls from some three or four muskets threw the dirt in my face but did not harm me.   well wee dident stay here long before wee were moved to Melen [Millen]   there wee had no chance for to escape   there we remained some 6 weeks or more and then old Sherman became dangerous then we were taken to Savannah and from there to Blackshere.   here wee remained 2 or 3 weeks when we were taken to Thomasville near the Florida line   here wee Remained some 2 weeks when wee were carried as they term it to Albany. but it wass the Darndest carying I ever seen. they marched us 5 days through the Swamps some time to our waste in water for 2 mile at a time, during the 5 days I had 6 crackers to eat.   when wee arrived at Albany wee took the cars for that Hell hole Andersonville and arrived there on Christmas eave   there wee were turned in the old stockade for the second time without blanket wood or shelter   I never will forget Christmas Eave   I spent it in an old well cold and wet and no fire to dry me   Christmas dinner was a cup full of cooked rice   thats all I eat for 36 hours   this wass a trying time   I would walk and run as best I could to keep warm.   there wass but one way to a void this suffering   that was to take the oath which many did but I could not see it in that light.   one oath is enough for me   well here I remained untill the 18 of March when we were taken out and started for the land of plenty.   Just 12 months to the day from the time I first went in there... on the 19 wee got to Collumbus   there wee changed cars and started for Montgomery on the Alabam R - here wee lay untill the eavening of the 20 when we took the Boat down the River to Selma.   there wee went in an other Bullpen and remained there untill the 22d when wee took the cars for Demopolis on the Tombigby R - there wee took the boat to McDowell's Landing and arrived there that night   there we remained untill the 23d when wee started on the cars for Maredian Miss and a rived there the same day and the next morning on the 24 started for Jackson and arrived there that night. on the morning of the 25 wee started on foot with a quart of meal each for Big Black then to reach our lines so off wee started. I felt as though I could march 50 miles as poor and week as I wass for I wass not very stout. when I was captured my weight was 175 lbs and when I wass released I weighed 106 or 105 lbs   Well our first days march wee reached Clinton some 23 miles from the River   the next morning wee started stiff and sore and reached within 5 miles of U S Lines wich wee reached on the morning of the 27th   one of the happyest days I ever experienced   there they gave us plenty of crackers to eat and Whiskey to drink.   here wee were Paroled and taken to the camp where I now remane   Well if God spares me to come I will give you all the particulars for I can tell you things you will think impoosable   thank God I am spared to return to the land of plenty   I hope this will find all of you in good health so I will Bring this to a close   hoping soon to see you all.   now I must goe to the Commissary and draw Ration for my mess for they are geting hungry

211

I have had this job to doe ever since I have been captured
  If you write to me while here
  Direct your Letters to
      T. W. (H)Oran
          Co B 4th Battalion
              Camp Fisk
                  Miss

Sill true to my Country
My Love to all   Good By
                        May God be with you as he has with me."[6]

On April 13, 1865, while still at Camp Fisk, Thomas wrote to his
brother-in-law Samuel Vickerstaff.

  April the 18 ' ' 65
Brother Vick, I again write to one and all to let you know that I am yet in
the land of the living and hope this will find you in better health than it
leaves me at present. I would like to hear from Some of you to know how
you are getting along but it seems as you dont want or are careless about
writing   but be as it may I think this is my last untill I hear from some of
you   every one gets a letter but me. I am a lone without Friends or money
but there is one thing I am not destitute of yet. that is Ambition   As for
Money I dont want any while in this place   I am yet in camp Fisk near
Vicksburg   how long I may be here I cant say   some are leaving every day
I hope we may go next   I doe not feel safe here   we are liable to an attack
at any time and no Forces to resist it. none but a few Negrow troops not
more than one or two companys   they you know woulden be a F.I high
Vick   I wish I could get home   I could tell you of some queer old times I
have spent in the Sunny South during my imprisonment   God Forbid I
should ever be taken in to bondage again.   tongue cannot express the
sufferings of a prisoner in the hands of the Rebbels. I will give you a full
detail of things if God spares me to return Home. I trust he will. God wass
with me when Starvation starred me in the face while hundreds fell daily
around me   with sickness and hunger but I thank my God I yet live and
have plenty to eat if I only was able to eat it but I often wish for someone
to talk with   I often wish for Old Jim Mc   you know the game is here
every one for them selves   but I think Molly or some of you can find time
to write me a few lines to let me know how you all are geting along   I
suppose things are greatly changed since I left Home.   well I must stop for
this time   write soon   give my love to all. My Poor Old Mother God bless
her.   Kiss the little ones   Direct to Camp Fisk near Vicksburg Miss
From your true Brother a Friend till Death
                        T W Horan"[7]

212

Within six days, on April 24, Thomas climbed aboard the vessel *SULTANA* headed north to his home in southern Indiana. The *SULTANA* left Vicksburg at 9:00 P.M. on the 24th and arrived at Helena, Arkansas the morning of the 25th. Within an hour the boat was bound north again and arrived at Memphis, Tennessee that same evening. Several of the men, almost all ex-prisoners of war, went ashore where they were fed and well received by the citizens of the city. All were back on board, however, when the steamer left its dock at midnight and crossed the Mississippi River to load over 1,000 bushels of coal in burlap sacks to fuel the vessel on its journey to Cairo, Illinois. This task took almost an hour and after 1:00 A.M. the journey north was continued.[8]

According to William McFarland, a relative and fellow passenger on the ill-fated steamer, Thomas Horan was sleeping next to the boiler room to keep warm, the night being rather chilly and Thomas having but few clothes. It was there that Thomas was believed to be sleeping when the boilers burst and the *SULTANA* burned and sank at 2:00 in the morning, April 27, 1865.[9]

{1}   Record Group 94, Office of the Adjutant General, Compiled Service records. Volunteer Soldiers, Horan, Thomas W. - Pension file & Service Record.

{2}   Frederick H. Dyer, *A Compendium of the War of the Rebellion - Two Volumes*. (Dayton, Ohio: National Historical Society. The Press of Morningside Bookshop. 1979), Volume #2, p. 1143

{3}   Record Group 94, Office of the Adjutant General, Compiled Service records. Volunteer Soldiers, Horan, Thomas W. - Pension file & Service Record.

{4}   Frederick H. Dyer, *A Compendium of the War of the Rebellion - Two Volumes*. (Dayton, Ohio: National Historical Society. The Press of Morningside Bookshop. 1979), Volume #2, pp. 990 & 1143.

{5}   Ibid., p. 1143

{6}   T. W. [h]oran to unaddressed. March 27th, 1865. Indiana Historical Society - Thomas W. Horan Letters.

{7}   T. W. Horan to "Brother Vick". April 18, 1865. Indiana Historical Society - Thomas W. Horan Letters.

{8}   Gene Eric Salecker, *Disaster on the Mississippi* (Annapolis, Maryland: Naval Institute Press, 1996), pp. 28, 35, 37, 64 - 80.

{9}   Record Group 94, Office of the Adjutant General, Compiled Service records. Volunteer Soldiers, Horan, Thomas W. - Pension file & Service Record.

Bibliography

BOOKS, JOURNALS AND MAGAZINES

Barnes, Surgeon General Joseph K, United States Army. *The Medical And Surgical History Of The War Of The Rebellion (1861 – 65) 12 Vols.* Washington: Government Printing Office 1870. Republished by Broadfoot Publishing Company, Wilmington, North Carolina 1990

Bayne, Frank L. *The View from Headquarters – Civil War Letters of Harvey Reid* Madison, Wisconsin – The State Historical Society of Wisconsin – MCMLXV)

Bearss, Edwin C. & Grabau, Warren. *The Battle of Jackson – May 14, 1863* Publication sponsored by The Jackson Civil War Round Table, Inc. – Gateway Press, Inc. 1981

Brown, D. Alexander. *Grierson's Raid – A Cavalry Adventure of the Civil War* Urbana: University of Illinois Press, 1954

Bryner, Cloyd. *Bugle Echoes: The Story of Illinois 47th Infantry* Springfield: 1981

Chaitlin, Peter M. and The Editors of Time-Life Books. *The Coastal War – Chesapeake Bay to the Rio Grand* Alexandria, Virginia: Time Life Books 1985

Clark, Champ and The Editors of Time-Life Books. *Gettysburg – The Confederate High Tide* Alexandria, Virginia: Time Life Books 1985

Clausius, Gerhard P. *The Little Soldier of the 95th* Journal of the Illinois State Historical Society – Winter, 1958

Dyer, Frederick H. *A Compendium of the War of the Rebellion – Two Volumes.* Dayton, Ohio: National Historical Society, The Press of Morningside Bookshop. 1979

Editors. *The History of Peoria County.* Chicago, Illinois: Johnson & Company, 1880

Fox, Lt. Col. William F. *Regimental Losses in The American Civil War 1861 – 1865* Dayton, Ohio: Press of Morningside Bookshop – 1974

Freund, Barbara. *Among The Things That Were – Letters of a Vermont Farm Family 1830 – 1874.* Fairfield, Pennsylvania: 2001

Futch, Ovid L. *History of Andersonville Prison* University of Florida Press – 1968

Gilson, J. H. *Concise History of the One Hundred and Twenty-Sixth Regiment, Ohio Volunteer Infantry.* Salem, Ohio: Walton, Steam Job and Label Printer, 183

Hennessy, John. *The First Battle of Manassas – An End To Innocence July 18 – 21, 1861.* Lynchburg, Virginia: The Virginia Civil War Battles and Leaders Series, H.E. Howard, Inc., 1989

Hennessy, John J. *Return to Bull Run – The Campaign and Battle of Second Manassas* New York, New York: Simon & Schuster, 1993

Hunt, Roger D. & Brown, Jack R. *Brevet Brigadier Generals in Blue* Gaithersburg, Maryland: Olde Soldiers Book, Inc. 1990

Ihling Bros & Everhard. Eds. *Record of Service of Michigan Volunteers in the Civil War 1861 – 1865. Vol#31* Kalamazoo, Michigan: 1903

Krick, Robert K. *Stonewall Jackson at Cedar Mountain* Chapel Hill, North Carolina: University of North Carolina Press, 1990

Lewis, Thomas A. and The Editors of Time-Life Books. *The Shenandoah in Flames – The Valley Campaign of 1864.* Alexandria, Virginia: Time Life Books 1987

Reece, Brigadier General J. N. *Report of the Adjutant General of the State of Illinois – 9 vols.* Springfield, Illinois: 1900

Rhodes, Robert Hunt, ed. *All For The Union: The Civil War Diary and Letters of Elisha Hunt Rhodes.* New York, New York: Orion Books, 1985

Salecker, Gene Eric. *Disaster on the Mississippi* Annapolis, Maryland: Naval Institute Press, 1996

Speers, Lonnie R. *Portals to Hell – Military Prisons of the Civil War* Stackpole Books, 1997

Stackpole, Edward J. *They Met at Gettysburg* New York, New York: Bonanza Books 1957

Stevens, Captain C. A. *Berdan's United States Sharpshooters in the Army of the Potomac 1861 – 1865* Dayton, Ohio: Press of Morningside Bookshop, 1984

Tucker, Glenn. *High Tide at Gettysburg: The Campaign in Pennsylvania* Dayton Ohio: Press of Morningside Bookshop, 1983

Unites States War Department. *War of the Rebellion, A Compilation of the Official Records of the Union and Confederate Armies. 128 Vols.* Washington: 1881 – 1902

Warner, Ezra J. *Generals in Blue* Louisiana State University Press, 1977

Wood, Wales W. *A History of the Ninety-Fifth Regiment Illinois Volunteers* Chicago, Illinois: Tribune Company's Book and Job Printing Office, 1865

NEWSPAPERS

Peoria Daily Transcript, Peoria, Illinois, June 22, 1863 – *The Death of Col. Cromwell*

Peoria Daily Transcript, Peoria, Illinois, June 23, 1863 – *Col. Cromwell*

Peoria Daily Transcript, Peoria, Illinois, July 31, 1863 – *The Death of Col. Cromwell*

Plainfield Union, Plainfield, New Jersey. December 12, 1865 – *The Late Col. Cromwell*

INTERNET SITES

Abruscato, Sue Skay & Abruscato, Mary Hara, *Harvey's Scouts*, 2001, http//www.rootsweb.com/~msmadiso/harveyscouts/

Wiley, Nash *Harvey's Scouts*, 1914 – Madison Co., Ms USGenWeb – http//www.rootsweb.com/~msmadison/harveyscouts/

Index

A

Acworth, Georgia, 162
Adams Express Company, 84,
    94, 105
Adams, General Wirt CSA, 36
Adkinson, Alice, 70
Adkinson, Alta, 70
Adkinson, Edward, 71
Adkinson, Henry, 66, 70, 71
Adkinson, Mary Hazzlewood,
    66, 71, 72
Adkinson, Joseph, 66, 71, 72
Adkinson, Private John H,
    USA, 66 - 72
Adkinson, Robert, 69 - 71
Admire, Lieutenant Jacob
    USA, 208
African Brigade, 183
Alexandria, Virginia, 20, 54,
    103, 141, 174, 175
Allatoona, Georgia, 161
Allatoona Hills, 162
Allatoona Pass (Ridge), 162
Albany, Georgia, 211
Anderson, General Richard
    CSA, 96
Anderson, Georgia, 190
Anderson, Private Robert USA,
    194
Andersonville Georgia National
    Cemetery, 147
Andrew, Governor John, 183
Antietam, Battle of, 41, 44, 109
Appomattox Court House, 124
Aqua Creek, Virginia, 55
Arizona Territory, 41
Arkansas Post, Battle of, 31
Armistead, General Lewis
    CSA, 59
Army of Kentucky, 150
    Mississippi, 34

Northern Virginia, 22,
    94, 96, 114,
    119
the Ohio, 191
Tennessee, 150, 163,
    166
the Cumberland, 104
the Potomac, 13, 44,
    52, 94, 96,
    113, 114, 119,
    124, 142, 174,
    176, 177
Virginia, 44
Athens, Alabama, 201
Atlanta, Georgia, 160, 162- 167
Atlantic Ocean, 175

B

Baker, Lieutenant Colonel
    Samuel USA, 34
Baldwin, Florida, 184
Ballou, Edgar Fowler, 10 - 12
Ballou, Hiram, 10
Ballou, Major Sullivan USA,
    10 - 13
Ballou, Sarah Hart Shumway,
    10 - 13
Ballou, William Bowen, 10, 12
Baltimore, Maryland, 93, 178
Banks, General Nathaniel
    USA, 16, 17, 133
Barnes, Major USA, 37
Barr, First Lieutenant Joseph
    USA, 31
Barton, Miss Clara, 147
Baton Rouge, Louisiana, 132,
    133
Battery Gregg, 184
Battery Park, 175
Battery Wagner, 184
Bayer, Private George USA,
    101

Bayne, Captain Andrew B.
USA, 93
Bayne, Private Donald B. USA,
93
Bayne, Jayne, 93
Bayne, John, 93
Bayne, Marianne, 93
Bayne, Second Lieutenant James
USA, 93 - 97
Bealton Station, Virginia, 174
Bean, Private Louis USA, 194
Bean Station, Tennessee, 208
Beaufort National Cemetery,
Beaufort, South
Carolina, 129, 187
Beaufort, South Carolina, 125,
126, 187
Beaver Guards, 141
Becker, Private Marcus USA,
155
Bell, Francis N. 61, 62
Benjamin, Secretary of War
Judah P. CSA, 198
Benton Barracks, St. Louis,
Missouri, 35
Bentonville, Battle of, 193
Berdine, Mirandy, 154
Berryville Canyon, 179
Berryville, Virginia, 16
Bermuda Hundred, 124
Big Foot, Wisconsin, 155
Blaine Cemetery, Boone County,
Illinois, 72
Bloody Angle, Virginia, Battle
of, 96, 119, 177
Blue Ridge Mountains, 16
Boonsboro, Maryland, 174
Boots, Horace, 145
Boots, Quartermaster Sergeant
Edward N. USA,
141 - 148
Boots, Reverend John, 141
Boots, Sylvia Coleman, 141
Boston, Massachusetts, 124, 125

Boyd's Neck, South Carolina,
185, 186
Brabazon, Private Bill USA,
153, 160, 163, 165
Bragg, General Braxton CSA,
150
Brandy Station, Virginia, 94,
118, 176, 177
Brattleboro, Vermont, 51 – 53,
60
Brentwood Station, Tennessee,
150
Briant Hall, Chicago, Illinois, 82
Brice's Crossroads, Battle of, 69
Bridgeport, Alabama, 88 - 90,
159
Brinkerhoff, Commander, USN,
145
Bristoe Station, Virginia, 94, 209
Bristoe Station, Battle of, 175
Bristol, Tennessee, 207
Brock, Sergeant David USA,
194
Brodhead, Archangela Macomb
Abbott, 15
Brodhead, Catherine Julie, 16
Brodhead, Colonel Thornton F.
USA, 15 - 21
Brodhead, Elizabeth Adams, 15
Brodhead, Ellen Macomb, 16
Brodhead, John (brother), 20
Brodhead, John Thornton (son),
15, 20
Brodhead, Josephine
Achangela, 15
Brodhead, Mary Jeanette, 16
Brown, Allen. 183
Brown, Annette Jane ("Sis"),
109, 110, 112, 117
Brown, Carlos Heath, 109, 117
Brown, Horace, 109 – 113, 117
Brown, Lavina, 183
Brown, Lemira, 52, 58, 62
Brown, Lydia Chandler, 109,
110, 113 - 117

Brown, Private Lyne USA,
      183 - 187
Brown, Private Thomas USA,
      109 - 120
Brown University, 10
Brown, Warren, 109, 117
Bruinsburg, Mississippi, 67
Bryner, Colonel John USA, 31
Buckland, General Ralph USA,
      136
Buford, General John USA, 17
Bull Run Creek, 15, 19, 55
Bull's Gap, Tennessee, 160, 209
Burmuda Hundred, 124
Burnside, General Ambrose
      USA, 12, 13, 44, 55,
      103, 104, 207
Burnside's Bridge, 44
Buzzard's Roost Gap, Battle of,
      105

C

Cahaba, Alabama, 190
Cahaba Hospital, 190
Cairo, Illinois, 69, 87, 213
Calhoun, John C. 127
California, 151
Callahan's Mill, 135
Campaign, Atlanta, 104, 105,
            159, 166, 191
      Bristoe, 94
      Central Mississippi, 83
      East Tennessee, 207
      Gettysburg, 103, 114
      Maryland, 51
      Mine Run, 84, 176
      Overland, 96
      Peninsula, 141
      Red River, 31
      Richmond, 119
      Shenandoah Valley,
            179
      Tullahoma, 191, 199
      Vicksburg, 35, 67, 68

Camp Brightwood,
      Washington, D.C. 13
Butler, Springfield, Il.
      132
Chase, Arlington, Va.
      53
Chase, Columbus, Oh.
      191
Clark, Washington,
            D.C.   10
Clear Creek, Ms. 33. 34
Covington, Covington,
      Ky, 25, 26
Curtin, Harrisburg, Pa.
      141
Decatur, Decatur, Al.
      200
Douglas, Chicago, Il.
      47, 82
Fisk, Vicksburg, Ms,
      190, 192 – 6,
      208, 212
Fuller, Rockford, Il. 24,
      25, 66
Irwin, Lexington, Ky.
      191
Keim, Norfolk, Va. 141
Lewis, Evansville, In.
      207
Lincoln, Brattleboro,
      Vt. 50, 51
Lyon, Detroit, Mi. 16
Lyon, Peoria, Il. 32
Meigs, Readville, Ma.
      183
New Meadow Bluff,
      Lewisburg,
      W.V. 42, 43
Parole, Annapolis, Md.
      192
Randall, Madison, Wi.
      151
Sherman, Big Black
      River, Ms. 86,
      87

Spear, Nashville, Tn.
 199
Steubenville,
 Steubenville,
 Oh. 172
Vermont, Hunting
 Creek, Va.
 53, 54
Canada, 66, 150
Canton, Ohio, 172
Carthage, Tennessee, 45, 46, 48
Cashier, Private Albert D. J.
 USA, 66
Cedar Creek, Virginia, Battle
 of, 16, 44
Cedar Mountain, Virginia, 17,
 19
Cedarville, Virginia, 113
Celle, Germany, 99
Cemetery Ridge, 59
Centerville, Virginia, 57
Chambersburg, Ohio, 41
Champion's Hill, Battle of, 69
Champlain, Lake, 51
Chancellorsville, Battle of, 103,
 113, 114
Charleston, Illinois, 135
Charleston, South Carolina, 32,
 93, 172, 174, 176, 184,
 186, 194
Charleston, West Virginia, 45
Chattanooga National Cemetery,
 Chattanooga,
 Tennessee, 79, 90
Chattanooga, Tennessee, 76 – 9
 87 – 90, 103, 104, 155,
 159, 163, 191
Cherubusco, Mexico, 15
Cheshire, Ohio, 207
Chesapeake Bay, 141, 144
Chicago, Illinois, 24, 47, 82, 83,
 153, 158
Chicago Mercantile Battery, 31,
 82
Chickasaw Bayou, Battle of, 31

Chickasaw Post, Mississippi, 84
Chickamauga, Georgia, Battle
 of, 44, 46, 75 – 77, 87
Churchill's Grove, Illinois, 24,
 66
Cincinnati, Ohio, 25 - 27, 150
City Point, Virginia, 124
Clark, Assistant Surgeon Anson
 USA, 88
Clarksburg, West Virginia, 45
Clay Chapel Cemetery, Gallia
 County, Ohio, 48
Clinton, Mississippi, 211
Cloyd's Mountain, Battle of, 44
Coburn, Private John USA, 156
Coburn, Private George USA,
 153, 156
Cold Harbor, Battle of, 96, 177
Collierville, Tennessee, 200
Columbus, Georgia, 37, 209
Columbus, Missouri, 134
Columbus, Ohio, 183, 191
Columbus, South Carolina, 209
Commerce, Missouri, 32
Congdon, Private John USA,
 162
Conrick, Second Lieutenant
 Oscar USA, 153
Conroy, Bird, 95
Contreras, Mexico, 15
Cook, Captain David L. USA,
 194
Cooke, Commander James W.
 CSN, 146
Coosawhatchie, South Carolina,
 185
Corbin, Private John USA, 167
Coren, Dr., 62
Corinth, Battle of, 33, 34
Corinth, Mississippi, 31 – 34,
 88
Cornwell, Captain Gabriel
 USA, 67, 68
Corps, 1st, 60, 95
 2nd, 95

3^{rd,} 95
5^{th,} 95
6^{th,} 95, 96, 178
8^{th,} 179
10^{th,} 183
11^{th,} 103, 104
12^{th,} 103, 104
15th, 36
16th, 134
18^{th,} 96
19^{th,} 179
20^{th,} 105. 106
Couch, General Darius USA, 142
Covington, Kentucky, 25 – 27, 150, 198
Crandle, Private Charles USA, 155, 157, 158
Crawfish Springs, Georgia, 75
Crawford, General Samuel USA, 19
Crutchfield Hotel, Chattanooga, Tennessee, 76
Cromwell, Charles H. 30
Cromwell, Jeremiah Wilson, 30
Cromwell, Colonel John N. USA, 30 - 38
Cromwell, Mr. & Mrs. Morris Nelson, 30
Cromwell, Sarah M. Brokaw, 30
Cromwell, William Nelson, 30, 37
Crook, Colonel George USA, 41
Cub Run, 12
Culbertson, Andrew, 82, 88
Culbertson, Eliza, 82, 88
Culbertson, Mary Ann, 82, 88
Culbertson, Private George USA, 82 - 88
Culbertson, Sarah, 88
Culpepper, Virginia, 19, 175
Cumberland Gap, 191
Cumberland, Maryland, 173

Cumberland Mountains, 159
Cumberland, Rhode Island, 10
Curritick Sound, 144
Curtis, Mary Jane, 24
Curtis, Private Elijah USA, 24 - 28
Custis family, 142
Cynthiana, Kentucky, 26, 27

D

Dabney, Chriswell, 18
Dallas, Georgia, 161
Dalton, Georgia, 161
Damkoehler, Agnus, 99, 101
Damkoehler, Clara, 99
Damkoehler, Ernst (son), 99
Damkoehler, Henry (Harry), 103, 106
Damkoehler, Mathilde, 99, 101 - 104
Damkoehler, Private Ernst USA, 99 - 106
Damkoehler, Walter, 99, 101
Daniels Hotel, Jackson, Mississippi, 36
Daniels, Mr., 36, 37
Danville City Cemetery, Danville, Kentucky, 28
Danville, Kentucky, 27, 150
Darien, Wisconsin, 167
Davis, President Jefferson CSA, 70, 163
Decatur, Alabama, 200
Decatur, Mississippi, 133
Dee, Lieutenant Maurice USA, 31
Delavan, Wisconsin, 150, 151, 153 – 155, 161, 164 - 6
Delaware, Ohio, 183
Demopolis, Alabama, 203, 211
Denison, Captain Charles E. USA, 30
Department of Ohio, 150
Department of the South, 183

Detroit Free Press newspaper, 16

Detroit, Michigan, 15, 16, 21

Diphtheria, 46, 47

Dover Light Guard, 172

Dover, Ohio, 172

Dover's Powder, 47

Douglass, Corporal Ora B. USA, 85

Duck, Private Charles H. USA, 83, 86, 87

Duckport, Louisiana, 36

Dudley, First Lieutenant Charles USA, 153, 163

Dugout Valley, 160

E

Eagle Brigade, 35, 36

Early, General Jubal CSA, 178

East Capitol Hill, Washington, D.C. 53

East Orange, New Jersey, 13

East Troy, Wisconsin, 99

Edmonds, Private John USA, 75

Edwards Ferry, Virginia, 57

Edwards, Private John "Jack" USA, 160, 163

Eighteenth United States Infantry, 30

Eighth Missouri Cavalry USA, 198

Eighth Missouri Infantry USA, 31

Eighth Wisconsin Infantry, 35

Eighty-fifth Indiana Infantry, 159

Eleventh Illinois Cavalry, 31

Eleventh Missouri Infantry (USA), 35

Elgin Battery, 82

Elgin, Illinois, 82, 85

Elizabeth, New Jersey Rifle Corps, 37

Elkhorn, Illinois, 24

Ellsworth, Colonel Elmer USA, 141

Elmwood Cemetery, Detroit, Michigan, 21

Emmittsburg, Pennsylvania, 57

Emmittsburg Road, 59

England, 30, 55, 66, 111, 142

Episcopal, 173

Evans, General Nathaniel CSA, 12

Evansville, Indiana, 207

Evergreen Cemetery, Plainfield, New Jersey, 37

Everingham, Mrs., 61, 62

F

Fairfax, Vermont, 51

Fairfax Court House, Virginia, 55

Fairfax Station, Virginia, 56

Fairmount, Virginia, 94

Fair Oaks, Battle of, 142

Falmouth, Virginia, 27, 111, 112

Farmington, Mississippi, 33

Ferguson, Champ CSA, 26

Ferguson, William C. 135

Fifteenth United States Infantry, 15

Fifteenth Vermont Infantry, 57, 58

Fifth Georgia Cavalry, 210

Fifth Minnesota Infantry, 35

Fifth New York Cavalry, 17

Fifth Vermont Infantry, 119

Fifty-eighth New York Infantry, 103

Fifty-fifth Massachusetts Infantry, 183 - 186

Fifty-fourth Massachusetts Infantry, 183, 186

Fifty-seventh New York Infantry, 93

First Georgia Cavalry, 210

First Manassas (Bull Run),
	Battle of, 10, 13, 19,
		99, 100, 141
First Massachusetts Cavalry,
	126
First Michigan Cavalry, 15 - 17,
	19
First Rhode Island Infantry, 13
First South Carolina Infantry
	US, 184
First Vermont Cavalry, 15, 19
First West Virginia Cavalry, 15,
	19
Fitzhugh, Major Norman CSA,
	17, 18
Flat Lick Ford, Kentucky, 191
Florida, District of, 124
Fleusser, Commander Charles
	E. USN, 146
Foley, Charles Preston, 191,
	192, 196
Foley, Mary Jane Wymore, 191
Foley, Sarah Catherine (Kate),
	191,195, 196
Foley, Sergeant Richard J.
	USA, 190 - 196
Folly Island, South Carolina,
	183 - 185
Ford, Private Gilbert USA, 203
Ford, Private William USA, 203
Forrest, General Nathan B.
	CSA, 134, 136, 150,
		194, 201
Fort Darling, Richmond,
	Virginia, 142
Fort Donelson, Battle of, 33, 82
Fort Drummer, Brattleboro,
	Vermont, 53
Fort Fribley (Redoubt), 184
Fort Henry, Tennessee, Battle
	of, 33, 82
Fort Pillow, Tennessee, 32, 134
Fortress Monroe, Virginia, 143
Fortress Rosecrans, Tennessee,
	154

Fort Sumter, Battle of, 32, 172,
	184
Forty-fourth Massachusetts
	Infantry, 125
Forty-fourth Wisconsin Infantry,
	150, 156
Forty-second Illinois Infantry,
	75, 76
Forty-second United States
	Infantry, 93
Forty-seventh Illinois Infantry,
	30 - 37
Foster, Captain Joseph W.
	USA, 75
Foster, General John G. USA,
	185, 186
Foster, Private Jim USA, 155,
	156, 164
Fosterville, Tennessee, 159
Fourteenth Vermont Infantry,
	51, 52, 54 – 60, 62, 63
Fourth Indiana Cavalry, 210
Fourth Massachusetts Cavalry,
	124, 125, 129
Fourth New York Cavalry, 15,
	19
Fourth United States Infantry, 41
Fourth South Carolina Infantry,
	12
Fox, William B. 44
Fox's Gap, Battle of, 44
Franklin, Illinois, 69
Franklin, Tennessee, 150, 191,
	199
Frederick, Maryland, 16, 57, 94
Fredericksburg, Battle of, 111,
	114
Fredericksburg National
	Cemetery,
		Fredericksburg,
		Virginia, 120
Fredericksburg, Virginia, 55,
	110, 111, 114, 119
Freeport, Illinois, 24
French Foreign Legion, 99

Front Royal, Virginia, 17
Frying Pan, Virginia, 57
Funk, Colonel Otto USA, 31
Fuhr, Private Wendel USA,
    164, 167

G

Gallipolis, Ohio, 207
Gangrene, 78, 79, 202
Garden Prairie, Illinois, 82, 90
Gardner, General Franklin
    CSA, 133
Garnett, General Richard CSA,
    59
Gaston, Virginia, 209
Gauley Bridge, West Virginia,
    45
General Hospital, Beaufort,
    South Carolina, 187
General Regimental Hospital
    #2, Danville, Ky. 27
Georgetown General Hospital,
    Washington, D.C., 43
Germantown, Tennessee, 134,
    135
Geronimo, 41
Gettysburg, Pennsylvania, 57,
    58, 60 – 62, 113, 174
Gettysburg, Pennsylvania, Battle
    of, 94, 174
Gettysburg, Pennsylvania
    National Cemetery, 62
Gilmore, General Quincy USA,
    176
Goodwin, Private Ed USA, 154,
    155, 158, 162, 164, 167
Gordon, General John B. CSA,
    179
Gorgas, Doctor, William USA,
    28
Grahamville, South Carolina,
    186
Grand Army of the Republic, 66

Grant General Lewis A. USA,
    119, 120
Grant, General Ulysses S. USA,
    33, 35, 69, 83, 86, 95,
    96, 118, 119, 123, 124,
    132, 177, 179, 193
Grand Gulf, Mississippi, Battle
    of, 67, 84
Grand Junction, Virginia, 209
Green Bay, Wisconsin, 100
Greenland Gap, Virginia, 94
Greenville, Tennessee, 207
Gregory, Private Myron USA,
    162
Grier, Colonel David P. USA,
    31
Grierson, Captain John USA,
    131, 132, 137
Grierson, General Benjamin
    USA, 132 - 134
Grierson's Raid, 133
Grizzle, Private Asariah USA,
    203
Grosse Isle, Michigan, 16
Gunboat, *BOMBSHELL*, 145
    MIAMI, 146
    SOUTHFIELD, 145,
    146
    WHITEHEAD, 145
Guilford Station, Virginia, 57
Gum Springs, Virginia, 114
Gurney, Colonel William USA,
    186

H

Haffensteff, Braunschweig,
    Germany, 99
Hall, Private Henry USA, 164
Hall, Oliver, 35
Halleck, General Henry USA,
    33, 34
Hamburg Landing, Tennessee,
    32
Hamilton, North Carolina, 146

Hampton Roads, Virginia, 175
Hancock, General Winfield S.
    USA, 58, 95, 119
Hancock, West Virginia, 45
Hardee, General William CSA,
    166, 167
Harmon, Adjutant Lewis CSA,
    20
Harper's Ferry, Maryland, 45,
    51, 94, 114, 174
Harper's Ferry, Battle of, 51
Harrison, President William
    Henry USA, 143
Harrison's Landing, Virginia,
    143
Hartwell, Colonel Alfred S.
    USA, 186, 187
Harvard Law School, 186
Harvard University, 15, 20, 186
Harvey, Lieutenant Addison
    CSA, 36, 37
Harvey's Scouts, 36
Hatch, General Edward USA,
    133, 134, 136
Hatch, General John P. USA,
    185
Hawaii, Chief Justice of the
    Supreme Court, 186
Hawes, Private Bradford USA,
    127
Heart, Private William USA,
    203
Helena, Arkansas, 36, 213
"Hell's Half Acre", 157
Hen and Chick Islands, 196
Henderson, Battle of, 207
Henderson, Kentucky, 207
Henry House Hill, 19
Hepburn, Lt. Colonel William
    USA, 135
Herod, Major Thomas G. S.
    USA. 132, 134, 135
Herndon, Virginia, 57
Herrick, Colonel Walter USA,
    136

Hewitt, Surgeon Henry S.
    USA, 36
Hilton Head, South Carolina,
    124 – 127, 129
Hines, Sergeant Joshua USA,
    203
Hingham, Massachusetts, 124
Hobbs, Sergeant Edwin USA,
    194
Hodgers, Jennie, 66
Hoke, General Robert CSA, 96,
    146
Holden, Private William USA,
    86, 89, 90
Holly Springs, Mississippi, 200
Honey Hill, Battle of, 186, 187
Hood, Bugler William USA,
    203
Hood, General John B. CSA,
    163, 166
Hooker, General Joseph USA,
    103, 161, 163
Hopkinsville, Kentucky, 194
Horan, Ellen, 207
Horan, Hanna Smith, 207
Horan, Hugh, 207
Horan, Private Thomas W.
    USA, 207 - 213
Horan, Rebecca, 207
Hough, John, 31
Hospital #8, Nashville,
    Tennessee, 47
Hospital #4327, Hilton Head,
    South Carolina, 129
Howard, General Oliver O.
    USA, 104
Hugo, Victor, 145
Humphrey, Colonel Thomas
    USA, 69
Hunt, Private Gibson USA,
    162
Hunt, Private Henry USA, 155
Huntsville, Alabama, 201
Hurlbut, General Stephan USA,
    136

Hurricane Creek, Battle of, 136

I

Illinois House of
     Representatives, 102
Indianapolis, Indiana, 25, 103,
     153
Ironclad, *CSS MERRIMAC*,
     141, 175
     USS MONITOR, 175
     USS MERRIMAC,
     175
Ironton, Battle of, 31
Island #10, Battle of, 32
Iuka, Battle of, 34
Iuka Springs, Mississippi, 89

J

Jackson, General Thomas
     "Stonewall" CSA, 17,
     19, 51, 113
Jackson, Mississippi, 36, 37, 86,
     192, 194, 211
Jackson, Tennessee, 66

Jacksonville East City
     Cemetery,
     Jacksonville, Illinois,
     137
Jacksonville, Florida, 184, 192
Jacksonville, Illinois, 131, 137
James Island, 185
Jaundice, 27
Jefferson, Wisconsin, 151
Jefferson City, Missouri, 32
Jeffersonville, Indiana, 153
Johnson, Vice President
     Andrew USA, 198
Johnson, General Edward
     CSA, 119

Johnston, General Joseph E.
     CSA, 36, 86, 142, 163,
     166, 193
Joliet Signal, newspaper, 102
Jones, Colonel William G.
     USA, 46

K

Kalarama Hospital,
     Washington, D.C. 43
Kanawha Valley, West
     Virginia, 43, 45
Kansas City, Missouri, 132
Kavanaugh, Corporal Thomas
     USA, 161
Keim, General William USA,
     141
Kellam, Captain Alphonso G.
     USA, 151
Kelly's Ford, Battle of, 115,
     175
Kelly's Ford, Virginia, 94, 175
Kemper, General James CSA,
     59
Kenhill, Private William USA,
     203
Kennesaw Mountain, 162
Kernstown, Virginia, 16
Keyes, General Erasmus USA,
     142
King, Private Sherwin USA,
     76, 78
King, Sergeant Martin USA,
     203
Kingery, First Lieutenant
     Ephraim USA, 26
Kingsport, Tennessee, 207
Kingston, Georgia, 135, 161
Knob School House, 141
Knoxville, Tennessee, 104, 160,
     207, 208
Kolb Farm, Battle of, 162

L

Lafayette, Georgia, 191
Lafayette, Indiana, 25, 153
Lafayette, Tennessee, 134, 192, 194
LaGrange, Tennessee, 87, 89, 134, 136
Lake City, Florida, 124
Lake Michigan, 82
Lake Providence, Louisiana, 67
Lang, Colonel David CSA, 59
Lansing, Michigan, 16
Laurel Hill, Virginia, 119
Lebanon, Kentucky, 191
Lee, General Fitzhugh CSA, 17, 18
Lee, General Robert E. CSA, 17, 51, 52, 70, 94, 96, 114, 118, 119, 124, 163, 174, 194
Leesburg, Virginia, 17
"Les Miserables", 145
Lewisburg, Battle of, 42
Lewis Farm, 15
Lewis Ford, 15, 19, 20
Lexington, Kentucky, 26, 27, 190, 193, 194
Lincoln, President Abraham USA, 51, 99, 102, 143, 157, 176, 177, 200
Little Big Horn, Montana, Battle of, 41
London, Kentucky, 191
Longstreet, General James CSA, 19, 104
Lookout Mountain, Chattanooga, Tennessee, 103
Lookout Valley, 159
Loomis, Lt. Colonel Reuben USA, 134, 135
Loranze Rifle, 54, 59
Lost Mountain, 162

Louisa Court House, Virginia, 17
Louisville, Kentucky, 102, 150, 153, 191, 194
Louisville, Mississippi, 132
Louisiana Tigers, 12
Love, Private William USA, 203
Lowe, Doctor Thaddeus, 143
Lung fever, 46, 47, 173
Lucken House Hotel, Germantown, Tennessee, 134
Lynchburg, Virginia, 209
Lyon, General Hylan B. CSA, 194

M

McClain, Private John "Jack" USA, 153, 158
McClellan, General George B. USA, 44, 142, 143
McClure, Colonel John D. USA, 31
McCutchenville, Indiana, 207
McDowell, General Irwin USA, 20, 21, 100
McDowell's Landing, 211
McFarland, Private William USA, 213
McKinney, Private Robert USA, 194
Madison, Wisconsin, 151, 153, 155, 156
Madisonville, Battle of, 207
Madisonville, Kentucky, 207
Malvern Hill, Battle of, 143
Manassas Junction, Virginia, 10, 12, 13, 17, 19, 141
Manufactory of Walsott and Campbell's New York Mills, The, 93
Marietta, Georgia, 163

Marietta National Cemetery,
    Marietta, Georgia, 167
Marshall House, 141
Martinsburg, Virginia, 173, 174
Martinsburg, West Virginia,
    94
Marye's Heights, Battle of, 111,
    120
Maryland Heights, 174
Mason, Captain J. Cass, 195
Mason, James M., 55
Masonic Lodge, 37
Matthew's Hill, 12, 13, 19
Maynardsville, Tennessee, 208
Meade, General George USA,
    119, 174
Memphis, Tennessee, 31, 35, 67,
    83, 84, 87, 89, 132 – 37
    195, 196, 204, 213
Menzie, Private Charles USA,
    153, 163
Meridian, Mississippi, 135, 211
Merrill, Private Nelson USA, 85
Mexican War, 15
Michigan City, Indiana, 25, 153
Middlebury, Vermont, 52
Military Asylum Cemetery,
    Washington, D.C., 43
Milliken's Bend, Louisiana, 67,
    84
Mill Springs, Kentucky, Battle
    of, 8
Milwaukee, Wisconsin, 99, 100,
    150, 151
Missionary Ridge, Battle of, 44,
    104
Mobile, Alabama, 174, 194
Monocacy, Battle of, 178
Montgomery, Alabama, 194,
    211
Morgan, General John Hunt
    CSA, 27, 207
Morgan, Colonel William H.
    USA, 134
Morrill,Hibbard 51

Morris Island, South Carolina,
    184
Morrison, Clarissa, 185, 192,
    209
Morrison, Elen P. Sweet, 151 – 6
    158, 159, 161 - 167
Morrison, Elsie, 151, 156, 167
Morrison, J. A. 167
Morrison, O. G., 114, 115
Morrison, Private Thomas
    USA, 151 - 167
Morristown, New York, 93
Morristown, Tennessee, 208
Morton, Captain Joseph, W.
    USA, 129
Mosby, Captain John S. CSA,
    18, 57
Moses, Doctor Israel USA, 76,
    77
Mott, Private William USA, 75,
    78
Moulton, Alabama, 201
Mount Vernon, 175
Mower, General Joseph USA,
    35, 136
"Mud March", 103
Mulberry Gap, Tennessee, 208
"Mule Shoe" Battle of the, 96,
    119
Munday's, Major Reuben, First
    Battalion Cavalry,
    190
Munford, Colonel Thomas T.
    CSA, 19
Munson's Hill, Virginia, 53
Murfreesboro, Tennessee, 7, 30,
    46, 150, 153, 154, 156,
    158, 191, 198, 199
Murfreesboro, Battle of (see
    Stones River)
Murray, Private Patrick USA,
    116

N

Nash, Doctor, 20
Nashville, Battle of, 165
Nashville National Cemetery,
    Nashville, Tennessee,
    153
Nashville, Tennessee, 31, 45, 47,
    48, 104, 150, 153 – 58
    165, 191, 199, 201
Natchez, Mississippi, 69 - 71
National Archives, 200
Neal, Ordinance Sergeant
    William USA, 194
New Bridge Road, 142
New Berne, North Carolina,
    144 - 146
New Creek, Virginia, 93
New Fork Mill Cemetery,
    Oneida, New York,
    97
New Hampton Institute, 51, 52
New Haven, Connecticut, 53
New Hope Church, Battle of,
    161, 162
New Hope Church, Georgia,
    161
New Madrid, Missouri, 32
New Madrid, Missouri, Battle
    of, 32
Newman, Reverend Hiram, 41
New Market, New Hampshire,
    15
New Orleans, Louisiana, 126,
    195
Newport News, Virginia, 124
Newton Station, Mississippi,
    133
New York, New York, 30, 37,
    53, 110, 174, 175
New York Times Newspaper, 21
Nibert, Private Hugh USA, 46
Nichols, Private Kosaklused
    USA, 203
Nicholasville, Kentucky, 26, 150

Ninety-fifth Illinois Infantry,
    66 - 69
Ninety-second Illinois Infantry,
    24, 25
Ninth Illinois Cavalry, 136
Ninth Indiana Cavalry, 201
Nord, Sergeant , USA, 194
Norfolk, Virginia, 141
North Africa, 99
Norton, Colonel Addison J.
    USA, 31

O

Occoquan Creek, Virginia, 56
Odd Fellow's Hall, 174
Officer's Hospital #1,
    Chattanooga,
    Tennessee, 76
Officer's Hospital #2,
    Chattanooga,
    Tennessee, 76
Ogdenburg, New York, 93
Okalona, Mississippi, 200
"Old Abe", the eagle, 35
Old Fort Comfort, Virginia, 144
Olustee, Battle of, 124
One hundred eleventh United
    States Colored
    Troops, 230
One hundred first Pennsylvania
    Infantry, 141 – 143,
    145, 146
One hundred sixth New York
    Infantry, 93 - 96
One hundred twenty-second
    New York Infantry,
    186
One hundred twenty-sixth Ohio
    Infantry, 172, 174, 175,
    177 - 179
One hundred twenty-seventh
    Illinois Infantry, 82, 83,
    85 - 88
Oneida, New York, 93, 94 - 97

Opequon Creek, 179
Opequon Creek, Battle of, 179
Orange Plank Road, 17
Orchard Knob, Battle of, 44, 104
Orphan Brigade, 198
Otterville, Missouri, 32
Overall Creek, 159
Overall, Private James USA, 42, 43, 46
Overall, Florence Virginia, 41
Overall, Jacob Asbury, 41
Overall, Jasper Newton, 41
Overall, John William, 41
Overall, Martha Jane Proctor, 41 – 46, 48
Overall, Private Isaac USA, 41 - 48
Overall, Sarah, 46
Overton Hospital, Memphis, Tennessee 31
Owens, Private Wartroop USA, 161, 163
Oxford, Mississippi, 136

P

Paducah, Kentucky, 134, 135
Palalka, Florida, 184
Palmer, Commander Archibald S. USA, 32
Palmer, Private George USA, 75
Palmyra, Wisconsin, 167
Panama Canal, 28
Parkersburg, Virginia (West Virginia), 172
Paris, Kentucky, 27
Parrish, Captain Ed USA, 194
Patterson, Judge, 198
Pawlet, Vermont, 75
Payne, Private Wiley USA, 203
Peach Tree Creek, 166, 167
Pea Ridge, Battle of, 99

Peck, Private Page P. USA, 155, 158
Pemberton, General John CSA, 69, 86, 132, 194
Peoria, Illinois, 30 – 32, 35
Peoria National Blues, 30 – 32, 37
Perry, General William CSA, 59
Perry, Private Lyman USA, 163
Perry, Sergeant William Norman USA, 158, 161, 163, 165
Perryville, Battle of, 99
Petersburg, Siege of, 124, 177
Petersburg, Virginia, 124, 177, 179, 209
Philadelphia, Mississippi, 133
Philadelphia, Pennsylvania, 47
Pickens, Governor William, Tennessee, 198
Pierce, President Franklin, 15, 16
"Pickett's Charge", 59, 60
Pine Mountain, 162
Pittsburg, Pennsylvania, 141
Plainfield, New Jersey, 30, 35, 37
Platte City, Missouri, 131
Plymouth, North Carolina, 145, 146
Plymouth Pilgrims, 146
Pneumonia, 46, 47
Point Pleasant, Missouri, 32
Polish Legion, 103
Polo, Illinois, 24
Pontatoc, Mississippi, 200
Pontiac, Michigan, 16
Poolsville, Maryland, 57
Pope, General John USA, 17, 19 – 21, 44, 100
Poplar Grove, Illinois, 66, 67
Port Gibson, Battle of, 67
Port Hudson, Battle of, 69, 133

Port-O-Plymouth Museum,
    Plymouth, North
    Carolina, 145
Portici House, 15
Pratt, Private Henry USA, 127
Preston, Captain Lyman USA,
    24, 26
Princeton, Indiana, 207
Prison, Andersonville, 93, 105,
            125, 146, 147,
            190, 192, 209,
            211
        Cahaba, 190, 192, 201
        Castle Morgan (see
        Cahaba)
        Sumter (see
        Andersonville)
Providence, Rhode Island, 10, 13
Prussian Army, 99

R

Racine, Wisconsin, 150
Railroad, Illinois Central, 83
        Louisville & Nashville
            27
        Nashville & Decatur
            200
        Orange & Alexandria
            55
        Savannah &
            Charleston,
            186
Raleigh, North Carolina, 209
Raymond, Captain Frederick A.
    USA, 89
Raymond, Enos, 124
Raymond, Margaret, 124
Raymond, Mary, 124
Raymond, Mary Jane Pratt, 124
Raymond, Mississippi, 88
Raymond, Private James USA,
    124 - 129
Raymond, Walter B. 125
Raymond, Walter F. 124, 125

Readville, Massachusetts, 124,
    128, 183
Reed, Major Walter USA, 28
**Regimental Losses in the
    American Civil War
    (1861-1865)**, 44
Republican Party, 102
Resaca, Battle of, 105, 160, 163
Richardson, Private Josiah
    USA, 13
Richmond, Battle of, 191
Richmond, Louisiana, 84
Richmond, Virginia, 70, 96, 119,
    135, 142, 177, 193,
    194, 200, 201, 209
Ricksecker, Adelaide (Addie),
    172, 173, 178
Ricksecker, Eugene (Genie),
    172
Ricksecker, First Lieutenant
    Rufus USA, 172 - 179
Ricksecker, Israel, 172
Ricksecker, Julius (Julie), 172
Ricksecker, Theodore (Thedie),
    172, 173, 175
Ridgeway Station, Tennessee,
    35
Rienzie, Mississippi, 34
Ringgold, Battle of, 105
River, Alabama, 190, 194
        Big Black, 86, 87, 190,
            211
        Broad, 185, 186
        Chattahoochee, 163 -
            166
        Chickahominy, 142
        Chowan, 145
        Chunky, 133
        Clinch, 207, 208
        Cold Water, 136
        Cumberland, 45, 82,
            191
        Gauley, 45
        James, 96, 141, 144,
            176, 209

Kanawha, 45
Little Harpeth, 150
Mississippi, 32, 36, 67,
    84, 132 – 134,
    196, 203, 212
New, 45
North Anna, 96
Ohio, 25, 26, 41, 48,
    150, 153, 191,
    207
Old, 67
Pamunkey, 96, 177
Potomac, 16, 57, 93,
    141, 175
Rapidan, 94, 96, 176
Rappahannock, 94
Roanoke, 145, 209
Rock, 66
St. Johns, 184
Stillwater, 172
Stones, 156
Sulphur, 201
Tallahatchie, 136
Tennessee, 82
Tippah, 135
Tombigby, 211
Totopotomoy, 96, 177
Wabash, 25
Yazoo, 136
Yohnapalaphia, 136
Roanoke Island, 146
Robilliard, Private John USA,
    165
Rockford, Illinois, 24, 25, 27, 66
Rock Island, Illinois hospital,
    47
Rockeport, Missouri, 131
Rocky Faced Ridge, Battle of,
    105
Rodes, General Robert CSA,
    179
Rohrback's Bridge, 44
Root, Sergeant USA, 194
Rose Bud, Battle of, 41

Rosecrans, General William S.
    USA, 34, 191, 199
Rowley, Private Silas USA,
    162
Ruff's Station, Georgia, 163
Rutland, Vermont, 109, 112
Rygate, Vermont, 109, 116, 120

S

Sabine Cross Roads, Battle of,
    31
Satterlee Hospital, Philadelphia,
    Pennsylvania, 47
Saunemin, Illinois, 66
Savannah, Georgia, 194, 210
Schmidt, Captain M. USA,
    103 - 105
Schurz, General Carl USA, 100
Scranton, Private Clark USA,
    166
Scurvy, 147
Second Iowa Artillery, 35
Second Iowa Cavalry, 132, 136
Second Manassas (Bull Run),
    Battle of, 15, 19, 44
Second North Carolina Infantry
    US, 184
Second Rhode Island Infantry,
    10, 13
Second United States
    Sharpshooters, 109,
        110, 113 – 16
    118, 119, 120
Second Vermont Brigade, 51,
    57, 58
Second Virginia Cavalry, 15, 19
Sedgwick, General John USA,
    95
Selma, Alabama, 190, 194, 211
Seminary Hospital, Gettysburg,
    Pennsylvania, 60 - 62
Seminary Ridge, 59, 60
Seven Pines, Battle of, 142
Seventh Illinois Cavalry, 132

Seventh Virginia Cavalry, 19
Seventeenth Illinois Infantry, 37
Seventy-seventh Illinois
    Infantry, 31
Shackelford, General James M.
    USA, 207
Sharpsburg, Maryland, 41, 44,
    45, 109, 110, 174
Shelbyville, Tennessee, 159
Sheridan, General Phil USA,
    178
Sheridan's Division Hospital, 77
Sherman, General William T.
    USA, 36, 83, 104, 159,
    166, 193, 211
Shiloh, Battle of, 31, 33, 99
Sigel Regiment, 100
Sigel, General Franz USA, 100,
    101
Simonds, Minerva Dayton, 79
Simonds, Private Merritt USA,
    75 - 79
Sixteenth Connecticut Infantry,
    145
Sixteenth New York Infantry,
    93
Sixteenth Vermont Infantry, 58
Sixth Illinois Cavalry, 162, 163,
    166 - 169
Sixth Kentucky Cavalry, 190 –
    192, 196
Sixth Tennessee Infantry, USA,
    198
Sixth United States Infantry,
    93
Sixth Virginia Cavalry, 19
Sixty-fifth Indiana Infantry, 207
Slidell, John, 55
Slocum, Colonel John USA,
    13, 104
Smith, Colonel Benjamin
    Franklin USA, 175,
    177
Smith, General William F.
    USA, 96

Smith, General William Sooy
    USA, 135
Smith J. (spy), 46
Smith, Private Julius USA, 160
Smithfield, Rhode Island, 10, 13
Smith, Postmaster Charles, 153,
    164, 165
Snicker's gap, Virginia, 16, 114
South Mountain, Battle of, 44
South New Market, New
    Hampshire, 15
Spencer Carbine, 125
Spotsylvania Court House,
    Battle of, 96, 119, 120,
    176, 177
Sprague, Governor William –
    Rhode Island, 13
Springfield, Illinois, 31, 132
Springfield, Missouri, 99
St. Joseph, Missouri, 132
St. Lawrence County Regiment,
    The, 93
St. Louis, Missouri, 32, 35, 85,
    150, 195
Stacy, Matthew, 169
Stannard, General George J.
    USA, 51, 59
Stanton, Secretary of War
    Edwin, USA, 51
Starksboro, Vermont, 51
Starr, Margaret, 131
Starr, Colonel Matthew H.
    USA, 131 - 137
Starr, Rebecca Kinney, 131
Starr, Reverend Thomas, 131,
    132
Steamer: *ALBEMARLE , CSS*,
    146
    CONTINENTAL, 53
    EMPRESS, 36
    PHEONIX, 144
    STATE OF MAINE,
    141
    SULTANA, 196, 204,
    213

TRENT, 55
WESTERN
METROPOLIS, 125
Stephen's Mounted Infantry,
    Captain, 190
Stewart, General Alexander
    CSA, 166
Steuart, General George H.
    CSA, 119
Stevensburg, Virginia, 17
Stevenson, Alabama, 76
Steinwehr, General Adolph von
    USA, 100
Stoneman, General George
    USA, 57
Stones River, Tennessee, Battle
    of, 30, 156, 157
Stoughton, Colonel Charles B.
    USA, 53
Stuart, General James Ewell
    Brown CSA, 17 - 19
Sturgeon Bay, Wisconsin, 99,
    100
Sudley Ford, 12
Sudley Ford Church, 13
Sudley Ford Road. 12
Suffolk, Virginia, 144
Sugar Creek, Wisconsin, 161
Sugar Loaf Mountain,
    Maryland, 57
Sulphur Springs, Virginia, 115
Summersville, West Virginia, 41
    - 43
Sunder, Private Frank USA, 75
Surber, Lieutenant James USA,
    194
Swan Point Cemetery,
    Providence, Rhode
    Island, 13
Sweet, Giles, 151, 163
Sycamore, Illinois, 75, 79

T

Taylor, Private Frank USA, 95
Tenth Wisconsin Infantry, 156
Third Maine Infantry, 116
Third Tennessee Cavalry, USA,
    198, 201, 204
Thirteenth Vermont Infantry, 58
Thirty-sixth Ohio Infantry, 41,
    43 - 46, 48
Thompson's Station,
    Tennessee, 150
Thorne, Laura, 82
Thrush, Colonel William A.
    USA, 31, 34
Tinker, Private William USA,
    155, 156
Tiptonville, Battle of, 32
Tower, Captain Levi USA, 13
Trenton, Michigan, 16
Tripler, Surgeon Charles S.
    USA, 147
Triune, Tennessee, 191
Tullahoma, Tennessee, 159
Tunnel Hill, Battle of, 104
Tunnel Hill Ridge, Georgia, 160
Tuscaloosa, Alabama, 194, 198
Tuscumbia, Alabama, 34
Twelfth Vermont Infantry, 57,
    58
Twelfth Virginia Cavalry, 19,
    20, 23
Twenty-fifth Indiana Infantry,
    165
Twenty-second Wisconsin
    Infantry, 150, 151, 154,
    156, 159, 160, 162, 164
    - 166
Twenty-sixth Wisconsin
    Infantry, 100, 103, 104,
    105
Tyler, Hospital Steward
    Edmond USA, 137
Typhoid fever, 129, 173

U

Union City, Tennessee, 134
Union Depot, Chicago, Illinois, 25
Union Mills, Virginia, 56
United States Civil War Center, 5
United States Colored Troops, 37, 199, 201
United States Military Academy, 41
United States House of Representatives, 56
United States Senate, 56
University of Wisconsin, 151
Upton, Colonel Emory USA, 96

V

Vanderburg, Battle of, 207
Van Dorn, General Earl CSA, 150
Van Meter, Private William H. USA, 32, 33, 37
Verdiersville, Virginia, 17
Vickerstaff, Samuel, 212
Vicksburg City Cemetery, Vicksburg, Mississippi, 72
Vicksburg, Mississippi, 31, 34 - 36, 67 – 70, 72, 83 – 7 132, 190, 192 – 196, 202, 203, 208, 212, 213
Vicksburg, Mississippi, Siege of, 85
Vicksburg National Cemetery, Vicksburg, Mississippi, 72
Vincent, Isabella Mary Adkinson, 66
Vincent, James John, 66
Vincent, Private James USA, 66, 69, 71, 72

Vincent, Joseph, 62
Volunteer Relief Corps, 93
Von Borcke, Major Heros CSA, 18

W

Walker's Ford, Tennessee, 208
Wallace, General Lewis, 178
Walnut Hills, Mississippi, 86
Walworth, Wisconsin, 157
Wapping Heights, Battle of, 94, 114
Ware, Reverend John Quincy Adams, 62
Warren, General Gouverneur K. USA, 95
Warrenton Junction, Virginia, 103
Warrenton, Mississippi, 102
Warrenton Pike, 12, 19
Washburn, General Cadwallader USA, 136
Washington, D.C., 10, 12, 13, 17,21, 43, 46, 53, 94, 95, 102, 109, 110, 141, 178, 200
Washington, President George, 173
Wauhatchie, Tennessee, 191
Wauhatchie, Tennessee, Battle of, 104
Weisher, Private Jacob, 155
Weiskoff, Private Peter USA, 167
Wessels, General Henry USA, 142, 146
West Point, Mississippi, 135, 200
West Point, New York, 41
Weymouth, Massachusetts, 124
Wheat, Major Robiedau CSA, 12

Wheaton, Lieutenant-Colonel
Frank USA, 13
Wheeler, Private Bob USA,
210
Whit, James, 111
White, Augustus, 60
White, Private Calvin USA, 24
White, Cornilia, 60
White, Emiline, 60
White, Private John USA, 24,
25
White, Julia Augustina Smith,
60
White, Private Pliny F. USA,
60 – 63
White, Sarah, 52 – 57, 62
White, Sidney, 61
White Oak Swamp, 143
Whiteside, Alabama, 104
Whiting, Vermont, 51, 52, 56,
62
Whitsit, Major Charles W.
USA, 134
Wilcox, General Cadmus M.
CSA, 59
Wild, General Edward A. USA,
183
Wilderness, Battle of the, 96,
119, 176
Wilkes, Captain Charles USN
55
William & Mary College, 142
Williams, Malinda, 199, 200
Williams, Mary, 200
Williams, Private Jason USA,
198, 199, 202
Williams, Private Nathan USA,
198
Williams, Second Lieutenant
Richard, USA, 157
Williams Private Spencer H.
USA, 198 - 204
Williamsburg, Virginia, 142
Wilmington, North Carolina,
194

Wilson, Colonel Joseph H.
USA, 142
Wilson's Creek, Battle of, 99
Winchester National Cemetery,
Winchester, Virginia,
179
Winchester, Virginia, 16, 179
Winchester, Battle of, 44, 94
Winchester, Third Battle of, 179
Wolf, Private James F. USA,
203
Wolf Run, Virginia, 55
Wolf Run Shoals, Virginia, 56,
57
Woodstock, Virginia, 16
Wood, Colonel W. B. CSA,
198
Woodword, Surgeon A. T.
USA, 60
Woodworth, Lieutenant J.
USA, 36
Worcester, Massachusetts, 10
Wright, General Horatio USA,
96
Wright, Private George W.
USA, 79

Y

Yale, 142
Yazoo, Mississippi Expedition,
83
Yellow Bluff, Florida, 184
Yorktown, Virginia, 141, 142
Young's Branch, 12

Z

Ziegler's Grove, 58
Zollicoffer, Tennessee, 207

ABOUT THE AUTHOR

FRANK CRAWFORD is a long time student of the American Civil War, having studied the subject since his high school years. He grew up on a farm in east-central Illinois with a horse named Traveller. With a family history involved with Abraham Lincoln, his interest in the era came naturally. A retired high school instructor of thirty years, Crawford has written several articles for many Civil War magazines as well as transcribed and printed *My Dear Wife*, the Civil War letters of Private Samuel Pepper of the 95th Illinois Infantry. He is an active member of the Northern Illinois, the McHenry County and the Lake County Civil War Round Tables in Illinois as well as the Sun Coast and Manasota Civil War Round Tables in Florida. He and his wife, Velma, live near Caledonia, Illinois. Their daughter, Nena, lives in Simpsonville, South Carolina, and their son, Charles, lives in St. Petersburg, Florida.